# Old West Lawmen

Happy Trails!
Kathy Weiser Alexander



Published by:

Roundabout Publications
PO Box 19235
Lenexa, KS 66285

800-455-2207

www.TravelBooksUSA.com

Published by Roundabout Publications, PO Box 19235, Lenexa, KS 66285
Phone: 800-455-2207 / www.TravelBooksUSA.com

Library of Congress Control Number: 2012936077

ISBN-10: 1-885464-41-X
ISBN-13: 978-1-885464-41-5

# Contents

# The Old West

The Old West, often referred to as the Wild West, encompasses the period after the Civil War, the rest of the 1800's, and the early part of the 20th century. During this time, thousands of pioneers pushed their way westward in search of land, better lives, gold and silver, and sometimes, to escape the law. Geographically, the "Old West" applies to those states west of the Mississippi River.

The Old West was often a lawless place, where outlaws frequently reigned supreme. However, as more and more families, women, and working pioneers headed westward, they demanded law and order. Marshals and sheriffs were in high demand in some of the most lawless settlements, such as Dodge City, Kansas and Las Vegas, New Mexico, as well as the numerous mining camps that dotted the west, such as Deadwood, South Dakota; Coloma, California; and Leadville, Colorado.

Many of the wild and rowdy places were initially populated by men and often attracted seedier elements of society to their many saloons, dance halls, gambling parlors and brothels. But, in any burgeoning community, there were also lawful businessmen and hard-working pioneers who craved a sense of stability, and demanding law and order, made efforts to hire peacekeepers. Where this was not possible or the lawmen were ineffective, invariably vigilante groups would form.

Though the vast majority of these Old West lawmen were honorable and heroic figures, ironically, many of them rode both sides of the fence and were known as outlaws as well.

# Code of the West

First chronicled by the famous Western writer, Zane Grey, in his 1934 novel *The Code of the West*, no "written" code ever actually existed. However, the hardy pioneers who lived in the west were bound by these unwritten rules that centered on hospitality, fair play, loyalty, and respect for the land.

Ramon Adams, a Western historian, explained it best in his 1969 book, *The Cowman and His Code of Ethics*, saying, in part:

"Back in the days when the cowman with his herds made a new frontier, there was no law on the range. Lack of written law made it necessary for him to frame some of his own, thus developing a rule of behavior which became known as the "Code of the West." These homespun laws, being merely a gentleman's agreement to certain rules of conduct for survival, were never written into statutes, but were respected everywhere on the range.

Though the cowman might break every law of the territory, state and federal government, he took pride in upholding his own unwritten code. His failure to abide by it did not bring formal punishment, but the man who broke it became, more or less, a social outcast. His friends 'hazed him into the cutbacks' and he was subject to the punishment of the very code he had broken.

Though the Code of the West was always unwritten, here is a "loose" list of some of the guidelines:

- Don't inquire into a person's past. Take the measure of a man for what he is today.
- Never steal another man's horse. A horse thief pays with his life.
- Defend yourself whenever necessary.
- Look out for your own.
- Remove your guns before sitting at the dining table.
- Never order anything weaker than whiskey.
- Don't make a threat without expecting dire consequences.
- Never pass anyone on the trail without saying "Howdy."
- When approaching someone from behind, give a loud greeting before you get within shooting range.
- Don't wave at a man on a horse, as it might spook the horse. A nod is the proper greeting.
- After you pass someone on the trail, don't look back at him. It implies you don't trust him.

- Riding another man's horse without his permission is nearly as bad as making love to his wife. Never even bother another man's horse.
- Always fill your whiskey glass to the brim.
- A cowboy doesn't talk much; he saves his breath for breathing.
- No matter how weary and hungry you are after a long day in the saddle, always tend to your horse's needs before your own, and get your horse some feed before you eat.
- Cuss all you want, but only around men, horses and cows.
- Complain about the cooking and you become the cook.
- Always drink your whiskey with your gun hand, to show your friendly intentions.
- Do not practice ingratitude.
- A cowboy is pleasant even when out of sorts. Complaining is what quitters do, and cowboys hate quitters.
- Always be courageous. Cowards aren't tolerated in any outfit worth its salt.
- A cowboy always helps someone in need, even a stranger or an enemy.
- Never try on another man's hat.
- Be hospitable to strangers. Anyone who wanders in, including an enemy, is welcome at the dinner table. The same was true for riders who joined cowboys on the range.
- Give your enemy a fighting chance.
- Never wake another man by shaking or touching him, as he might wake suddenly and shoot you.
- Real cowboys are modest. A braggert who is "all gurgle and no guts" is not tolerated.
- Be there for a friend when he needs you.
- Drinking on duty is grounds for instant dismissal and blacklisting.
- A cowboy is loyal to his "brand," to his friends, and those he rides with.
- Never shoot an unarmed or unwarned enemy. This was also known as "the rattlesnake code": always warn before you strike. However, if a man was being stalked, this could be ignored.
- Never shoot a woman no matter what.
- Consideration for others is central to the code, such as: Don't stir up dust around the chuckwagon, don't wake up the wrong man for herd duty, etc.
- Respect the land and the environment by not smoking in hazardous fire areas, disfiguring rocks, trees, or other natural areas.
- Honesty is absolute - your word is your bond, a handshake is more binding than a contract.
- Live by the Golden Rule.

# Organizations

## Arizona Rangers

By James Harvey McClintock in 1913. ***Note***: The article is not verbatim as spelling errors and minor grammatical changes have been made.

The organization of the Arizona Rangers was on the recommendation of Governor Murphy to the Legislature of 1901. The first Captain appointed was Burton C. Mossman, a Northern Arizona cattleman, who proceeded with an organization of a company that at first consisted of only twelve men, with Dayton Graham of Cochise County as first lieutenant. Mossman made his organization wholly non-political and men were sought for enlistment on account of their records as efficient officers, good shots and good frontiersmen, well acquainted with the country. In some cases, men were enlisted whose previous records would not have entitled them to distinguished consideration in a Sunday school, but who had a reputation for courage and endurance. Such men usually gave a very good account of themselves. According to Mossman: "I have never known a body of men to take a more intense interest in their work. They were very proud of the organization, proud of the record that they were making, and there was great emulation among the men to make good." Every section of the territory had its representatives so that wherever the command might be called there would be some ranger familiar with the country, water holes, trails, etc. During the first twelve months after organization, 125 arrests were made of actual criminals, who were sent to the penitentiary or back to other states to answer for crime. The deterrent effect of these many captures was great, serving to drive from the territory a large percentage of its criminal population.

Organized in August, the rangers proved effective from the first. In November, two of its members, Carlos Tafolla and Dean Hamblin, reinforced by four Saint Johns cattlemen, chased the Jack Smith band of outlaws into the Black River country south of Springerville. The outlaws were headed for Mexico with a band of stolen horses and were surprised while in camp.

After apparent surrender, they dodged behind trees and opened fire. Tafolla and a cattleman named Maxwell were killed and two of the outlaws wounded. The latter escaped in darkness, on foot, leaving their camp outfit and horses behind. Captain Mossman, with three more rangers, soon was on the trail, but the gang, stealing fresh

Arizona Rangers in 1903

horses, managed to escape in the snows of the New Mexican mountains. Tafolla's widow was pensioned by the Legislature.

Captain Mossman early established amicable relations with the Mexican authorities and an agreement was entered into with Lt. Col. Kosterlitsky of the Mexican Rurales that either should have the privilege of chasing outlaws across the border and they should work in unison with the definite objective of ridding the Southwest of the "rustler" element.

In 1903 the force embraced twenty six officers. Six years after organization a report was made that the rangers in that time had made 4000 arrests of which 25% had been for serious felonies. The best work was against horse and cattle thieves.

Special value was found in the fact that the Rangers were independent of politics and were not controlled by considerations that often tied the hands of local peace officers. This very feature, however, led to occasional trouble with disagreeing sheriffs.

After Governor Brodie assumed office, a change was made in the leadership of the Arizona Rangers, to the position being appointed T.H. Rynning, who had been a lieutenant of Rough Riders. Under him the organization did splendid work, especially in the labor troubles in Bisbee and Morenci. At the latter point, one episode most worthy of mention was when a band of several hundred rioters, coming over the divide from Chase Creek, encountered a few rangers, commanded by Sergeant Jack Foster. Foster was hailed and a demand was made upon him for his guns. The sergeant, remembering his experience in the Rough Riders, deployed his men along the crest of a ridge and laconically answered:" If you want the guns, come and get them." The rioters concluded to move on and Foster saved both his rifles and his self-respect.

The history of the rangers under whatever leadership, was one of devotion and of rare courage, well worthy of a separate volume. Some of it is told in this work but much is left unchronicled. There is the story how Ranger Frank Wheeler, with Deputy Sheriff

John Cameron, killed Herrick and Bentley, former convicts wanted for horse stealing, in the course of a battle in the rocks, after the fugitives had been tracked for five days. There might be mentioned, as typical, the encounter in Benson of Captain Harry Wheeler with a desperado named Tracy wherein the latter died with four bullet holes in his body and Wheeler received wounds that disabled him for months. There was the case of Willis Wood, an outlaw of the worst type, who was taken by [Thomas] Rynning from a roomful of the prisoner's friends.

Rynning resigned to become superintendent of the territorial prison during the period of its reconstruction at Florence and March 21, 1907, was succeeded by his lieutenant, Harry Wheeler, later sheriff of Cochise County. Wheeler notably was successful in handling difficult border conditions. But politics finally caused the disbandment of the rangers.

***Note***: As McClintock's writing of the Arizona Rangers occurred in 1913, he couldn't have known that they would be revived. In 1957, the group was re-established by several original Arizona Rangers. The present day Arizona Rangers are an unpaid, all volunteer, law enforcement support and assistance civilian auxiliary. Currently, they work co-operatively at the request of and under the direction, control, and supervision of established law enforcement officials and officers. They also provide youth support and community service and work to preserve the tradition, honor, and history of the original Arizona Rangers.

Arizona Rangers in front of Bisbee Bank, 1902

## California State Rangers

California's first state-wide law enforcement agency, the Rangers were formed in 1853 when the legislature authorized a body of some 20 men to kill or capture the Mexican bandit, Joaquin Murrieta and his gang called the Five Joaquins. Led by former Texas Ranger, Captain Harry Love, the men tracked down the gang and allegedly killed Murrieta and his right-hand-man Manuel Garcia, known as "Three Fingered Jack." Later, the Rangers were disbanded; however, Captain Love and another ranger stayed on at the State Capitol and helped to form the California State police. Over the years, the organization was reorganized several times and was eventually merged with the California Highway Patrol in 1995.

## Lighthorse Police

The Indian Police in Oklahoma were given the name Lighthorse by the Five Civilized Tribes when the state was still Indian Territory. As early as 1808, when the Cherokee were still located in the southeast, they appointed "regulators" to stop crime, protect widows and orphans, and kill those who resisted authority. The tradition continued after the Cherokee were forced on the "Trail of Tears" to Indian Territory and was taken up by the other "civilized" tribes including the Chickasaw, Choctaw, Creek, and Seminole tribes. The police force got its name from Revolutionary War hero, General Henry Lee, who was called "Lighthorse Harry" due to how quickly his cavalry responded to conflicts. The first official Lighthorse Company was formed in 1844 by the Cherokee National Council. Composed of a captain, lieutenant and twenty-four horsemen, the men were tasked with the pursuit and arrest of all fugitives from justice before turning them over to the Indian courts for trial and punishment. Though history tends to focus on the U.S. Deputy Marshal's activities in Indian Territory, the Lighthorse Police were just as important and their tales, unfortunately remain mostly "unsung." When the Five Civilized Tribes lost their tribal lands in the late 19th century, the Lighthorse Mounted Police were disbanded. However, today, some tribes still use the Lighthorse name for elements of their police forces.

## Pinkerton Detective Agency

Founded by Allan Pinkerton, a Scottish immigrant in 1850, the Pinkerton Agency quickly became one of the most important crime detection and law enforcement groups in the United States. Born in Scotland on August 25, 1819, Allan Pinkerton worked as a barrel maker before immigrating to the United States in 1842. Settling near Chicago, Illinois, he went to work at Lill's Brewery as a barrel maker. However, Pinkerton soon determined that working for himself would be more profitable for his family and they moved to a small town called Dundee, some forty miles from Chicago.

Making barrels once again, he quickly gained control of the market due to the superior quality and low prices of his product.

Allan Pinkerton in 1867

Always thrifty, Pinkerton thought that he could save some money by not paying someone else for poles to make barrel hoops. Before long, he found a small deserted island in the middle of the Fox River and rowed out to cut down a supply of his own.

However, when he got to the island, he found signs that someone had been there and knowing that counterfeiters had been working in the area, he wondered if the island might be their hideout.

When he returned, he notified the local sheriff of his suspicions and the two teamed up to stake out the island which soon led to the arrest of the counterfeit band. However, they failed to catch the ringleader. Soon, Pinkerton found himself involved in the search for the leader and soon tracked him down, as well.

This accidental involvement in justice led to Pinkerton's appointment as a deputy sheriff for Kane County and in 1850 he became Chicago's first police detective. That same year, he, along with Chicago attorney, Edward Rucker, founded the North-Western Police Agency.

In the meantime, Allan's brother, Robert, had formed his own business called "Pinkerton & Co" as early as 1843. Robert's organization was originally established as a railroad contractor, but somewhere along the line, he began to work as a railroad detective.

Through his contacts in the railroad business, Robert had also secured a number of contracts with Wells Fargo to provide guards on stage coaches. Robert's business grew so rapidly that he hired several men as railroad and stage coach detectives and guards.

When Allan and Rucker's business dissolved a year after it was formed, Allan joined his brother Robert in his already established company and the name was changed to the Pinkerton National Detective Agency. The "new" company provided a variety of detective services, from private military contractors to security guards, but specialized in the capture of counterfeiters and train robbers. Though there were a few other detective agencies at the time, most had unsavory reputations and the Pinkerton Agency was the first to set uniform fees and establish practices which quickly earned respect for the organization.

In 1861, while investigating a railway case, the agency uncovered an assassination plot against Abraham Lincoln, where conspirators intended to kill Lincoln in Baltimore during a stop on his way to his inauguration. However, with Pinkerton's warning, Lincoln's itinerary was changed. During the Civil War, President Lincoln hired the Pinkerton Detective Agency to organize a "secret service" to obtain military information on the Confederates and sometimes act as Lincoln's bodyguard. Working diligently, Allan Pinkerton traveled under the pseudonym of "Major E.J. Allen."

After the war, Allan Pinkerton returned to his duties at the detective agency, which was often hired by the government to perform many of the same duties that are now regularly assigned to the Secret Service, the FBI, and the CIA. The agency also worked for the railroads and overland stage companies, playing an active role in chasing down a number of outlaws including Jesse James, the Reno Brothers, and Butch Cassidy and his Wild Bunch.

On their three story Chicago building, their logo, a black and white eye, claimed "We Never Sleep." This was the origin of the term "private eye."

When Robert Pinkerton died in 1868, Allan assumed full control of the Pinkerton Detective Agency. However, just a year later, in the autumn of 1869, Allan suffered a paralyzing stroke which nearly killed him. Both Robert and Allan's sons then took on most of the responsibilities of running the business. However, there was rivalry between them, and the agency struggled without leadership. At the same time, the agency began to suffer financially.

Despite the challenges, by the early 1870s, the agency had the world's largest collection of mug shots and a "criminal database." During the height of its existence, the Pinkertons had more agents than the standing army of the United States of America, causing the state of Ohio to outlaw the agency, due to the possibility of its being hired out as a "private army" or militia.

Fortunes were to decrease once again for the agency when, in 1871, Chicago suffered the Great Fire which began on the evening of October 7th. Before it burned itself out three days later, the entire business district was destroyed, including the Pinkerton buildings and many of their records. When the fire was finally extinguished, martial law was declared in Chicago and guards from the Pinkerton Detective Agency were hired to prevent looting. Robert's widow, Alice Isabella Pinkerton, and his dependents were also left homeless. When she approached Allan for assistance, he encouraged them to return to Great Britain. Offering to pay for the journey, Alice and her sons accepted his offer and sailed for Liverpool, leaving the agency entirely in the hands of Allan and his sons.

Early Pinkerton Agents

When Allan Pinkerton passed away in 1884, the agency was taken over by his sons, Robert and William. They soon became involved in the labor unrest of the late 19th century when they were hired by a number of businesses to keep strikers and suspected unionists out of their factories.

However, the rapidly expanding agency soon became known for less admirable activities as they often became the "law" in and of themselves. Accused of using heavy handed tactics, such as firebombing Jesse James' mother's home and using intimidation against union sympathizers, the public support began to turn away from the agency.

Many labor sympathizers accused the Pinkertons of inciting riots and their reputation continued to suffer. The most notorious example of this was the Homestead Strike of 1892, when Pinkerton agents killed 11 people while enforcing strikebreaking measures. In order to restore order, two brigades of state militia had to be called out.

Continuing their involvement against the labor movement into the 20th century, their reputation was harmed for years in the public consciousness.

However, the agency endured. In 1907, the agency was inherited by the founder's grandson, Allan Pinkerton II and his great-grandson, Robert II, in 1930. However, when Robert Pinkerton II died in 1967, without a male heir, family direction of the corporation came to an end.

However, Pinkerton's Inc. has since grown to a $1.5 billion organization that provides a wide range of security services. The company has its U.S. headquarters in Westlake Village, California, and is a subsidiary of the Securitas Group of Stockholm, Sweden, a world leader in the security industry.

## Texas Rangers

The second oldest state level law enforcement agency in the United States, the Texas Rangers got their start in 1823, only two years after white settlement in Texas formally began. Following the Mexican War of Independence, some 600 to 700 families moved to Texas; however, it had no regular army to protect its new citizens. New Empresario Stephen F. Austin soon began to organize experienced frontiersmen as "rangers" in informal groups to protect the settlers against Indian attacks and other criminal elements.

It was not until October 17, 1835 that Texas formally constituted the force that has since been known as the Texas Rangers, and on November 24, 1835, Robert McAlpin Williamson was chosen to be the first Ranger Major.

Beginning with a complement of fifty-six men in three companies, the Rangers grew quickly as their numbers increased to more than 300 by 1837. Though officially sanctioned and their numbers increased, the Rangers served sparingly in their first few years.

During Texas' fight for independence from Mexico, the Rangers sometimes served as scouts and couriers. Other menial tasks were also assigned to them such as retrieving cattle, escorting refugees, and destroying supplies and equipment left behind by the Mexicans.

Once independence was gained and the land became the Republic of Texas, the lawmen continued to see very little duty under President Sam Houston. However, when Mirabeau B. Lamar became President in 1838, he rejected Houston's frontier policies of friendship with the Indians and engaged the Rangers in war against the tribes. Congress allowed him to recruit eight companies of mounted volunteers and maintain a company of fifty-six Rangers. A month later, he then provided for five similar companies in Central and South Texas. Over the next three years the Rangers waged all-out war against the Indians, successfully participating in a number of battles including the Council House Fight in San Antonio, the raid on Linnville, and the Battle of Plum Creek. By the time that Lamar's administration was over, Texans had severely damaged the strength of the most powerful tribes.

When Sam Houston was re-elected to the presidency in December, 1841, he saw the effectiveness of the Rangers and on January 29, 1842, approved a law that officially provided for a company of mounted men to "act as Rangers." As a result, 150 Rangers under Captain John Coffee "Jack" Hays, were assigned to protect the southern and western portions of the Texas frontier. Houston's foresight in this decision proved successful in helping to repel the Mexican invasions of 1842, as well as shielding the white settlers against Indian attacks over the next three years.

Texas Rangers

Hays was also responsible for improving the quality of recruitments and initiating tough training programs for the new Rangers, as well as initiating an "esprit de corps" within his command. From this group came a number of celebrated ranger captains including, W. A. A. "Big Foot" Wallace, Ben and Henry McCulloch, Samuel H. Walker, and Robert Addison "Ad" Gillespie.

Texas officially became part of the United States in 1846, which also started the Mexican War when the U.S. attempted to establish the boundary at the Rio Grande River. During the two year affair, the Texas Rangers were called on to assist the American Army and soon achieved worldwide fame as a fighting force. Superbly mounted with a large assortment of weapons, the Rangers were found to be so successful against Mexican guerillas, that they soon earned the name "los diablos Tejanos" or the " Texas Devils."

When the Mexican War ended on February 2, 1848, the United States assumed responsibility for protecting the Texas frontier. Having no official function, the Rangers soon lost a number of its famous captains and frontier defenders. A decade later in the Spring of 1858, they briefly saw combat again when they were sent north to the Red River to settle a band of Comanche Indians.

After Texas seceded from the United States during the Civil War in 1861, an organization was formed in Houston called Terry's Texas Rangers. Under the leadership of Colonel Benjamin Franklin Terry, many of the former Rangers enlisted under his command.

During the reconstruction period of 1865-1873, the Rangers were designated as state police. A dark period in their history, they were charged with enforcing unpopular new laws that came with rejoining the United States. Among the war weary Texans, the Rangers fell into disrepute. During this period, the Rangers acted as a military type police unit when enforcing the new laws or fighting Indians or Mexicans. However, when hunting down outlaws, they functioned more as lawmen and posses.

Their role changed once again in May, 1874, when the state Democrats returned to power and Governor Richard Coke, along with the Legislature, appropriated $75,000 to organize six companies of 75 Rangers each. By this time, Texas was overrun with outlaws, Indians ravaging the western frontier, and Mexican bandits pillaging and murdering along the Rio Grande River. The new troops were stationed at strategic points over the state and were known as the Frontier Battalion. During this era, the Ranger Service held a place somewhere between that of an army and a police force.

Texas Rangers in Presidio County, El Paso district, in 1890

In 1877, the Texas Rangers found themselves on the outlaw trail, pursuing John Wesley Hardin. Hardin, who had killed Charles Webb, a deputy sheriff in Brown County in 1874, left the state when he began to be relentlessly pursued. However, one Texas Ranger by the name of John Barclay Armstrong, better known as "McNelly's Bulldog," received permission to pursue Hardin across state lines. Finally catching up with the notorious outlaw on a train in Pensacola, Florida, the inevitable shoot-out occurred. When the smoke cleared, Hardin had been knocked unconscious, one of his gang members killed and the rest were arrested on July 23, 1877.

In the spring of 1878, Sam Bass and his gang held up two stage coaches and four trains within twenty-five miles of Dallas. The gang quickly found themselves the target of a spirited chase across North Texas by a special company of Texas Rangers headed by Junius Peak. Bass eluded his pursuers until one of his party, Jim Murphy, turned informer. As the Bass Gang rode south intending to rob a small bank in Round Rock, Murphy wrote to Major John B. Jones, commander of the Frontier Battalion of Texas Rangers.

In Round Rock, Texas, a fierce battle between the gang and the Rangers took place on July 19, 1878. In the melee, Bass' sidekick, Seaborn Barnes, was killed and Sam was wounded, though he was able to ride away on his horse. The next morning he was found lying helpless in a pasture north of town and was brought back to Round Rock where he died on July 21st.

Over the next several years, the Frontier Battalion captured more than 3,000 Texas outlaws, but by 1882 the "frontier" was beginning to disappear.

Texas Rangers

Over the next three decades, the Rangers' prominence and prestige waned, although they continued to occasionally intercept cattle rustlers, contended with Mexican and Indian marauders along the Rio Grande River, and at times protected blacks from white lynch mobs. By the turn of the century, critics began to urge the curtailment or abandonment of the Texas Rangers. As a result, the Frontier Battalion was abolished in 1901 and the Ranger force was cut to four law enforcement companies of twenty men each.

Ranger activities were soon redirected towards law enforcement among Texas citizens, but when violence increased along the Rio Grande River, the Rangers participated in numerous bloody brush fights with Mexican nationals.

In 1914, during the early days of World War I, the Rangers had the daunting task of identifying and rounding up numerous spies, conspirators, saboteurs, and draft dodgers. In 1916, Pancho Villa's raid on Columbus, New Mexico, intensified already harsh feelings between the United States and Mexico. As a result, the regular Rangers, along with hundreds of special Rangers appointed by Texas governors, killed approximately 5,000 Hispanics between 1914 and 1919, which soon became a source of scandal and embarrassment.

In order to restore public confidence, the Texas legislature overhauled the force in January 1919, but not before a number of sordid tales of ranger brutality emerged. Soon the four companies of Ranger recruits was cut from twenty to fifteen per unit. The legislature also established higher salaries in order to attract men of higher character and established procedures for citizen complaints.

After the enactment of Prohibition in 1920, the Ranger's primary function was patrolling the Rio Grande River against tequila smugglers and cattle rustlers.

During the Great Depression, the Ranger force was reduced to just 45 men. Adding fuel to the fire, the Rangers openly supported Governor Ross Sterling against Miriam A. "Ma" Ferguson in the Democratic primary in the Fall of 1932. As a result, when Ferguson took office in January, 1933, she fired every ranger for his partisanship, salaries were slashed and the budget further reduced the force to thirty-two men. Without the protection of the Rangers, Texas soon became a haven for outlaws such as Raymond Hamilton, George "Machine Gun" Kelly, and Clyde Barrow and Bonnie Parker.

In 1934, Frank A. Hamer, a long-time Ranger who had been let go during Ferguson's cutback, was asked by the head of the Texas prison system to utilize his skills to track down Bonnie and Clyde. Previously the pair successfully broke out a member of their gang from the Huntsville Prison, killing a guard in the process.

After tracking the Barrow gang across nine states, Frank Hamer, in conjunction with law enforcement in Louisiana, learned that Bonnie and Clyde had visited Bienville Parish on May 21, 1934, and that Clyde had designated a rendezvous point near there with gang member Henry Methvin. Unknown to Bonnie and Clyde was that Methvin, cooperating with law enforcement, participated in assisting with an ambush along the route to the rendezvous.

Led by former Texas Rangers Hamer and Manny Gault, a posse including two Louisiana lawmen, and two more Texans, lie in wait on Highway 154, between Gibsland and Sailes. In place by 9:00 p.m., they waited all night and through the next day with no sign of Bonnie and Clyde. However, around 9:10 a.m. on May 23, 1934, the posse, concealed in the bushes and almost ready to concede defeat, heard Clyde's stolen Ford V-8 approaching. When he stopped to speak with Henry Methvin's father, planted there with his truck that morning to distract Clyde and force him into the lane closest to the posse, the lawmen opened fire, killing Bonnie and Clyde while shooting a combined total of approximately 130 rounds.

It is not clear what legal authority there was to kill Bonnie Parker, who was not known to have killed anyone, but Hamer made it clear that he had intended to kill her. He had a reputation for not being overly solicitous with regard to law details. Hamer and others from the posse kept for themselves some of the stolen guns from Bonnie and Clyde's vehicle, and the United States Congress awarded him a special citation for trapping and killing the outlaws.

In 1935, James Allred became the Texas governor after having run on a platform of better law enforcement. The legislature soon established the Texas Department of

Public Safety, of which the Texas Rangers became a part of on August 10, 1935. Also in this new department was the Highway Patrol and a scientific crime laboratory and detection center known as the Headquarters Division.

Over the years, the Texas Rangers have investigated crimes ranging from murder to political corruption, kept the peace during riots, protected the Texas governor, tracked down fugitives, and functioned as a quasi-military force.

Today's Texas Rangers are an investigative division of the Texas Department of Public Safety. More than 100 highly trained men and women are posted across the State of Texas and are one of the most effective investigative law enforcement agencies in the world.

## The Three Guardsmen

This name was given in Old West literature to describe the three effective U.S. Deputy Marshals, Bill Tilghman (1854-1924), Chris Madsen (1851-1944), and Heck Thomas (1850-1912). In 1889, this trio began the "cleaning up" of Indian Territory, which at the time, was known as a wild and lawless place. Working under Judge Isaac Parker in Fort Smith, Arkansas, the three men arrested more than 300 outlaws in the next ten years and killed many others. Their main claim to fame was their relentless pursuit of the members of the Doolin-Dalton Gang, eliminating many of them systematically, and apprehending those that would surrender.

Heck Thomas

Bill Tilghman

## U.S. Marshals

Invoking an image of weathered cowboys riding hard on the range, chasing outlaws in a running gunfight, are the U.S. Marshals of the Old West. While those images were "real," especially with many of the brave men working in Indian Territory under the jurisdiction of "Hanging Judge" Isaac Parker, or in the fledgling western territories of Arizona, New Mexico, Montana, Wyoming and others; many may not know that the U.S. Marshal Service is more than 200 years old.

The U.S. Marshal Service was created by the first Congress in the Judiciary Act of 1789, the same legislation that established the federal judicial system. When George Washington set up his first administration and the first Congress began passing laws, both quickly discovered an inconvenient gap – there was no agency established to represent the federal government's interests at the local level.

Part of the problem was solved by creating specialized agencies, such as customs and revenue collectors, to levy the tariffs and taxes, but there were numerous other jobs that needed to be done.

Many of these tasks fell to the U.S. Marshal Service. Given extensive authority to support federal courts, congress, or the president, these marshals and their deputies have served subpoenas, warrants, made arrests, and handled prisoners for more than two centuries.

And though these are the most well-known of their tasks, they had numerous others as well, including the disbursement of money. The Marshals paid the fees and expenses of the court clerks, U.S. Attorneys, jurors, and witnesses. They rented the courtrooms and jail space and hired the bailiffs, criers, and janitors. They made sure the prisoners were present, the jurors were available, and the witnesses were on time.

But this was only a part of what the Marshals did. The Marshals have also taken the responsibility for a number of other tasks over the years, such as taking the national census through 1870, distributing Presidential proclamations, registering enemy aliens in times of war, capturing fugitive slaves, and protecting the American borders.

Their motto is "Justice, Integrity, and Service," and through the years, their heroics in the face of lawlessness have often become famous, especially in the days of the Wild Old West, which has so often been portrayed in popular films, and invoking the many images we have of these courageous men today.

In the second half of the 19th century, the U.S. Marshals became synonymous with the "Wild West" as they made their mark on history in the many lawless frontier towns. In many of these places, the marshals were the only kind of law that was available, and knowing this, numerous outlaws made their livelihoods in these fledgling towns that had not yet become structured enough to provide for their own authorities. Here, in "wicked" places like Deadwood, South Dakota; Tombstone, Arizona; and the plains of Indian Territory, U.S. Deputy Marshals became famous as they pursued such notorious outlaws as Billy the Kid in New Mexico; Bill Doolin, the Dalton Gang, Belle Starr, and the Rufus Buck Gang in Indian Territory; Jesse James in the Midwest; and Butch Cassidy's Wild Bunch in Wyoming; and hundreds of others.

These deputy marshals were sent from the federal court at Fort Smith, Arkansas to capture Ned Christie. Front row, l-r: Charles Copeland, Gideon S. "Cap" White. Back row, l-r: Bill Smith, Bill Ellis, Paden Tolbert, 1892.

Though popular western films generally showed these fearless men as forming a posse, pinning on their silver star-shaped badges, and pursuing the outlaws in a running gunfight, that the marshals always won, this was in truth, not the norm. In fact, in Indian Territory (which later became Oklahoma) alone, 103 deputies were killed between 1872 and 1896, roughly a quarter of the number slain throughout the marshals' history. The territory, controlled by Judge Isaac Parker in Fort Smith, Arkansas, was described by a Fort Smith newspaper as the "rendezvous of the vile and wicked from everywhere." Some of the true courageous men who made names for themselves here were Heck Thomas, Bass Reeves, Bill Tilghman, Chris Madsen and dozens of others.

In other areas of the west, more men who made names for themselves included Seth Bullock in South Dakota; Bat Masterson in Kansas; Joseph Meek in Oregon; William Wheeler in Montana; and again, dozens of others. Two of the most recognizable men who served as U.S. Deputy Marshals were Wyatt Earp and Wild Bill Hickok. However, they gained their notoriety primarily through their own exaggerations and film depictions, rather than the courageous acts shown by many more deputy marshals.

Once the Wild West was tamed, the U.S. Marshal service began to suffer in the 20th century as their star faded and the FBI flourished. Though they protected the home front during World War I and were heavily involved in enforcing Prohibition laws, they had essentially lost their "specialty," and by the 1950s found themselves acting as bailiffs for the federal courts and requesting background checks. In the 1960s, their importance again rose as they enforced court-ordered racial desegregation and the Federal Witness Security Program was established in the 1970s.

Today, the Marshal Service still has responsibility to enforce federal laws and orders issued by the court, as well as prevention of civil disturbances, continued protection of federal witnesses, terrorist events, hostage situations, and numerous other duties directed by the Department of Justice, such as airline security after the terrible attack in New York on September 11, 2001. Current Deputy Marshals are required to carry firearms and to become proficient in the latest electronic communications equipment and security devices. Their work continues to hold the constant threat of violence involving personal risk to the many men and women who pledge to protect the justice system.

Over the years, some 400 marshals have been killed in the line of duty. Their famous five-sided star is the oldest emblem of federal law enforcement in our country.

# The Lawmen

## Burton "Burt" Alvord

*Lawman Turned Outlaw*

Alvord was born in Arizona Territory in 1866. The son of a justice of the peace, he often traveled with his father. When he was just 15 years old he was working as a stable hand at Tombstone's O.K. Corral, where he witnessed the famous gunfight. Three years later, he also was present when vigilantes lynched John Heath, a convicted thief and murderer.

Burton Alvord

In 1886, at the age of twenty, Alvord was appointed Deputy Sheriff of Cochise County by the newly-elected Sheriff, "Texas" John Slaughter. Within no time, Alvord earned a reputation as an excellent tracker as he brought in a number of cattle rustlers and other wanted fugitives.

For the next three years, Alvord served with Slaughter in many a shoot-out with outlaws, rustlers, and gunmen of all kinds. However, Alvord's sterling reputation as an efficient lawman began to slip in 1889, when he began to drink heavily.

Frequenting the many saloons of Tombstone, Alvord started to socialize with some of the criminal elements and was known to get into frequent scuffles. As Slaughter began to chastise his actions, Alvord soured on both the Sheriff and the law.

Alvord moved to Fairbank, Arizona in the early 1890's and became a town constable. Continuing to drink heavily and cavort with known outlaws, he was soon asked for his resignation and he moved once again, this time, to Pearce, Arizona. There, he worked briefly as a deputy marshal for George Bravin in 1896, who was looking for a "tough nut" to make sure his growing mining camp didn't get out of hand. However, after just six months, Bravin decided that there was no longer a need for the toughened lawman and Alvord moved on to Willcox. Little did Bravin know that the two would meet again under far different circumstances.

Again he obtained work as a town constable but commanded very little respect as by this time he had become a serious alcoholic. By the turn of the century, Alvord had given up on being a lawman and joined with the many outlaws he had befriended over the years. Starting with cattle rustling, he later formed a gang with Billy Stiles and began to commit armed robberies. After a foiled attempt to rob a Fairbank train and a run-in with tough lawman Jeff Milton, Alvord was arrested and taken to the Cochise County Jail. By that time, his former boss, George Bravin, was working as a lawman in Tombstone and the two came face to face once again.

However, on April 7, 1900, as Bravin had some 25 prisoners housed in his jail, Billy Stiles went to visit Alvord and other gang members who were in the jail. He then held a gun to Bravin demanding the release of all of the prisoners and ended up shooting the lawman taking off two of his toes. The prisoners, including Alvord, then escaped.

The gang continued their criminal ways until both Alvord and Stiles were arrested in December, 1903. Again they were incarcerated in the Tombstone Jail and again they escaped. Shortly later, Alvord got the idea that they would fake their deaths in order to get the law off their trail. The pair either killed two Mexicans or unearthed them from recent graves and sent them in sealed coffins to Tombstone. Spreading the word that the coffins contained their own outlaw bodies, the lawmen were suspicious and opened the coffins. Finding the moldering remains of the Mexicans, rather than the outlaws, they went after them again.

The Arizona Rangers, pursued the men into Mexico in February, 1904 and trapped them near Naco. When Alvord and Stiles went for their guns, the Rangers returned fire hitting Alvord twice in the leg and Stiles in the arm. Though Stiles was somehow able to get away, Alvord was captured and sent to the Arizona Territorial Prison at Yuma, where he served two years for robbery. Released in 1906, he then traveled to Central America. He was last seen in 1910 working as a canal employee in Panama.

## David Monticello "Bud" Ballew

*Gunfighter & Lawman of Oklahoma*

Though not nearly as well known as other Oklahoma lawmen, such as Heck Thomas or Bill Tilghman, Bud Ballew was just as colorful and respected as both a gunfighter and lawman.

Born David Monticello Ballew, to Bryant and Mary Turban Ballew in Fannin County, Texas in 1877, Ballew inherited his father's nickname "Bud" from an early age. When he was a young boy, he helped his father on the family ranch and became extremely adept as a horseman as well as handling firearms. While still no more than a boy, Bud left the family in 1890 and made his way to the Ardmore area in Indian Territory. Three years later, his father and the rest of the family would follow him and also settle in the area. Bud started a small ranching operation and before long met a girl named Fannie Mariah Harper. The two married on April 17, 1901 and settled on his ranch at Lone Grove, Oklahoma.

By 1910, Bud had a stable ranching operation and the couple had two sons. In the Spring of 1914, his ranch was running so smoothly that he began to look around for something else to do.

By this time, the area was filled with oilfields and the rough characters that often worked in them. When Carter County Sheriff, Buck Garrett, offered him a job as a deputy sheriff, Bud accepted. For the next 12 years, Ballew would work as a lawman, as well as continuing his ranching operation, and also speculated in oil leases.

During this time, Bud was described as being 5'11" tall, stockily built, with a shock of curly red hair, and a hearty booming laugh. He was fond of the gambling dens and saloons, where he was often spied wearing a wide brimmed cowboy hat, high topped cowboy boots, a pistol on each hip, and a large diamond tie-tack. His cherubic looking face and ready laughter often belied his character. He feared no man and would be credited with killing as many as eight men over the next 12 years.

Ballew first made headlines on November 19, 1915 when he killed Pete Bynum who was in the middle of holding up a liquor joint in Wirt, Oklahoma. Catching Bynum in the act, Bud intervened, and Bynum shot him in the stomach. Ballew returned fire, and not only killed Bynum, but also a man named Alison, who was unlucky enough to be sleeping in an adjoining room. Though the bleeding was no doubt, profuse, Ballew's wound was not serious.

After Ballew had fully recovered, he was sent to arrest a wanted outlaw named Steve Talkington. However, when Talkington resisted arrest, Ballew shot and killed him. He was then sent to retrieve the commission from City Marshal Highnote of Wirt. However, Highnote had been fired and refused to vacate his position or hand over the reward. As a result, Ballew killed him too.

The next killing occurred when Deputy Ballew, along with fellow officer, Fred Williams, were escorting a prisoner, a black man named James Perle, on a train. Unfortunately, when the prisoner jumped from the train in an attempt to escape, both officers fired, and he was killed. In another incident, Ballew and a fellow officer were involved in a shooting with a man named Arch Campbell in an Ardmore barber shop.

Bud Ballew on the left,
Sheriff Buck Garrett on the right.

On another occasion, Ballew saved Buck Garrett's life when the Sheriff was trying to apprehend two highway men who had robbed a man named Jim Taliafero. As the bandits, Charlie Thomas and Arthur "Dusty" Miller, were fleeing east of Ardmore, Garrett overtook the pair and a fight ensued between Thomas and Garrett. As Dusty Mills circled the two men, trying to get a clean shot at the sheriff, Bud arrived. Mills whirled on him, but a fraction of a second too late, as Bud shot first and the outlaw fell victim to his .45.

Ballew's most famous gunfight was with former U.S. Deputy Marshal Dow Braziel on January 31, 1919. The two apparently had a long standing feud because Buck Garrett and Bud Ballew had not enforced the Prohibition laws as aggressively as Braziel. Very early in the morning, Ardmore Chief of Police Les Segler met up with Bud Ballew in the east part of the city, where gunshots had been heard. After talking for a time, the two headed to the California Cafe, at the corner of Main and Mill Streets for breakfast. As the pair entered the cafe, they noticed Dow Braziel standing on the east side of the room. Before they knew it, Braziel fired two shots at Bud Ballew. The deputy immediately returned fire, emptying his pistol and hitting Braziel six times, leaving Braziel dead on the floor. Bud was then arrested by the Police Chief, taken to the police station, and later transferred to the county jail. However, Chief Segler made a formal statement as to the facts and Bud was released.

Though there were numerous headlines during Ballew's career, it would be the Clara Smith case that would popularize both Buck Garrett and Bud Ballew across the country. On November 21, 1920 Ardmore oil king and potential political power, Jake L. Hamon, stumbled into Hardy Sanitarium with a gunshot wound.

The prominent oil king claimed he had been cleaning a gun when it went off. He died six days later. Despite the fact that the incident had occurred in a very small town north of the Red River, it gained national attention because Hamon was not only a rich oilman, but also a Republican National committeeman and was slated for a post in President Warren Harding's cabinet.

Irregardless of the statement made by Hamon before he died, his secretary and lover, Clara Smith, quickly became a murder suspect. It was alleged from the beginning that she had fired the fatal shot to protect herself from his brutality. However, others said that she shot him because he was going to break off their scandalous love affair. In any case, she was tried for murder in March, 1921. After seven days of testimony, the verdict was given to the Jury on March 17th. After only 39 minutes of deliberation, the jury filed into the court and handed a verdict of not guilty.

Though the trial itself was big news, the reporters also made big news out of Sheriff Buck Garrett and his Deputy Bud Ballew. Feeling as if they had been transported back into the days of the Wild West, they wrote many a story about the two lawmen, which were published throughout the world.

This did not prove well for Deputy Bud Ballew. Although he had long been respected and feared as a lawman, he was far from being heralded by the locals as a hero. Unfortunately, he had a habit of frequently making drunken rides through town, yelling and shooting off his gun. Though no one was ever hurt during his escapades, citizens had grown tired of them, especially in light of the fact that he was supposed to be holding up the law. Unfortunately, the notoriety he earned from the newspaper articles seemed to make him work hard to live up to the Wild West image, and his obnoxious drunken rides increased.

But, his lawman days were almost over. In early 1922, an investigation began against Carter County and Ardmore officials for a number of charges. On February 17, 1922, Buck Garrett was ousted from his office for non-enforcement of the laws and unlawfully releasing prisoners. In support of the sheriff, all of his deputies, including Bud Ballew, resigned that very day. The scandal rocked the city and the county. Three days later, a fistfight broke out at the Carter County Courthouse, which escalated into a shooting spree between three of Garrett's ex-deputies, and two newly appointed officers. When the smoke cleared, no one had been killed, but Bud Ballew had taken a shot in his thigh.

By the first week of May, 1922, Bud had mostly recovered from his leg wound and he and his 18 year-old son went to Wichita Falls, Texas to attend a rodeo. On May 4th, Captain Tom Hickman of the Texas Rangers informed Wichita Falls Chief of Police, J.W. McCormick, that Ballew was in town, drinking, armed, and raising hell. The next day, Ballew was continuing his drunken antics and in the afternoon, the police were called to quell a disturbance at the Denver Domino Parlor. McCormick, along with another officer, arrived at the domino parlor at about 1:30 p.m., where they found Ballew standing at the bar. The two officers approached Ballew, flanking him on each side, and advised him he was under arrest for disturbing the peace. The former deputy responded by saying, "You're out of luck," and when he reached to his side, McCormick fired five shots into him. Ballew was dead before he hit the floor.

Chief McCormick was arrested by a Texas Ranger captain, but, soon made bond and was never prosecuted for the killing. Immediately afterwards, his body was taken to an undertaker and embalmed. In an unusual move for the day, his remains were flown back to Ardmore where mourners, including ex-sheriff Garrett, Bud's wife, Fannie; and his son, Dorris, greeted the plane. His body was then taken to Dr. Herbert Harvey, who made an examination. His results led to several questions including the fact that the shots were made from the back, and at least one came from a different caliber pistol than Chief McCormick's.

Buck Garrett then made the statement: "Bud Ballew was murdered. Five shots and all from the back – he didn't have a chance." Soon, articles like "Noted Killer Of Ardmore Slain By Ex-Ranger," which appeared in the May 6, 1922 issue of the Houston Post, added fuel to the fires of controversy. To this day, questions still exist about Ballew's death.

Upon the deputy's death, it was widely reported in newspapers from the previous "fame" he had achieved. Even the New York Times ran an article. David Monticello "Bud" Ballew is buried in the Lone Grove Cemetery, just outside of Ardmore, Oklahoma.

## Judge Roy Bean

*The Law West of the Pecos*

Judge Roy Bean

Roy Bean was born in Mason County, Kentucky around 1825 to Phantley Roy and Anna Henderson Gore Bean. The youngest of three sons, the Kentucky family was very poor.

At the age of 15, he left Kentucky to follow his two older brothers west. With his brother, Sam, he joined a wagon train into New Mexico, then crossed the Rio Grande River and set up a trading post in Chihuahua, Mexico in 1848.

After killing a local man, Roy fled to San Diego, California where his brother, Joshua, lived.

On February 24, 1852, Bean was in a duel on horseback with a Scotsman named Collins. In the gunfight, Collins was shot in his right arm and both men were arrested for assault with intent to murder. Bean, who was considered brave and handsome by the local women, received numerous visits and gifts during his six-week stay in jail. When one of his admirers slipped him knives hidden in some tamales, Bean used them to dig through the cell wall and escaped on April 17th.

Next, he wound up in San Gabriel, California, where his brother Joshua owned a saloon called the Headquarters. When Joshua was killed in November, 1852, Bean inherited the saloon and began to operate it.

While there, Bean killed a Mexican official during an argument over a woman. Friends of the official soon hauled Bean off, lynched him and left him to die. However, he was saved by the young woman who had been the cause of the dispute. For the rest of his life, he sported a permanent rope burn on his neck, which constantly felt stiff.

Before long, he was back in New Mexico where he again lived with his brother Sam who had become the sheriff in Mesilla.

During the Civil War, the Texas army invaded New Mexico and Bean soon joined them, hauling supplies for the Confederates and living in San Antonio. On October 28, 1866, he married eighteen-year-old Virginia Chavez, but the couple was not happy together. Just a year into the marriage, Bean was arrested for aggravated assault on his wife. However, despite their differences, the couple would eventually have four children. For the next decade, the family lived in a Mexican slum area on South Flores Street in

San Antonio that soon earned the name of Beanville. During these years, he worked at a number of professions including teamster, saloon operator, running a dairy business, and other entrepreneurial enterprises that were obviously not very successful, as he became known for circumventing creditors, business rivals, and the law.

By the early 1880's, Bean and his wife were separated and he sold all his possessions and left San Antonio, wandering about the railroad camps before finally landing in west Texas near the Pecos River. In the early 1880's the Southern Pacific Railroad was working hard to overcome its last obstacle of completing its transcontinental route – crossing the Pecos River. A construction camp formed near the railroad bridge site, which was called Vinegarroon, named for a type of scorpion found in the area, that emits a vinegar-like odor when it is alarmed. The community was founded in 1881, serving as a temporary home for thousands of railroad workers and Roy Bean quickly established a small saloon in the tent city.

On July 5, 1882, Texas Ranger Captain T. L. Oglesby penned a note to his commanding officer General King describing the area:

> Eagle Nest, Pecos County, Texas
> July 5, 1882
>
> Upon my arrival here on June 29th, I proceeded to visit all the railroad camps and scout the country thoroughly. There is the worst lot of roughs, gamblers, robbers, and pick-pocketed, collected here I ever saw, and without the immediate presence of the state troops, this class would prove a great detriment towards the completion of the road.
>
> There is nothing for Rangers to do but hold this rough element in subjection and control them. The majority of the railroad camps are in Pecos County. This immediate section being 200 miles from Fort Stockton, the nearest jurisdiction Court of Justice and the consequent minor offences go unpunished; but, I hope to remedy that in a few days by having a Magistrate appointed for the precinct.

When it became known that a Justice of the Peace was wanted for the area, Roy Bean was quick to volunteer and on August 2, 1882, he became the only "legal authority" in the area. He first operated his "justice" out of his tent saloon in Vinegarroon, Texas another railroad camp to the south of Langtry. With the nearest court 200 miles away at Fort Stockton, he quickly became the self-proclaimed "Only Law West of the Pecos."

An unusual sort of "judge" from the beginning, one of his first judicial acts was to shoot up the saloon of a Jewish competitor. Holding court in his saloon, he utilized a single law book – the 1879 edition of the Revised Statutes of Texas. His methods of justice, carried out in his combination saloon/courtroom, were somewhat odd and always final.

During construction of the bridge at Vinegarroon, a structure collapsed and ten workers fell. Judge Roy Bean was called to the site to hold an inquest. Riding on a mule to the accident, he pronounced all ten men dead; however, only seven of them had actually been killed. When questioned on this point, the judge reasoned that the others would soon die and that he did not want to make the trip twice. Fortunately, for the three men, he was wrong, and they survived to tell the tale.

By December, 1882, railroad construction had ended on the bridge and Vinegarroon was abandoned. Bean then headed northwest to the railroad camp of Eagle Nest (later called Langtry.) There, he quickly set up another tent saloon on railroad land, to the chagrin of Cezario Torres, who owned most of the land beside the railroad right-of-way. He later built a wooden structure for his saloon, which he called the "Jersey Lilly," after the well-known British stage actress Lillie Langtry. Her real last name was actually Emilie Le Breton and she was not related to George Langtry, of whom the town was named. Bean used the saloon as his headquarters and courtroom, and continued his eccentric judicial antics.

On one occasion when the body of a dead cowboy was found in the area, which held $40 and a six-gun, he charged the corpse with carrying a concealed weapon and fined it $40. On another case, when an Irishman named Paddy O'Rourke was going to be tried for shooting a Chinese laborer, a mob of 200 angry Irishmen surrounded the courtroom and threatened to lynch Bean if O'Rourke was not freed. In response, Bean ruled that "homicide was the killing of a human being; however, he could find no law against killing a Chinaman" and the case was dismissed.

Despite the protest of Texas Rangers, Bean thought it preposterous to forbid a man to carry a weapon. One man who was arrested and accused of carrying a concealed weapon was released by Bean with the following logic.

"That charge won't stick," pronounced the judge. "If he was standing still when he was arrested he wasn't carrying weapons because he wasn't going no place. And, if he was not standing still, he was traveling, and it's legal for travelers to carry weapons. Case dismissed."

Jurors for his cases were chosen from his best bar customers and Bean allowed no hung juries or appeals. Because Langtry had no jail, all cases were settled by fines, most of which just happened to be the amount the accused had on his person. Of these fines collected, he was never known to have sent any of the money to the state, but, rather pocketed the cash.

Though later portrayed in Western films and books as a "hanging judge," Bean only sentenced two men to hang, one of which escaped. And, in fact, when it came to horse thieves, who were often sentenced to hang, they would be let go under Judge Roy Bean if they returned the horses, and of course, paid a fine. Bean also made money from granting divorces, which he didn't have the jurisdiction to do, and married numerous couples, always ending the wedding ceremonies with the words, "and may God have mercy on your souls."

Bean was defeated in the election of 1886, but the very next year a new precinct was created after Langtry had become part of Val Verde County and he was appointed once again as the new justice of the peace. He continued to be elected until 1896, when he was finally defeated. However, in typical "Bean" fashion, he refused to surrender his seal and law book and continued to try all cases north of the railroad tracks.

In 1896, Judge Roy Bean made national headlines by setting up a boxing match in Langtry. Because Texas had outlawed boxing, he scheduled the heavyweight fight between Robert James Fitzsimmons and Peter Maher, to be held on a sandbar on Mexico's side of the Rio Grande River, just south of Langtry. Bean then made arrangements for the press, spectators, and Texas Rangers to travel by train from El Paso to Langtry. Fitzsimmons knocked Maher out in 95 seconds, winning the heavyweight title.

For years, he boasted of his "acquaintance with Miss Langtry," telling anyone and everyone that he would one day meet her. When he built a home for himself behind the saloon, he even called it the "Opera House" in anticipation of a visit by the famous actress. Though he never met Lillie Langtry, he often wrote her, and she allegedly wrote him back and sent him two pistols, which he cherished for the rest of his life. He also claimed credit for naming the town after her, even though it was not the case.

As he aged, Bean spent much of his time on his porch with a shotgun in his arms and doing a lot of drinking and boasting. However, he was also known to help the poor in the area.

After a heavy bout of drinking, Bean died in his saloon on March 16, 1903 of lung and heart ailments without ever having met his fantasy woman Lillie Langtry. He was initially buried in Westlawn Cemetery in Del Rio, Texas, but due to the numerous visitors to his grave, he and his son, Samuel, were later re-interred behind the Whitehead Memorial Museum.

Almost a year after his death, Lillie Langtry finally visited his old home. En route from New Orleans to Los Angeles, she stopped to listen to the townspeople tell the stories of Judge Roy Bean. Of the visit, she would later write, "It was a short visit, but, an unforgettable one."

The Jersey Lilly Saloon still stands in Langtry, Texas today, along with his home and a museum.

## Johnny Harris Behan

*First Sheriff of Cochise County, Arizona*

Hailing from Westport (now Kansas City,) Missouri, Behan made his way to California as a young man, working as a freighter and a miner. He later joined the California Column and fought with them at Apache Pass near Fort Bowie, Arizona on July 15, 1862.

Johnny Harris Behan

In 1863, he decided to settle in Arizona and first worked as a freighter at Fort Lowell, then at the Cerro Colorado Mine in Pima County, before moving on to the Prescott area, where he worked in various jobs. While prospecting along the Verde River, he and about five other men were attacked by Indians, but successfully fought them off on February 28, 1866.

That same year, he became the under sheriff of John P. Bourke in Yavapai County, Arizona where he gained a reputation as a brave and honest lawman.

During this time, he also joined with civilian groups in investigating Indian attacks and married Victoria Zaff in 1869. The couple would have two children.

By 1871, he was made the sheriff of Yavapai County, a position he held for two years. In 1873, he was the Prescott representative in the Seventh state assembly. In 1875, he and his wife divorced and Behan moved to Mohave County, where once again he was a state assembly representative, this time for Mohave County in 1879.

When mining in Tombstone began, he moved south and in 1880, became a deputy under Sheriff Charles A. Shibell of Pima County. When Cochise County, which included Tombstone, was organized in 1881, Behan became its first sheriff. Working for him as deputies were Frank Stilwell, William Breakenridge, Harry Woods, W.I. Perry, Bill Soule, H.L. Goodman and others.

Shortly after Behan became sheriff, Virgil Earp became the city marshal of Tombstone and recruited brothers Wyatt and Morgan as "special deputy policemen." The Earps almost immediately came into conflict with the Clantons and the McLaurys, to whom Behan was an advocate. This naturally pitted him against the Earps. Adding further fuel to the fire, was Behan's interest in Josephine Sarah Marcus, who was quickly becoming enamored with Wyatt Earp.

After the gunfight at the O.K. Corral on October 26, 1881, Behan arrested Virgil, Wyatt, and Morgan Earp, as well as Doc Holliday for the murder of Billy Clanton, Tom McLaury and Frank McLaury. However, the judge decided that the Earps and Holliday had been justified in their actions.

In September, 1882, after the Earp Vendetta Ride, Behan had a feud with his own deputy, William Breakenridge, which made him unpopular with Cochise County citizens. At the same time, investigations discovered that Behan had somehow banked some $5,000 during his tenure as sheriff. Where the money came from was never discovered.

In the end, public criticism of Behan resulted in his showing last on the ballot of possible sheriff nominees for his own party, an unusual result for a seated sheriff. Losing the nomination, he was forced out of office in November, 1882. He would never serve as a peace officer again.

In 1888, Behan became the Deputy Superintendent of the Territorial State Prison at Yuma, which prompted former Tombstone resident and writer George Parsons to suggest Behan was on the wrong side of the bars. Later, he served as a U.S. agent in El Paso, Texas, tasked with controlling area smuggling.

John Harrison Behan died of Brights Disease in Tucson on June 7, 1912 and was buried at a now-lost site in Tucson's Holy Hope Cemetery.

## Hamilton Butler Bell

By Frank W. Blackmar in 1912

From thirty to forty years ago the name "Dodge City" was almost a synonym for outlawry of every description. Today [1912] Dodge City is one of the thriving and prosperous towns of southwestern Kansas, a city of peace and order, of good homes, good schools and churches, and a citizenship that for worth and enterprise will equal that of any town of similar size in the state. The transformation and reformation have been accomplished through the efforts of men stout of heart and of noble purpose, who truly desired a better order of things and bent their energies to attain it.

Hamilton Butler Bell

### *Transforming Wicked Dodge City*

Of the work of these men, that of Hamilton B. Bell stands out prominently. He was born July 31, 1853, on a farm in Washington County, Maryland. Death deprived him of a mother the year of his birth and nine years later, or in 1862, his father died, leaving him the youngest of three orphaned children.

For a few years he lived with an uncle at Hagerstown, Maryland, where he received limited educational advantages, and at the age of fourteen went out into the world to make his own way. At Waynesboro, Pennsylvania, he secured employment as a salesman in a jewelry store and remained there five years.

In 1872 he started west, working his way by repairing and cleaning clocks. He reached Lawrence, Kansas in June and from there went to Abilene and then to Ellsworth. July found him at Great Bend. After several months' employment there as a hack driver he gave up that work and engaged in the ice business on his own account. That proved a profitable venture. In September, 1874, he moved to Dodge City and with five teams began to fill a contract he had secured to haul cross ties for the Santa Fe railroad, then being built through to Colorado. This occupied his attention for several months, but in 1875 he returned to Dodge City, where he opened a livery business and conducted it for twenty-four years.

Shortly after his removal to Dodge City his bravery and fearlessness caused him to be made deputy sheriff, in which capacity he served three years. Afterward he was made sheriff and served in that office in the "cowboy" days, when that section was a wild frontier and tried men's souls to live in it. For twelve years he was a deputy United States marshal and for many years was sheriff of Ford County, having been elected to the latter office for twelve years in succession prior to January, 1911. He is a Democrat and each victory was won in a county that is strongly Republican. During his service as sheriff of Ford County he made a great many important captures and arrests of desperate frontier characters—old outlaws who had for years defied arrests—such as cattle thieves, bank and train robbers, etc. He was a terror to these notorious characters, who in the early history of western Kansas reigned in bands in that part of the state and along the border of the old Indian Territory. Dodge City was for many years a rendezvous for this undesirable element, and to Mr. Bell's tact and ability as an officer is largely due the credit for eradicating the "bad men" in that section.

He made Dodge City be good and is now esteemed by all for his good work in this direction. Unlike many men who occupied the office of sheriff in those "wild days," Mr. Bell was never accused of shooting a man or of using drastic means in effecting an arrest.

Today he remains a link connecting the old order with the new, well and popularly known from the Rio Grande in Texas to the British possessions among cattlemen and cowboys as "Ham" Bell, respected by them as a fearless officer, and by all as a public-spirited citizen.

When the government abandoned Fort Dodge as a military post, there was a lack of decision among the people as to the best use to be made of the grounds and buildings. It was Mr. Bell who originated the idea of converting the place into a State Soldiers' Home. He broached the project to John McEvalla and Captain Howard, old soldiers of Dodge City, who secured a favorable resolution from their Grand Army Post.

He has always manifested a great regard and kindness for the old veterans of the Civil War, and was not only the means of securing the State Soldiers' Home at Fort Dodge, but when the district reunion of soldiers was held there Mr. Bell, almost wholly alone, secured and collected about $1,000 to defray expenses, besides which he contributed largely of his own means to their entertainment and comfort. It was through his efforts that the reunion was held there.

In 1910 he was appointed chief of police of Dodge City. That same year he erected one of the most modern automobile garages in Kansas, and has a large and well equipped auto livery, with an elegantly furnished ladies' rest room, one of the few of its kind in the West and a haven for auto tourists to Colorado.

Mr. Bell is a member of the American Auto Association and of the Touring Club of America. The penniless boy of forty-four years ago is today a wealthy man. He has made it in Kansas, by brawn, brain and intelligent and industrious effort. Besides his garage he has an 8,000-acre ranch near Dodge City, where he raises horses and is extensively engaged in the cattle business.

Mr. Bell was married on August 1, 1874, to Miss Josephine Dugan, a daughter of James Dugan, a farmer of Barber County, Kansas. To this union was born one son, Hamilton B. Bell, Jr., born November 22, 1876, who is now a traveling salesman, with headquarters at Salt Lake City, Utah. Mrs. Bell died on October 7, 1900. Mr. Bell is a Knight Templar Mason, a Noble of the Mystic Shrine, and a member of the Benevolent and Protective Order of Elks. During the thirty-five years or more of his residence at Dodge City no citizen has been more closely identified with its upbuilding and with the development of southwestern Kansas than has Mr. Bell. Generous to a fault, he has both made and spent fortunes, but he still remains an active and energetic business man, wealthy, popular, and occupying an enviable position in the love and esteem of his fellow citizens.

*Note*: After this 1912 account, Hamilton Bell continued to live in Dodge City until his death in 1947. He was the longest living Old West Sheriff and Marshal in the history of the American West and outlived all his Western associates. Living in lawless Dodge City during its boisterous cattle days, he was acquainted and or friends with such men as Wyatt Earp, Doc Holliday, Luke Short, Bat Masterson and numerous other colorful characters of the Old West. The rigid, stand-up lawman who seldom drew his guns and never shot a man during his 30 years of law enforcement, arrested more outlaws, with a warrant, than any other lawman in the West. He retired about 1911 and, at the age of ninety, was operating a pet shop in Dodge City, selling canaries, his favorite bird.

## George Bravin

*Tombstone's British Marshal*

George Bravin was born in Devon, England in March, 1860, the 13th child of Richard and Catherine Bravin. His father died when he was three years old. By the time he was just nine years old, he was dependent upon his own resources and worked at a number of jobs.

When he was 18, he immigrated to the United States and began to roam the West. He first settled in Cripple Creek, Colorado, where he worked as a miner for a time before moving southwest to Tombstone, Arizona in 1882.

Once again, he was employed in the mines of Tombstone until 1888, when he was almost asphyxiated in one of the mines. That same year, he married a 19 year-old local girl named Mary Ellen Butler, who just happened to be the daughter of another British immigrant. The couple would eventually have ten children. For a couple of years, Bravin ran a livery barn and invested his money wisely into a number of mining claims.

In 1891, Bravin, who had a friendly disposition which earned him many friends in Tombstone, was elected county assessor and also purchased the Arcade Saloon on Allen Street. Three years later, in 1894, though he certainly didn't look the part of a lawman, but rather, more like a schoolmaster, he took the position of deputy sheriff. Working hard at the position, he quickly gained the respect of the locals.

The following year, on September 25, 1895, he was appointed as a U.S. Deputy Marshal and in 1896 was working as the first elected constable in Pearce, Arizona. Though the new mining camp, east over the Dragoon Mountains, was never as tough as Tombstone, Bravin was determined that it wouldn't be. He soon hired a tough deputy to work with him – Burton Alvord. At this time, Alvord had not yet turned to his lawless ways and had a reputation as solid lawman. However, just six months later, Bravin decided that there was no longer a need for the tough deputy and let him go. Little did he know that the two would meet again under far different circumstances.

Alvord then moved on to Willcox, where he worked as a deputy constable once again and gained a reputation as both a killer and an alcoholic. But, Alvord would change his ways by the turn of the century, partnering up with Billy Stiles and forming the Alvord-Stiles Gang, who began by rustling cattle but soon advanced to robbing trains.

In the meantime, Bravin returned to being a lawman in Tombstone. In 1900, the Alvord-Stiles Gang attempted to rob a Fairbank train, but instead, ran into tough lawman Jeff Milton. Alvord was arrested and taken to the Cochise County Jail, where he came face to face with his former boss, George Bravin.

On April 7, 1900, as Bravin had some 25 prisoners housed in his jail, Billy Stiles went to visit Alvord and other gang members who were in the jail. He then held a gun to Bravin demanding the release of all of the prisoners and ended up shooting the lawman taking off two of his toes. The prisoners, including Alvord, then escaped.

Bravin continued his duties as a lawman and on June 20, 1908 was involved in a gunfight with a Mexican man named Marcello Mendez. When the shooter blasted a local woman three times, the shots brought Bravin and another constable named Kelly running. Searching for the shootist, they found him hiding under the bed and as the lawmen crouched down, the shots rang out again. Though the men received only powder burns, Mendez was hit in the head and the heart. The woman who had been shot survived.

For the next nine years, Bravin continued to serve as a Tombstone lawman until at the age of 55, in 1917, he became ill and entered the hospital in Douglas. He never recovered and died at his daughter's home in Douglas on October 21, 1918. His body was returned to Tombstone where his funeral was one of the largest ever held. He was buried at the Tombstone Cemetery (not Boot Hill.)

## William Milton Breakenridge

*Lawman, Surveyor & Author*

Known as one of the most courteous and modest peace officers who ever worked in the lawless town of Tombstone, Breakenridge however, was not to be trifled with. Born on December 26, 1846 in Watertown, Wisconsin, he traveled to the Pike's Peak mining area when he was just 15. Three years later, in 1864, he joined Company B of the Third Colorado Cavalry for service in the Civil War, where he fought in the Battle of Sand Creek, as well as several other skirmishes.

Around 1876, he headed for Arizona Territory, ending up in Tombstone by 1880. There, he went to work for Sheriff Johnny Behan. That same year, he was also appointed as a U.S. Deputy Marshal, a position he would hold until 1889. This designation gave him more authority than what was allowed by Cochise County, helping him to become one of Tombstone's most effective lawmen.

William M. Breakenridge

Though he put several outlaws in the Boot Hill cemetery, Breakenridge used a gun only as a last resort. But, when necessary, use it he would, in a fast and accurate manner. Before long, his skills with a gun earned him a reputation as a lethal gunfighter and few outlaws even challenged him.

He was present in Tombstone during the famous Gunfight at the O.K. Corral. He was said to have been on friendly terms with the Clanton faction, and of course, working under Johnny Behan, is generally perceived to have sided with those opposing the Earps. Many years later, when he wrote his memoirs, he would say that Wyatt Earp was a desperate character.

Though many outlaws would not challenge him, this would not be the case on March 26, 1882. The night before, two men by the names of Zwing Hunt and Billy Grounds, attempted to rob the Tombstone Mining and Milling Company in Charleston, Arizona.

After being challenged, they shot and killed a man before panicking and taking off without a dime. Before long, Breakenridge deputized three men to ride with him in a posse and they began to track the two killers. Finding them at the Jack Chandler Ranch near Tombstone, a gunfight ensued. Though it lasted only seconds, when the smoke cleared, Breakenridge had killed Billy Grounds and Zwing Hunt had been wounded. Unfortunately, one of the deputized men, John Gillespie, was also dead. The other two posse members were wounded but would recover. Outlaw Zwing Hunt would also recover and escaped, but was killed by Apache Indians a short time later.

In 1888, Breakenridge changed tactics completely, accepting a position as a surveyor for Maricopa County. In this capacity, he was soon tasked with surveying the Salt River for potential dam sites. After examining several sites, he returned with a party from Phoenix in July, 1889, which included James McClintock, William J. Murphy, and John R. Norton to examine the sites Breakenridge recommended and conduct a feasibility study. Traveling on horseback it took the men a week to reach Box Canyon, near the confluence of Tonto Creek and the Salt River. Breakenridge insisted that this would be the best place for a dam and he was right. Though it would be more than a decade later before construction would start in September, 1906, Breakenridge had accurately predicted the perfect site of what is now Roosevelt Dam, completed in 1911.

Later, James McClintock would become one of Arizona's official historians, writing the three volume book series, *Arizona: The Youngest State*.

Breakenridge would eventually return to "looking after the peace," when he accepted a position as a detective with the Southern Pacific Railroad

In 1895, the railroad had been held up or attempted to be robbed several times by outlaws, Grant Wheeler and Joe George. Breakenridge, along with a posse, wasted no time tracking the men and trailed Wheeler into Colorado, near Mancos on April 25th. The next morning the outlaw was surrounded and briefly resisted with a few shots from his gun, but sure that he would be taken to jail or killed, Wheeler chose instead, to take his own life.

When the ex-lawman was in his seventies, he began to write his memoirs which includes the lawless days in Tombstone, the Gunfight at the O.K. Corral, numerous accounts with outlaws and Indians, and his days working for the railroad. In 1928, his book, *Helldorado: Bringing the Law to the Mesquite*, was published. Three years later, the Arizona pioneer and lawman would die in Tucson, Arizona on January 31, 1931. Before his death, he said he would gladly do it all again.

## Jack L. Bridges

*Kansas Lawman*

Born in Maine in 1838, Bridges moved westward where he landed in Kansas City. There he served as a lawman for 15 years before becoming a U.S. Deputy Marshal in 1869. Working under U.S. Marshals, Dana Houston and William S. Tough, out of the Wichita, Kansas Court, he was first assigned to Hays City, Kansas.

Since Bridges worked the western part of Kansas, he was often called to work with the Cavalry at Fort Supply, Oklahoma curtailing Indian attacks on white settlers and arresting Indians who had violated laws. In this capacity, he often worked with famed frontier marshal, U.S. Deputy Ben Williams, who was respected among the Comanche, Cheyenne and Arapaho tribes.

Jack L. Bridges

A few years later, he was sent to Wichita, where he became involved in one of the most serious altercations of his life. On February 28, 1871, Bridges got the opportunity to arrest an infamous train robber, horse thief, and murderer by the name of J.E. Ledford. The U.S. Deputy Marshal harbored a deep resentment against Ledford for having pistol-whipped him some months earlier and looked forward to taking his "revenge." Taking no chances, Bridges rounded up some 25 soldiers of the Sixth United States Cavalry to accompany him on the arrest. The men approached the Harris House Hotel, where Ledford was the proprietor, but were told he was not on the premises. They then scouted the area, seeing a man run into an outhouse behind the hotel. Bridges, a cavalry scout named Lew Stewart, and Lieutenant Hargis were approaching the outhouse when Ledford came charging out with his pistol blazing. He shot Bridges, but the men emptied their guns into him, hitting him four times. Ledford died a few hours later.

Severely wounded, Bridges returned to his birthplace in Maine to recuperate from his wounds. Once he was healed, he headed west again, first to Colorado and then back to Kansas, where he settled in Dodge City. On July 8, 1882, he became the city marshal and a few days later the Dodge City Times commented on his appointment:

"Jack Bridges was installed as City Marshal on Saturday last. Marshal Bridges was for a number of years Deputy U. S. Marshal in Western Kansas. He is a cool, brave and determined officer, and will make an excellent city marshal. Jack's friends speak highly of him and of his integrity and bravery. He has done some fine service for the government, and upon every occasion, has acquitted himself with honor. He is a pleasant man socially, and has courage for any occasion."

In the wicked little town of Dodge City, Bridges had a number of altercations with hard case cowboys, and in the spring of 1883, found himself caught in the middle of the "Dodge City War." As city marshal, he was directly responsible to Mayor L. E. Deger who was one of the protagonists in the affair. However, Bridges declared that he was "as much the marshal for one party as the other" and though he did his duty as city marshal, he did not take sides in the bloodless battle between the Dodge City Peace Commission and City Administrators.

When Bill Tilghman replaced Bridges as marshal of Dodge City in 1884, Bridges left town. He was later known to have lived in Blasedell, Arizona, where his son was shot dead. He then moved on to Texas. He died in 1915 and was buried in Briggs Estate in Barstow, Texas.

## William "Billy" L. Brooks, aka: Buffalo Bill

*Lawman and Horse Thief*

Born in Ohio about 1832, Brooks moved westward where he grew up and became such a successful buffalo hunter, that he earned the nickname of "Buffalo Bill," which has often gotten him confused with the more famous William "Buffalo Bill" Cody, or the original Kansas buffalo hunter, William "Buffalo Bill" Mathewson, who had been called such as early as the 1860's.

William "Billy" L. Brooks

At the same time, he was gaining a reputation as a gunfighter and by 1870 was working as a stage driver for the Southwestern Stage Company between Wichita, Kansas and Fort Sill, Oklahoma. Later, he began to drive the stage to the wild cattle town of Newton, Kansas, where he was made the city marshal in 1872 at a salary of $75 per month. In June of that year, several Texas cowboys were having a drunken spree at a local dance hall when Brooks ran them out of town. However, the cowboys turned on him as they were leaving and fired three shots into him, hitting him once near his collar bone and twice in his limbs. The fearless Brooks; however, continued to pursue the cowboys for about ten miles, before finally returning to Newton, to have his wounds looked after.

Brooks recovered from the gunshots, which were obviously minor, resigned his position as city marshal and next appeared in Dodge City, Kansas in early 1873, where he again worked as a lawman. Though in his first year, he cleared many of the town's seedier elements, it was also felt that he was too quick on the trigger. In his first month alone, it is said that he was involved in 15 gunfights. In one instance, he was said to have killed four men who were looking to take revenge on Brooks after he had killed their brother. However; Brooks killed all four instead. Before long, Dodge City officials began to wonder about several men who had been killed in questionable circumstances, including a man Brooks killed in an argument over a local dance hall girl. After backing down from gunfighter Kirk Jordan, Brooks left the position and returned to his old job as a stage driver for the Southwestern Stage Company.

However, in early 1874, the stage company lost their mail contract to a rival company and Brooks lost his job. In June, several mules and horses owned by the rival company were stolen, allegedly by Brooks and several other men in an attempt to weaken the rival company and get their jobs back. The following month; however, Brooks and two other men, by the names of L.B. Hasbrouck and Charlie Smith, were arrested and jailed to await trial near Caldwell, Kansas. They would not get their day in court. On July 29th, a lynch mob stormed the jail and Brooks and the other two men were taken to a large tree to be hanged. Despite their pleas for mercy and a fair trial, all three were hanged. Reportedly, Brooks struggled violently after the rope failed to break his neck and strangled to death.

## Henry Newton Brown

*Outlaw Marshal of Kansas*

Born in 1857, Henry Newton Brown was orphaned at an early age and raised by relatives in Rolla, Missouri. When he was seventeen, he headed west to become a cowboy, working on Colorado ranches before drifting south to Texas. There, he killed another cowhand in a gunfight outside a Texas panhandle town and moved on to Lincoln County, New Mexico, where he soon became involved in the Lincoln County War. Fighting on the side of the McSween-Turnstall faction, known as the "Regulators," he befriended Billy the Kid.

Henry Newton Brown

He rode with Billy the Kid's Gang, rustling cattle, and continued on with the gang when they went to the Texas Panhandle in 1878 to steal horses.

When the Kid returned to New Mexico, Brown decided to stay in Texas, which probably saved his life for a few more years.

He then took a job working as a deputy sheriff in Oldham County, Texas, but was soon fired for picking fights with drunks. He then moved on to Oklahoma, where he worked on several ranches before making his final move to Caldwell, Kansas.

In 1882, he was hired as an assistant marshal in Caldwell and later was promoted to marshal. Brown hired his friend Ben Wheeler, aka: Ben Robertson, to work as a deputy and the two men "cleaned up" the tough town quickly. When Brown felled two outlaws in the streets of Caldwell in 1883, the Caldwell Post bragged that Brown was "one of the quickest men on the trigger in the Southwest." So taken were the town citizens, that they presented him with a new, engraved Winchester rifle.

The marshal continued to serve the city well and the Caldwell Commercial lauded him as "cool, courageous and gentlemanly, and free from vices." In early spring of 1884 he married a local woman, purchased a house and furnishings, and seemingly settled down. However, unbeknownst to his wife and the citizens of Caldwell, Brown had been living beyond his means and the debts were mounting.

Falling back on his old outlaw skills, Brown, along with his deputy, Ben Wheeler, and two other former outlaw friends named William Smith and John Wesley, planned to rob the bank in Medicine Lodge, Kansas. The lawmen, under the ruse of traveling to Oklahoma to apprehend a murderer, left Caldwell, met up with the two other would-be bank robbers, and headed to Medicine Lodge. On April 30, 1884, they entered the bank just after it opened and demanded the cash. When Bank President E.W. Payne reached for his gun, Brown shot him to death. Though Chief Cashier George Geppert had his hands up, he too was shot. However, before he died he staggered to the vault and managed to close the door.

Their robbery attempt failed, the gang quickly mounted their horses and fled with an angry posse right behind them. Just outside of town the posse trapped them in a box canyon and after a two hour shoot-out, the outlaws finally surrendered. Taken to the Medicine Lodge jail, a mob outside chanted "Hang them! Hang them!"

The outlaws were given a meal, their photo taken, and told to write letters to their families.

At about 9:00 p.m. the mob broke into the jail, demanding the prisoners. The sheriff refused but was overpowered by the mob of men and the jail doors opened. As the prisoners attempted to dash for freedom, Brown was shot and killed, his body riddled with bullets. Wheeler was also wounded but was dragged along with Wesley and Smith to a nearby elm tree and hanged.

## Seth Bullock

*Finest Type of Frontiersman*

Seth Bullock was born in Amherstburg, Ontario, Canada on July 23, 1849 to George Bullock, a retired British Major, and his Scottish wife, Agnes Findley Bullock. By the time Seth was five, the family had moved to Sandwich, Ontario when his father became involved in politics.

Little is known of his boyhood, except that he was frequently at odds with his father's strict discipline. No doubt, his father's military like attitudes concerning politics, discipline, and other view points ultimately led to Seth's personal "code of honor." At the age of 16, Seth ran away from home, ending up in Montana where his older sister lived. However, she quickly sent him home to his parents.

Seth Bullock

Not to be deterred for long, as soon as Seth was 18 he left home for good. By the time he was twenty, he was back in Montana, arriving in Helena in 1867. Following in his father's political footsteps, he ran for the Territorial Legislature, but was defeated. However, he did manage to get himself elected as a member of the Territorial Senate, where he served for two years in 1871-1872. During this time, Bullock was instrumental in creating the first ever United States National Park – Yellowstone.

After serving on the Montana Territorial Senate, Bullock was elected Sheriff of Lewis and Clark County in 1873. Quickly making his presence known, he not only acted as a lawman, but also as an auctioneer and entrepreneur, entering into a hardware business with Sol Star. In 1874, Bullock married his childhood sweetheart, Martha Eccles in Salt Lake City, Utah. But when the hardware partners saw a better opportunity in Deadwood, South Dakota, he sent his wife and newborn baby girl back to the security of her family home in Michigan.

Arriving in Deadwood on August 1, 1876, in wagons filled with hardware goods, including picks, pans, shovels, dynamite, cooking utensils, and more, Seth and Sol immediately set up their hardware store in a tent. Later, the entrepreneurial pair bought a lot and built a false front building to house their business, advertising furniture, wall paper, lamps, and hardware.

By the time they arrived, Deadwood had already gained a reputation as a hell-raising camp, filled with miners, transients, gamblers, outlaws and prostitutes. The day after their arrival, Wild Bill Hickok was shot by the coward Jack McCall. Outraged, the camp began to demand law enforcement in the ungoverned territory.

Though it is commonly thought that Bullock served as Deadwood's first marshal, that is incorrect. Actually, the camp's first marshal was a man named Isaac Brown who was elected by the Miner's Court after the trial of Jack McCall on August 5, 1876. However, when Isaac Brown, along with the Reverend Smith, and two other men named Charles Mason and Charles Holland were traveling between Crook City and Deadwood, they were ambushed and killed on August 20th. Leaving an open position, the miner's court soon met again, this time electing Con Stapleton as the new sheriff.

However, in March, 1877, Seth Bullock was appointed by Governor Pennington as the Lawrence County Sheriff.

Undaunted by the county's lawless and dangerous nature, he wasted no time appointing several fearless deputies to help him "clean up" the town. Before long, order had been established in the former hell-raising camp.

Bullock never killed a man while serving as the Lawrence County Sheriff. According to his grandson, he could "outstare a mad cobra or a rogue elephant" which was generally enough to convince the rowdy elements to settle down before any violence ever took place.

With Deadwood becoming more stable, Bullock sent for his family. Seth's wife Martha soon became a pillar of the community. With Seth having more time on his hands, he spent much of it ranching and raising horses on a section of land he and Sol had purchased at the divergence of the Belle Fourche River and Redwater Creek. Bullock also dabbled in mining and politics while continuing to serve as Deputy United States Marshal.

In 1884 while bringing a horse thief named Crazy Steve into Deadwood for trial, Bullock encountered Theodore Roosevelt for the first time. Roosevelt was then the Deputy Sheriff from Medora, North Dakota, and the two shared coffee and beans over the tailgate of a chuck wagon on the rangelands near Belle Fourche. The pair quickly formed a friendship that would last through Bullock's lifetime.

In the late 1880s Bullock persuaded the Fremont, Elkhorn and Missouri Valley Railroad to build across the ranch, free of charge. Located three miles northwest of the town of Minnesela, the railroad arrived in 1890, and Seth founded the town of Belle Fourche. Bullock and Star offered free lots for any building moved from the town of Minnesela and the new settlement soon took over the county seat. Belle Fourche would later become the largest livestock shipping point in the United States.

In 1894, the hardware store in Deadwood was struck by fire and Bullock decided to build Deadwood's first hotel over the original store and warehouse. At a cost of $40,000, the three-story, 64 room hotel boasted steam heat and a bathroom on each floor. Completed in 1896, the Bullock Hotel quickly became the most sought after luxury hotel of its time. This historic hotel still stands today, continuing to provide lodging as well as a 24-hour casino.

When the Spanish-American War broke out in 1898, Bullock volunteered as one of Roosevelt's Rough Riders and was named a Captain of Troop A in Grigsby's Cowboy Regiment. However, the outfit never saw combat as they sat out the short war in a Louisiana training camp. After his short stint in the war, Bullock was from thereon referred to as "Captain."

When Theodore Roosevelt was elected president, Bullock organized a group of 50 cowboys, including Tom Mix, to ride in the President's inaugural parade in 1905. Later that year, Roosevelt appointed Seth Bullock as the United States Marshal for South Dakota, a position he held for the next nine years.

When Roosevelt died in January, 1919, it was a terrible blow to Bullock. Soon he enlisted the help of the Society of Black Hills Pioneers and erected a monument to the deceased president. Dedicated July 4, 1919 it was the first monument to the president erected in the country.

Just a few months later, Seth Bullock died of cancer on September 23, 1919 at his ranch near Belle Fourche. He was buried in Mount Moriah Cemetery along with several other colorful characters of Deadwood's past including Wild Bill Hickok and Calamity Jane. The gravesite once faced toward Mount Roosevelt across the gulch, but the view is now obscured by a half-century growth of ponderosa pines.

## Rufus "Rufe" Cannon

*Important African-American U.S. Deputy Marshal*

U.S. Deputy Marshal commissioned on September 15, 1892 in the Western District at Fort Smith, Arkansas serving under Marshal Jacob Yoes. Cannon was one of the most important black lawmen of the Oklahoma territorial era. Though not as well known as other African-American peace officers in Oklahoma, such as Bass Reeves and Grant Johnson, he was notable for participating in the capture of several notorious outlaws. Cannon was of both Cherokee and African-American descent and was familiar with many of the Cherokee native customs and the language, which helped him greatly in his position. One of Cannon's first notable captures was the arrest of the notorious African Creek outlaw Captain Willie, who had murdered Oklahoma City U.S. Deputy Marshal George Thornton in 1891.

Rufe was riding with fellow U.S. Deputy Marshal Ike Rogers in January, 1893, when they encountered Jesse Jackson, Henry Starr and George "Slaughter Kid" Newcomb near Bartlesville, Oklahoma. The outlaws resisted arrest and in no time, a gun battle ensued, in which more than 100 rounds were fired. Cannon shot Jesse Jackson in the side and right arm. The wounded Jackson surrendered but Henry Starr and George Newcomb escaped.

In 1895, Cannon arrested William Christian of the Christian outlaw gang, but unfortunately Christian was able to later escape, fleeing to Arizona and continuing his life of crime.

Cannon was with the posse led by Heck Thomas that tracked down and killed Bill Doolin on August 24, 1896. Though some accounts actually say that Cannon was the one who shot Bill Doolin, Thomas got the credit for it. Interestingly; however, all the posse men were rewarded for Doolin's demise, except for Cannon. It is not known why Cannon was not paid, but it is believed that Heck Thomas shared part of his reward with Cannon.

Later, Cannon left the Fort Smith region and moved to Kansas City where he lived to be 105 years old.

## William "Bill" H. Carr

*Heroic Deputy or Outlaw?*

U.S. Deputy Marshal commissioned in the Western District court at Fort Smith, Arkansas in 1887. He was later commissioned in the Southern District of Indian Territory at Paris, Texas and in the Kansas District Court at Wichita. In April, 1889, he arrested Harris Austin, a Chickasaw Indian charged with murder. When Austin resisted arrest, gunplay erupted and the outlaw was wounded three times. He would be hanged at Fort Smith, Arkansas the following year.

Later that year, in August, Carr confronted a gang of whiskey runners crossing the Red River Bridge into Indian Territory. The outlaws quickly turned around escaping back into Texas. However, one of them who was left behind, a man named Lewis Jackson, was shot and killed by Carr.

In 1892, Carr, along with three other previously commissioned deputy marshals, were arrested and charged with arson and murder for a fire in Lexington, Indian Territory where a man had lost his life. However, Carr was evidently cleared of the charges, as he was back in action in April, 1894, when he and Marshal Evitt Nix confronted the Doolin-Dalton Gang near the Sacred Heart Mission in the Pottawatomie Reservation. When a gun battle erupted, Bill Dalton, and George "Bitter Creek" Newcomb were badly wounded, but able to escape. Carr was also shot three times and left for dead by the outlaws, but he survived. By this time, Carr had become so well known, he was called "King of the Chickasaws" by the New York Times, who ran a feature article on his deeds of daring in April, 1895 (see article below).

Though Carr had a solid reputation as a U.S. Deputy Marshal, he was also allegedly friends with outlaws, Will and Bob Christian. When the Christians, along with several other outlaws, broke out of jail in Oklahoma City in June, 1895, killing Chief of Police, Milt Jones and wounding the jailer and two innocent bystanders, Carr would soon be implicated in assisting the outlaws with their escape. Though the vast majority of lawmen who were acquainted with Carr felt Oklahoma County Sheriff C. H. Deford made the charges against Carr in an attempt to clear his office of any negligence, Carr would later be arrested anyway.

In the meantime, he continued to serve as a U.S. Deputy Marshal as on October 17, 1895, he arrested four murderers, who were wanted for the murder of John Swilling near Tecumseh, Indian Territory.

As the investigation into the escape of the Christian brothers continued, some of Carr's friends attempted to get him out of the country. However, Carr was eventually indicted by a Grand Jury for assisting the outlaws. The lawman then raised the $14,000 bond by selling his property and personal possessions. Then, for reasons unknown, he skipped his bond and was "officially" never heard from again. Some speculated that he went to Texas while others thought he remained in Indian Territory.

The newspapers of the day then tried to link Carr with a number of wanted fugitives. In 1896, the Beaver County, Oklahoma Territory newspaper reported that Carr was with Bill Doolin when Doolin attempted to make terms with lawmen and give himself up. Later that year, the Guthrie Daily Leader reported: "while playing with an old revolver, the 5 year old son of Bill Carr, the noted outlaw, shot himself through the stomach, dying in a short time."

In the meantime, another man named John Reeves, with the help of a woman, was charged with secreting the guns to the Christian Gang which allowed them to escape and was sentenced to the Kansas penitentiary on December 21, 1896. However, William Carr was still a wanted man.

The last report of his existence was on June 1, 1900 when the Tecumseh Republican reported that a man who was called Dad Feagin had visited Bill Carr, who was using an alias of "Bill Evans," about 65 miles east of Shawnee, Oklahoma. Feagin also said that Carr was in the presence of a former deputy marshal named George Elkins. He further added that Carr had been hiding out with the Christian brothers in southwest Texas prior to returning to Oklahoma.

After this unsubstantiated statement, nothing more was ever heard about William Carr.

### ***New York Times Article***

New York Times, April 20, 1895 - King of the Chickasaws - "Fighting Bill Carr" and His Many Deeds of Daring

Wichita, Kansas, April 29, 1895 - The man who goes down into the Chickasaw Indian country and says he never heard of "Fighting Bill" Carr is considered the greenest king of tenderfoot.

"A man who don't know Carr should not be permitted to live in the Territory," Rowdy Kate Daniels used to say while holding court in the Red Light Saloon in Purcell, [Oklahoma,] in 1889.

"Never heard of Bill Carr?" says Jim Davis, who has been in the country "since their days of Sam Bass." "Wal, stranger, you'd better git acquainted with him. Jist now he's laying up at the Clifton House nursing a sore arm. One uv ther Rogers gang shot him last week.

"Who is Bill? He's a double-distilled rattler, a bunch of catmounts, a whole herd of Texas longhorns, and a grizzly bear all tied together with chain lightning. By profession he's a Deputy Marshal in this yer district, and he's a killer from way up near the head waters of Bitter Creek.

"You can jest yell that he is a daisy," continued the old man. "Bill civilized this heathen country. He's the chap who made angels of the Franklins and Washingtons and Christianized the Indians, and he dun it with cold lead, the only simon-pure religion of any use on the border."

"Is he the man they call the King of the Chickasaw Nation?" asked an interested tenderfoot, while the gang strolled up and took a drink of chain lightning.

Carr, the officer in question, is a handsome Pennsylvanian with a record as a Deputy Marshal that is little short of miraculous. The story, as stated by old man Davis, would appear, in the vernacular of the border, "durned fishy" were it not backed up by the testimony of United States Marshals Nix and Walker.

"Billy Carr came here before the Oklahoma boom" resumed Davis reflectively, as he shot a mouthful of saliva at a crack in the floor. "Yep! I believe he's called the King of the Chickasaw country. He first came into notice on the 4th of July in 1887. Down there in the bottom a lot of sharks were fleecing suckers. A pretty girl was in one of the crowds trying to induce her foot brother to quit a brace game, but the grinning sharp only gave her the laugh and joked the fool boy into playing until all his money was gone.

"Then he insultingly ordered them to 'clear out and let him alone.' the girl cried bitterly over her brother's losses and the tough gang stood about and laughed. Nobody knowed Bill Carr them days, and so he didn't cut much figger. The man who had robbed the boy was 'Coyote Dave,' and he had killed a man or two, and had a private graveyard down in No Man's Land. Well, Bill, he sorter stood 'round awhile after the pretty girl and her brother had left, and then he began to play. 'Coyote Dave' won some his money and when Carr accused him of cheating, he said:

"''Course I did, tender. W'at you going to do about it, hey?'

"The camp turned out an' buried Dave next day," and here the old-timer's face took on a contented frown, as his mind traveled back to that delightful occasion.

"Yes, Billy put three holes in David's carcass inside a second, and as he walked away I heard him say, 'That's for that pretty girl with blue eyes; durn his ugly picture.'

"Well, a day or two after this a wild and woolly chap from the Brazos country plugged a hole through our City Marshal and then skipped out for Oklahoma. There wasn't any one to foller him, and no one wanted the job of Marshal till Bill Carr said he'd take it if he could have an assistant, and he chose Joe McNally. (Poor Joe was killed by Sheriff Throttler at Fort Smith a month or so ago.) while Joe held down the town Bill Carr mounted his horse and chased the murderer down to where Oklahoma City now stands. The skunk turned on Bill, and there was another killing. A durned fool United States Marshal arrested Carr and took him to Wichita for trial, but he beat the case, and when he came back to the Territory the boys lynched 'Horse Thief Johnny," a witness agin Bill, just to show their goodwill. Bill said he'd a-knowed their hearts was all right without this proof, but he couldn't bring Johnny back to life, so he helped plant him.

"Bill and Joe had their prison about three miles out of town, in the hills. They dug a hole back into a bank and staked their prisoners out in a pen till they had a load for Fort Smith. They made a camp up on a hill where they could overlook this pen, and if any of them durned murderers, horse thieves, whisky peddlers, or outlaws generally thought they could skip out, they were usually brought to their senses with a bullet in their carcasses.

"About this time Harris Austin, a full-blooded Chickasaw Indian who had been killing people worse than the Bender family for about ten years, did some new devilment, and the Fort Smith officers wanted him captured. The old heathen had the whole country 'buffaloed' except Bill Carr, and some of the boys said he didn't have sense enough to know when he was a fool. So Bill he got on his old sorrel pony and rode out to this Indian's lair in the mountains. He laid for him at daylight, and when the old red man came out to the spring for water Bill popped out and tried to arrest him, but the chief wouldn't have it that way and slid behind a tree. Bill and him banged away at one another from under cover for about an hour, and then Bill put three bullets into the old rascal. That night he landed him into town across his horse's back. The Indian recovered, and was afterward hung at Fort Smith.

"But the very worst fight Billy ever had was with the Franklins and Washingtons. They was nigger hoss thieves, and lived in a cabin back in the hills. When Bill went after them he took a posse along, and when they reached the cabin a posse man, a personal friend of Bill's, rode up and pounded on the door. Then those heathen niggers just opened a crack and stuck out their guns and killed that posse man. Bill vowed then and there that he would kill every one of them for murdering his pard. So he set fire to the woods back of the house, and when those heathens came running out with their guns in their hands he shot them all down. There were five in the party. Three he killed and two were taken to Fort Smith and hanged.

"Whisky peddling was one of the tough crimes about now, and a gang of outlaws along the Red River district took to sending in their red liquor by the gallon. You see, the boys rather liked the poison, and didn't think the traffic ought to be curtailed by law, so that when Bill started in to stop the supply the boys were agin it. One night Bill corralled three members of a gang of smugglers near Dennison, [Texas.] They were Lewis Jackson, his brother, and Walter Keene, a full-blood Injun. Together with a Sheriff's posse Carr sat down to watch a bridge. About dark the posse went to supper, and Bill just staid on guard. While his friends were gone them chaps sneaked across the bridge, and when Carr halted them they began to shoot. Talking about hell a popping wasn't in it. When the Sheriff heard the firing and run back they found Bill wounded and two of the gang dead. The next day they followed a trail of blood and run into Lewis Jackson's body in a cave.

"As Carr was returning to Purcell, [Oklahoma] he was thrown from his horse and had a leg broken. He was carried into a ranch house, and who do you think he found there?" and Jim glanced eagerly into the faces of his interested audience. "Why the girl whose brother had been plucked by 'Coyote Dave." When Bill's leg got well his heart was gone to the girl, and he married her soon after. All the boys turned out to Bill's wedding, and after it was over he rode out to his ranch with his bride. While they were riding along in that moonlight one heathen coyote that had it in for Bill tried to shoot him, and they had a running fight, but Bill was too much for him, and Cherokee Ned was buried next day. Some of the boys found him along down the trail with a bullet between his cross eyes.

"After Bill had been spliced a while and had been shot two or three times, his better half got him to quit and go down to Violet Springs, Oklahoma and buy a grocery. The idea of Bill Carr a-selling peas, and corn, and taters, like a common clerk!" and old Jim wiped his mouth and squinted up his eyes to show his utter contempt for such a proceeding. "Es I was a-saying, Bill turned clerk, but he didn't like it, and neither did the boys. Arter a little a papoose was born, and then Bill was happy. At this time Bill Dalton and Bill Cook and other tough gangs was a cavorting around, and I often said that if Bill Carr hadn't got married and settled down he'd made them fellers hard to ketch. Sure enough, Bill got into it last Spring year ago. Course you seen it in all the papers. Marshal Nix dun heered that Bill Dalton was down near Violet Springs, so he sends Carr a warrant for him and Slaughter Kid. Bill felt just like getting into the harness again. One arternoon along come two galoots on horseback. Bill seen 'em a-coming and watched them hitch their horses to the old rack. His wife and kid were in the store when they came in and eyed Bill.

"'Be you Bill Carr?' asked one of the chaps.

"'Recon I be,' said Bill, bold as brass, as he slid along the counter toward a six-shooter. 'Who be you'ns?'

"'I'm Bill Dalton, and this is Slaughter Kid,' said one of the strangers. 'Heard you'd a warrant for us and thought we'd come in,' with a laugh.

"'Yes, she is red-hot and still a hottin,' said Bill, as he raised his gun. Just then his two-year-old kid run in atween them and his wife run in arter it. This spoiled Bill's aim, and afore he could pull a second time the two geisers begin to bore holes in him. But he was game and drove 'em out arter they had shot him three times. They got on their horses and escaped, but poor Bill lay about dead on the floor. When the outlaws heered that Bill wasn't dead they threatened to finish the work, so a lot of the boys from Oklahoma City went down and guarded his house till he got better. Shortly after this Dalton was killed. When Bill got well he sold out his grocery and since then he's making it hot for the balance of the gang. Someone shot him last week during the Rogers fight, but they can't kill Bill Carr," and old Jim took a drink with a tenderfoot and went off up to the Clifton House to see how the "King of the Chickasaw Country" was getting along.

## Scott Cooley

*Texas Ranger Turned Killer*

Born in 1845, Cooley was an honorable man for the first 30 years of his life and served as a Texas Ranger but that would later change when he got involved in the Mason County War and befriended notorious outlaw, Johnny Ringo.

Born in Texas in 1845, Cooley was unofficially adopted and raised by a rancher named Tim Williamson, who, along with his wife, nursed him through Typhoid as a child. Cooley grew up to have tremendous respect for the couple, which would later come into play at the eruption of the Mason County War.

As a young man, he joined the Texas Rangers, serving in Captain Cicero R. Perry's Company D, and earned recognition for his relentless pursuit of outlaws. However, by 1875, he had resigned his position and was farming and ranching near Manardville, Texas. During this time, he and his benefactor, Tim Williamson, made two cattle drives to Kansas.

Scott Cooley

Cooley's life changed on May 13, 1875 when his friend, Tim Williamson was arrested by Deputy Sheriff John Worley on the suspicion of cattle rustling. While Worley escorted Williamson to jail, an angry mob of German cattlemen abducted the prisoner and shot him to death. This incident marked the beginning of the Mason County War in Texas, that pitted the German cattlemen against the native-born Texans.

Scott Cooley blamed Worley for Williamson's death, believing him to have been in collusion with the German ambushers. However, he waited for the ambushers to be arrested, but when no indictments were made against them, he took matters into his own hands.

He soon recruited several men to help him, including John and Mose Beard, George Gladden, and Johnny Ringo and began to avenge the death of Tim Williamson.

Cooley and his "posse" first went to Worley's home where he found the deputy working on his well with an assistant, who had been lowered over the side. Cooley shot Worley dead, and the well worker, clinging to the rope, tumbled to the bottom of the well. Cooley then cut scalped Worley, proudly displaying his prize to the Germans.

They then killed Peter Bader, who was believed to have been Williamson's killer, before tracking down and murdering another man named Daniel Hoerster, whom they suspected of having been part of the ambush group. The Germans retaliated when a posse led by Sheriff John Clark, ambushed Mose Beard and George Gladden, killing Beard and seriously wounding Gladden. The posse included Charles Bader, brother to Cooley's second victim, Peter Bader.

Cooley and his allies then began to kill a number of the ambushers, which was retaliated by the hanging of two of Cooley's confederates. The killing continued in both directions for the next several months and the Texas Rangers did little, as many of them were friends of Cooley's.

Finally in December, 1875, Scott Cooley and Johnny Ringo were arrested by Sheriff A. J. Strickland, but they later escaped from the Lampasas County, Texas jail with the help of friends.

Cooley escaped from a posse at the Llanno River and was thought to have fled into Blanco County where he was sheltered by friends and died a short time later, supposedly of brain fever. Only a few minor gunmen were ever charged, one of which was Johnny Ringo, but he was acquitted. He would later turn up in Tombstone, Arizona to tangle with the likes of Wyatt Earp.

## The Daltons

*Lawmen & Outlaws*

Though the Dalton brothers are best known for making their livings robbing trains and banks in Kansas and Oklahoma, this was not always the case, as one of them – Frank Dalton, lived and died a heroic death as a lawman. During Frank's tenure as a U.S. Deputy Marshal, he would often work with brothers Bob and Grat, aggressively pursuing outlaws in Kansas and in Indian Territory. Unfortunately, for Frank's younger brothers that would later change, as they became notorious outlaws, best known for their numerous robberies and being killed in the Coffeyville, Kansas, raid.

The Dalton brothers were part of a large family headed by parents Adaline Younger Dalton and James Lewis Dalton. Lewis Dalton came west from Kentucky to Missouri during the late 1840's and in the 1850's he was trading horses and running a saloon in Westport, Missouri (now Kansas City) when he married Adeline. Adeline's brother was the father of Bob, Cole and James Younger.

Most of their fifteen children were born in Missouri before the family migrated to Indian Territory (now Oklahoma) in 1882.

In 1886, the family moved again to a place near Coffeyville, Kansas. In this rough and wild area, the Dalton brothers inherited a tradition of violence on the bloody ground of the Missouri – Kansas border, where Quantrill's raiders and other guerilla bands operated during and after the Civil War.

Frank Dalton, U.S. Deputy Marshal

When the Oklahoma Territory opened for settlement in 1889, the family headed south again. However, Lewis died along the way leaving Adaline to raise the younger children alone. Adaline continued on, placing a claim on the banks of Kingfisher Creek in Indian Territory, where initially she and the family lived in a dugout. By this time the older Dalton brothers were on their own.

### The Family Hero - Frank Dalton

Frank Dalton (1859-1887) – The older brother of the infamous Daltons who would later form the Dalton Gang, Frank was always an upstanding citizen. Born in Missouri on June 8, 1859, he was commissioned as a U.S. Deputy Marshal at Fort Smith, Arkansas, in

1882. During his short tenure as a Deputy Marshal, he was involved in a number of dangerous episodes and was described as “one of the most brave and efficient officers on the force.” Frank even enlisted his brothers, Bob and Grattan Dalton, who would later become the leading members of the Dalton Gang, to also become lawmen and work for him on several posses as he rounded up outlaws. His career and his life would end on November 27, 1887 when he and Deputy Marshal James R. Cole, went to the Cherokee Nation to arrest a man named Dave Smith on charges of horse theft and whiskey running.

Dalton made a fatal mistake when he expected no trouble from Smith and approached the camp where Dave Smith, his brother-in-law, Lee Dixon, Dixon’s wife, and a man named William Towerly were camped near the Arkansas River. The outlaws were not to be taken easily and as the two deputies approached the camp, Smith immediately shot Dalton in the chest, driving the officer to the ground. Deputy Cole, reacting quickly, returned the fire, killing Dave Smith.

Though one of the outlaws then hit Cole in the side, the officer continued to fire, hitting both Dixon and his wife. Cole, believing that Frank was dead, escaped and made his way back to Fort Smith for assistance. However, Dalton was still alive and after Cole left the area, Will Towerly, a noted murderer and horse thief, approached Frank, who was conscious and begged Towerly not to shoot him as he was already mortally wounded. However, the outlaw blasted him in the head twice with his Winchester before he, too, made his escape.

By the time Deputy Cole returned with a posse, Smith, Dalton, and Dixon’s wife were already dead. Lee Dixon, though seriously wounded was alive and soon transported to Fort Smith, Arkansas, where he died before he could stand trial.

Towerly’s escape was brief, as lawmen were quickly on his trail. Locating him near his home at Atoka, Choctaw Nation, he was shot and killed by a man named William Moody, who was assisting another deputy marshal in his arrest.

Frank Dalton was just 28 years-old at the time of his death. He was buried in the Elmwood Cemetery in Coffeyville, Kansas, and is remembered by the U.S. Marshal’s service on their Roll Call of Honor.

**Lawmen Turned Outlaws - Bob and Grat**

Robert “Bob” Reddick Dalton (1868-1892) – The very same Bob Dalton that was part of the Dalton Gang and killed at the Coffeeville, Kansas, raid was also a U.S. Deputy Marshal for a time. Born in 1868 in Missouri, Bob was one of fifteen children. The family moved to Indian Territory in 1882 and when Bob’s older brother Frank became a U.S. Deputy Marshal, Bob Dalton served on several of his posses. Some accounts say that he was with his brother, Frank, when he was killed by a gang of horse thieves in November, 1887. Bob, himself was later commissioned in the Western District at Fort Smith, Arkansas, and assigned to work out of the Wichita, Kansas, Court. Bob Dalton also served as Chief of Police for the Osage Indian Nation when he worked out of the Kansas court.

Bob Dalton, leader of the outlaw Dalton Gang

On August 26, 1889, Bob was sent to Coffeyville, Kansas, to arrest a man named Charley Montgomery, who was charged with peddling whiskey and stealing horses in Indian Territory.

However, when the outlaw resisted arrest and drew his guns, Montgomery died at the end of Dalton's pistol. Bob did not receive any payment for Montgomery when he delivered him to Fort Smith because there was not a reward on his head for "Dead or Alive." Unfortunately, no one claimed the outlaw's body, and as was the custom of the time, Bob had to pay for his burial.

In April, 1890, both Bob and Grattan Dalton were sent to Claremore, Oklahoma, to arrest a man named Alex Cochran who had killed U.S. Deputy Marshal Cox. When they came upon a rider who fit the description of the fugitive, they began to follow him, who quickly tried to outdistance himself from the deputies. When the man would not stop, Bob shot both the horse and rider from a distance of some 300 yards. Unfortunately, the dead man was not Alex Cochran, but his son.

Bob continued to work in the Osage Nation under the Wichita court for a time. However, rumors soon began to abound that he and Emmett Dalton were selling whiskey to the Indians and that the Dalton brothers were involved in a noisy disturbance with the natives. When U.S. Commissioner Fitzpatrick received word of these events, he called in Bob Dalton, demanded his badge and discharged him from service. An angry Bob insisted that he resigned claiming that court had cheated him out of several expenses.

In any event, in 1891, Bob, Grattan and Emmett traveled to California, where they robbed a Southern Pacific Railroad of $60,000 and began a life of crime. With Bob as their leader, they soon formed the Dalton Gang, recruiting a number of outlaws, which included Dick Broadwell, George "Bitter Creek" Newcomb, Bill Power, "Black-Faced" Charlie Bryant, and Bill Doolin. These tough characters, along with Bob, Grat, and Emmett, then robbed banks and trains throughout Oklahoma for the next 18 months. However, the Dalton Gang came to an end in 1892, at Coffeyville, Kansas, when they attempted a double bank robbery on October 5, 1892. Spotted by locals, a shootout followed the attempted robbery, which claimed the lives of Grat and Bob Dalton, Dick Broadwell and Bill Power as well as four Coffeyville residents. Emmett Dalton, though seriously wounded, was the only one to survive and wound up serving 14 years in prison.

Deputy Marshal Heck Thomas remembered Bob Dalton as the most accurate shot he had ever seen. He was buried at the Elmwood Cemetery in Coffeyville, Kansas, under a marker for himself, his brother Grat, and Bill Power.

Grattan "Grat" Dalton (1865-1892) – Also serving as a U.S. Deputy Marshal before he turned outlaw, Grattan Dalton was born in 1865 near Lawrence, Kansas, one of fifteen children. The family moved to Indian Territory in 1882. Grat took his brother, Frank's job as a U.S. Deputy Marshal after Frank was killed on November 27,1887. The following year, he took a bullet in the left arm when he was trying to serve an arrest warrant on an Indian outlaw. In August, 1889, he was working as a Deputy Marshal for the Muskogee court in Indian Territory.

For the next year, he assisted in arresting a number of fugitives. However, when Grat forced a young black boy to place an apple on his head, then shooting it off, Marshal Jacob Yoes got wind of the incident. He then dismissed Grat for misuse of his authority.

By 1891, he had turned to a life of crime with his brothers and other members of the Dalton Gang. He was killed on October 5, 1892, when the gang attempted a double bank robbery in Coffeeville, Kansas. He is buried at the Elmwood Cemetery in Coffeyville, Kansas, under a marker for himself, his brother Bob, and Bill Power.

Grattan "Grat" Dalton

**Bill Dalton - Riding With the Doolin Gang**

William "Bill" Dalton (1866-1894) - Bill, who was once a member of the California legislature, became fed up with politics and robbed a train with his brothers just outside of Los Angeles, California, in 1891. After the death of his brothers at the Coffeyville,

Bill Dalton

Kansas, raid in 1892, he joined Bill Doolin's gang and soon became one of the leaders of the Doolin-Dalton Gang. Obsessed with the idea of making his own name more prominent than that of his brothers, he and Doolin vowed to take East Texas by storm. For three years, the gang specialized in robbing banks, stagecoaches and trains in Arkansas, Oklahoma, Texas, and Kansas becoming the terror of the Wild West. But it was not to last.

On June 8, 1894, a posse of lawmen approached Bill's home near Ardmore, Oklahoma. Bill, with a pistol in hand, jumped out of a window and ran toward the posse, ignoring orders to halt. He was killed immediately. His wife identified the body and shipped him to California for burial.

**The Only Survivor**

Emmett Dalton (1871-1937) – Born in Missouri in 1871, Emmett Dalton was the youngest of 15 children. Though he never served as a U.S. Deputy Marshal, like his brothers, Frank, Bob, and Grat, he was known to assist on several of their posses.

Emmett Dalton

It was Emmett, who was working as a cowboy on the Bar X Bar Ranch in Oklahoma, that met most of the other men who would become part of the Dalton Gang, including Bill Doolin, Bill Power, Charley Pierce, George "Bitter Creek" Newcomb, Bill EcElhanie, Charlie Bryant, and Richard (Dick) Broadwell. Emmett participated in the Coffeyville, Kansas, raid that killed his brothers, Bob and Grat, as well as Bill Power and Dick Broadwell. Though Emmett was wounded, he survived to stand trial in Independence, Kansas, five months after the robbery.

He plead guilty to murdering a Coffeyville citizen and was sentenced to life in prison at the Kansas State Penitentiary at Lansing. After fourteen and one-half years in prison, Emmett Dalton was pardoned by E. W. Hoch, governor of Kansas, in 1907. On September 1, 1908 Emmett married Julia Johnson Gilstrap Lewis in Bartlesville, Oklahoma, before settling in Tulsa. Emmett worked as a police officer in Tulsa for a couple of years before the pair moved to California. In California, Emmett worked as a building contractor and later would write a book about the exploits of the Dalton Gang entitled "*When The Daltons Rode*." Written in collaboration with Jack Jungmeyer, a Los Angeles newspaperman, the book was published in 1931. Emmett died quietly at his home in Long Beach, California, on July 13, 1937. Emmett was cremated and his ashes returned to Kingfisher, Oklahoma, for burial.

The bodies of Bill Power, Bob Dalton, Grattan Dalton and Dick Broadwell

## Frederick "Fred" James Dodge

*Undercover Detective*

Wells Fargo Detective, constable of Tombstone, Arizona, and Texas cattleman, Dodge was born in Spring Valley, California on August 29, 1854 and raised in Sacramento. When he grew up, he went to work as an undercover agent for Wells Fargo, working in California, Nevada and Arizona. In December, 1879, he was working in Tombstone, Arizona and recommended that Wyatt Earp be hired as a guard and messenger for the stage line. The two quickly became good friends and Dodge supported Wyatt and his brothers in their troubles in Tombstone after the Gunfight at the O.K. Corral and during the Earp Vendetta Ride. He and Wyatt remained friends the rest of their lives.

Dodge was an integral part in the investigation into the "Bisbee Massacre," on December 8, 1883, where six desperados left four people dead inside the Goldwater and Castenada Store in Bisbee.

In the end, five of the killers would be legally hanged, and when the sixth man, John Heath, was sentenced to life in prison, a vigilante group descended upon the Tombstone jail, where Heath was being held, and lynched him.

Later, Dodge was elected constable of Tombstone, while still working under cover for Wells Fargo, where he solved a number of train and stage robberies. In December, 1890, Dodge went to work "openly" for Wells Fargo in Texas, where he worked on a number of cases, not only in the Lone Star State, but also in Oklahoma. He was known to have teamed up with U.S. Deputy Marshal, Heck Thomas, in the pursuit of the Doolin-Dalton Gang.

While he and his wife, Patsy, and daughter, Ada, were vacationing in Leon Springs, Texas, they fell in love with the hill country and in 1906, Dodge purchased 2,000 acres, which he called the Dodge Ranch near Boerne, Texas. He retired from Wells Fargo in 1917 and settled down on his ranch. After his first wife died, he remarried a woman named Jessie in 1917 and the couple had a son named Fred James Dodge, Jr. the following year. Dodge continued to live on his ranch until his death at the age of 84 on December 17, 1938. He was buried at the Boerne Cemetery in Kendall County, Texas.

During his long career as a detective, Dodge was described as an intelligent and determined investigator. He was also an extremely meticulous man, who kept a daily diary of his activities and travels, collecting some 27 journals over the years. These would later be used as research for two books – *The Life and Times of Wyatt Earp* and *Undercover for Wells Fargo*.

## Virgil Earp

*Upholding the Law of the West*

Though living a life of as much adventure as did his younger brother, Wyatt, Virgil Earp never obtained the same kind of fame, perhaps due to Wyatt's better skills at self-publicity.

Virgil Earp

Virgil Walter Earp was born on July 18, 1843 in Hartford, Kentucky, the second son of Nicholas Earp and Virginia Ann Cooksey. By the time Virgil was 17 years-old, his family was living in Pella, Iowa, where he eloped with a Dutch immigrant by the name of Magdalena C. "Ellen" Rysdam on September 21, 1861. Though her parents severely disapproved of her choice in a husband, the pair remained together. When the Civil War broke out, 18 year-old Virgil enlisted in the Union Army, eventually serving with the 83rd Illinois Infantry from July 26, 1862 - June 24, 1865.

Virgil and Ellen had a baby girl on January 7, 1862, naming her Nellie Jane Earp. It was the only known child that Virgil would have in his lifetime. He went off to war when she was only two weeks old.

While Virgil was off fighting the war, Ellen received word in the summer of 1863, that Virgil had been killed. Soon after, she remarried a man named John Van Rossem and the couple, along with Virgil's daughter, Nellie, moved to Oregon Territory.

Alas, when Virgil was discharged from the army on June 26, 1865, he arrived back in Pella to find his wife and daughter gone. In the meantime, the rest of his family had moved westward to San Bernardino, California. A year later, he joined them in California. Though he had probably learned where Ellen and his daughter had gone, he evidently did not go looking for them.

In 1866, Virgil was working with younger brother, Wyatt, as a freighter-teamster between Wilmington and Prescott, Arizona. Later, the pair also worked on railroad construction in Wyoming.

In 1868, the Earps returned to the Midwest, settling in Lamar, Missouri, where Virgil helped his father, Nicholas, farm and operate a grocery store. While there, Virgil took a second wife named Rosella Dragoo on August 28, 1870. But, Virgil was obviously having no luck in the love department as the marriage lasted just three years.

Shortly afterwards, Virgil left Lamar, settling in Council Bluffs, Iowa, for a short time. There he met a waitress named Alvira "Allie" Sullivan. Though some say they married in 1874 in Los Angeles, California, others surmise that they never made it official. In any case, Virgil would spend the rest of his life with her.

Over the years, Virgil would most often work as a lawman, but also held a number of other jobs, including farming, prospecting, driving a stagecoach, rail construction, and working at a sawmill.

In 1877, Virgil was in Dodge City, Kansas, along with his brother, Wyatt. However, no records indicate that he ever worked as a lawman there. From Dodge City, he and his wife moved on to Prescott, Arizona, where he worked in a sawmill. However, in October, 1877, he was deputized by Yavapai County Sheriff, Ed Bowers, during a gunfight in the street. Fighting robbers who were trying to make off with their loot, Virgil shot one of them twice through the head with a Winchester Rifle. The next year, he served as a night watchman in Prescott for a couple of months before becoming a constable.

On November 27, 1879, Virgil was appointed as a U.S. Deputy Marshal for Arizona Territory and traveled from Prescott to Tombstone, along with brother Wyatt. Less than a year later, on October 30, 1880, Virgil became the acting town marshal after Fred White was shot and killed by outlaw and gunman Curly Bill Brocius.

He continued to hold his federal law enforcement position, as well as the marshal's appointment. However, it wouldn't be for long, as elections were held just two weeks later for the "open" marshal slot. Virgil was narrowly defeated by Ben Sippy.

The next year, on June 6, 1881, Virgil would find himself appointed as acting city marshal again when Ben Sippy requested a temporary leave of absence. During his appointment, Tombstone was devastated by a fire on June 22nd and Virgil was left to help manage the issues. Less than a week later, the City of Tombstone discovered $3,000 in financial improprieties in the marshal's office. Ben Sippy, who had known financial problems, was then permanently replaced by Virgil, on appointment of Tombstone Mayor John Clum.

Later that year, on October 26th, Tombstone and the Earps would become famous for the well publicized Gunfight at the O.K. Corral. When Virgil, temporarily deputizing brothers, Wyatt and Morgan, and Doc Holliday, went to disarm the McLaurys and Billy

Clanton, all hell broke loose resulting in the most famous gunfight of the Old West. The affair made Wyatt a legend, but it was actually Virgil who was the most experienced. Up to that point, Wyatt had only been in one gunfight, Morgan in none, while Virgil had years of lawman experience plus that of the Civil War. When the smoke cleared, Frank and Tom McLaury and Billy Clanton were dead. Virgil Earp took a shot to the leg and Morgan suffered a shoulder wound.

Sheriff John Behan arrested Virgil Earp, Wyatt Earp, Morgan Earp and Doc Holliday for murder of Billy Clanton, Tom McLaury and Frank McLaury. Three days later, the city council suspended Virgil, pending the outcome of the shooting investigation. After a trial, all of the members of the Earp faction were found to have acted within the law.

Over the next few months, the Earps struggled to retain control over Tombstone, as word was spreading that the Cowboy faction would take their revenge on the Earps for the killings. For safety, Virgil moved to the Cosmopolitan Hotel. A couple of months later, on December 28th, when Virgil was walking from the Oriental Saloon to the hotel, he was ambushed. Shots were fired from the second story of a building across Allen Street, hitting the Crystal Palace Saloon and the Eagle Brewery, breaking windows and narrowly missing customers. Virgil was hit in the back and left arm by buckshot. Though his arm would be permanently crippled, he would survive. The shooters were never positively identified. Though Ike Clanton's hat was found at the shooting site, one of his friends gave him an alibi and no arrests were made.

Upon learning of Virgil's mishap, territorial U.S. Marshal Crawley P. Dake appointed Wyatt Earp as a U.S. Deputy Marshal.

On March 18, 1882, the cowboy gang struck again while Morgan Earp was playing pool at Campbell and Hatch's Saloon. A shot was fired from the darkness of the alley striking Morgan in the back. Morgan's body was dressed in one of Doc Holliday's suits and shipped to the parents in Colton, California for burial. The entire Earp party, including Virgil and his wife, Allie, accompanied Morgan's body. Also accompanying them out of town were a number of "body guards," including Sherman McMasters and "Turkey Creek" Jack Johnson.

However, in Tucson, Wyatt, Warren and Doc Holliday hopped off the train in search of Frank Stilwell, who supposedly worked in the railroad yards. The train went on to California without them.

In Tucson, Wyatt and Warren Earp, along with Doc Holliday, Sherman McMasters, and "Turkey Creek" Jack Johnson, saw the train safely off. Afterwards; however, they spied Frank Stilwell, a member of the Cowboy faction, near the train tracks and Wyatt shot him. He and the others then began what is known as the Earp Vendetta Ride, chasing down those they felt were responsible for Morgan's death, killing them one by one, or running them out of the territory. Though the five men were indicted for the killing of Stilwell, none were brought to trial, all having fled the territory after their vengeance ride.

After settling in Colton, California and recovering from his injuries, Virgil worked as a railroad agent for a couple of years and was also said to have gambled heavily. In 1886, he opened a detective agency for a brief time, before becoming a constable in July, 1886. A year later, when Colton was officially incorporated, Virgil became the city's first elected marshal on July 11, 1887.

In March, 1889, he resigned as city marshal and became a boxing matchmaker and gambling hall operator in San Bernardino, California. By the spring of 1893, the restless Virgil had moved on again, establishing an Earp's Hall in the mining camp of Vanderbilt, California. The two-story saloon provided dances, prizefights and church services in its upstairs hall, while downstairs held the typical saloon fare. Even though he was well liked in the town, he lost a constable election in 1894.

Virgil and Allie briefly returned to Colton in early 1895 but was soon headed to another booming mining town – Cripple Creek, Colorado. But, Virgil didn't stay long, soon moving back to Prescott, Arizona and working in the mines. In the fall of 1896, he was injured in a mining accident and took up ranching south of Prescott.

In the fall of 1898, Virgil Earp received a letter from a Mrs. Levi Law of Portland, Oregon, in which she asked if he was the same Virgil Earp who had married Ellen Rysdam in Pella, Iowa, in 1861. Obviously he was and the two soon began a correspondence. In April, 1899, Virgil and Allie traveled to Portland to see her for the first time in 37 years and his two grandchildren. They maintained a relationship for the rest of his days.

In 1900, he ran for Yavapai County, Arizona, Sheriff, but his health was suffering and he was forced to drop out of the race.

By 1904, Virgil was back in Colton, California, but by that time the city had an anti-saloon sentiment and a liquor ordinance that limited the number of saloons in the city. When Virgil was unable to get a license, he and Allie struck out for yet another mining camp – Goldfield, Nevada.

There, he became a Deputy Sheriff on January 26, 1905. However, his health continued to fail him and on October 19, 1905, he died in Goldfield of pneumonia.

His daughter Nellie made arrangements for her father's body to be transported to Portland, Oregon, where she lived, and he was buried at Riverview Cemetery. Allie returned to California where she spent the rest of her life, dying at the age of 98.

## Wyatt Earp

*Frontier Lawman*

Wyatt Earp is the best known of all the frontier lawmen of the American West. Soft-spoken, with nerves of steel, he survived countless gunfights due to his extraordinary patience and resolute manner. But, Earp wasn't just the famous lawman of Dodge City and Tombstone fame; he was also a buffalo hunter, a miner, card dealer, stagecoach driver, saloon owner, and much more throughout the years.

Wyatt Earp

Wyatt Berry Stapp Earp was born to Nicholas Earp and Virginia Earp in Monmouth, Illinois on March 19, 1848. His father was a lawyer and a farmer who had formerly served in the Army. The would-be lawman was named for his father's former Army captain. Older brothers James and Virgil were ages seven and five by the time Wyatt came along. He also had an older sister named Martha who was three.

Just two years later, the family moved to Iowa where Nicholas established a farm. Soon three more siblings would join the rapidly growing family – Morgan in 1851, Warren in 1855, and Adelia in 1861. Nicholas Earp always had a high regard for land and for the law, instilling in his children the same respect.

In 1864 the family moved to Colton, California near San Bernardino. Along the way, Wyatt was given his first weapon – a combination shotgun and rifle, to help protect the family against attacking Indians. Young Wyatt soon acquired a six-gun and practiced every day, becoming a deadly marksman.

When he arrived in California, he worked as a teamster and a railroad worker for a time. But soon he began to work his way back east as a buffalo hunter, wagon train scout, and a railroad hand.

By 1870 Wyatt had worked his way to Lamar, Missouri, where he fell in love and married Urilla Sutherland. However, their time together was to be brief, when Urilla died within a year of their marriage. Historical facts vary as to the cause of her death – some saying she died in childbirth, while others indicated that she died of typhoid fever.

Heartbroken, Wyatt headed to Indian Territory (now Oklahoma,) working as a buffalo hunter and stagecoach driver. However, he and two travel companions were soon accused of stealing horses. Paying his bail, Wyatt fled to Kansas before the case ever came to trial.

In 1871 Earp met Wild Bill Hickok in Kansas City, along with other western legends including "Buffalo Bill" Cody, Jack Gallagher, Billy Dixon and Jim Hanrahan. Wyatt would later say of Wild Bill Hickok, "Bill Hickok was regarded as the deadliest pistol shot alive as well as being a man of great courage. The truth of certain stories of Bill's achievements may have been open to debate but he had earned the respect paid to him." Wild Bill helped Wyatt to become a better buffalo hunter, where Wyatt met Bat Masterson on the open Kansas prairie.

August, 1873 found Wyatt in Ellsworth, Kansas. It was here that the Earp legend began. Ellsworth, a railhead where huge herds of cattle were driven north from Texas, was wild with drunken cowboys shooting up the town. Two of these cowboys were Billy and Ben Thompson, lethal gunmen who would rather resort to gunplay than talk out an argument.

Wyatt had heard of the two killers and chose not to play at the same gaming tables with the unpredictable men. But before long he got caught up with them on August 15, 1873. While Earp was standing across the street from Brennan's Saloon, he heard the sounds of an argument coming from the gambling house. The Thompsons had started a dispute with two other gamblers named John Sterling and Jack Morco, a local lawman. The disturbance soon brought Sheriff Chauncey B. Whitney and two deputies.

Sterling and Morco charged at the Thompsons, guns blazing, but Ben Thompson drove them off with a volley of shots. Then Billy Thompson, a homicidal maniac and hopeless alcoholic, turned his gun on Sheriff Whitney, who prior to this had been a drinking companion and friend to the two brothers. At point-blank range, he shot the sheriff down.

Wyatt, at first, watched the events without interfering as he saw Ellsworth Mayor, James Miller, enter the saloon and demand that Thompson surrender his guns. When Thompson refused, Miller went in search of Whitney's deputies who had inexplicably disappeared from the scene after the sheriff was shot.

Dismayed when Wyatt spotted the two deputies cowering on the sidelines, he remarked to the passing Mayor Miller, “It’s none of my business but if it was me I’d get me a gun and arrest Ben Thompson or kill him.” Miller then tore the badge off of Deputy Norton’s chest and walking back to Earp, said: “I’ll make it your business.”

Wyatt watched, stunned, as Ben Thompson swaggered out of the saloon and mounted his horse, as brother Bill waved him goodbye. “What kind of a town is this?” he snapped at the deputies and mayor, who now stood meekly across the square.

Borrowing a pair of six shooters, he followed Ben Thompson, who was now about a block away. When he caught up with him he demanded that Thompson throw down his gun. Thompson, who knew of Earp, complied and Wyatt marched him to jail. Ben Thompson was fined $25 for disturbing the peace and a warrant for murder was issued for his brother Bill.

So impressed was Mayor Miller that he offered Wyatt the job of town marshal at $125.00 a month. But Earp declined, handing Miller back the badge, and saying that he intended to go into the cattle business with his brothers.

Ben Thompson, who would later turn lawman himself, would say to Bat Masterson in subsequent years, that he had a powerful hunch that Wyatt would have killed him if he hadn’t thrown down his gun. The story of how Earp had backed down Ben Thompson soon spread up and down the Chisholm Trail and the Wyatt Earp legend was born.

In the spring of 1874, Wyatt moved on to Wichita, Kansas, yet another Wild West town. In Wichita, Wyatt worked as a part-time lawman and city maintenance man, making about $60.00 per month. However, he was fired from the police force after getting into a fight with William Smith, who was running for city marshal against Mike Meagher, who was a friend of Wyatt’s.

Furthermore, Wyatt was almost arrested himself for discharging his weapon in public. Though the incident was an accident, it didn’t speak well of a lawman. When he was sitting in a local saloon with his feet up on a table, his pistol fell out of it’s holster and hit the floor and the gun went off. The bullet went through his coat and into the wall. Before moving on to Dodge City, Wyatt and his brother, James, were almost arrested for vagrancy and some reports have it that Wyatt stole city tax money before hightailing it to Dodge.

### *Dodge City*

By the spring of 1876 the cattle trade had shifted west to Dodge City and soon Wyatt was offered the position of Chief Deputy Marshal from Dodge City’s mayor.

In the burgeoning settlement, Dodge City had already acquired its infamous stamp of lawlessness and gun slinging. As the many buffalo hunters, railroad workers, drifters and soldiers streamed into the town after long excursions on the prairie, they quickly found the many saloons, gambling houses and brothels in the lawless town. Inevitably, gunfights were common and the people of Dodge feared for their lives.

Marshal Larry Deger, the last of a long line of officers who had been run out of town or shot in the back by the lawless forces of Dodge, was overwhelmed and heartily welcomed Wyatt. Soon, four assistant deputies were hired – Bat Masterson, Wyatt's old buffalo hunting friend; Charlie Basset; Bill Tilghman; and Neal Brown.

Intending to restore order, one of the first things the new lawmen did was to initiate a "Deadline" north of the railroad yards on Front Street to keep the commercial part of the city quiet. On the north side, the city passed an ordinance that guns could not be worn or carried. On the south side of the "deadline", those who supported the lawlessness continued to operate as usual, with a host of saloons, brothels, and frequent gunfights. The gun-toting rule was in effect around the clock and anyone wearing a gun was immediately jailed. Soon, Dodge City's jail was filled.

Wyatt Earp and Bat Masterson in 1876

In his new role, Earp would go after famed train robber, Dave Rudabaugh, following the outlaw's trail for 400 miles to Fort Griffin, Texas. When he arrived, Wyatt went first to the largest saloon in town, Shanssey's, asking about Rudabaugh. Owner John Shanssey said that Rudabaugh had been there earlier in the week, but didn't know where he was bound. He directed Wyatt to Doc Holliday who had played cards with Rudabaugh.

Wyatt was skeptical about talking to Holliday, as it was well known that Doc hated lawmen. However, when Wyatt found him that evening at Shanssey's, he was surprised at Holliday's willingness to talk. Doc told Wyatt that he thought that Rudabaugh had back-trailed to Kansas. Wyatt wired this information to Bat Masterson, Sheriff in Dodge City, and the news was instrumental in apprehending Rudabaugh. The unlikely pair formed a friendship in Shanssey's that would last for years.

In the fall of 1876, Wyatt and his brother, Morgan, left Dodge for awhile, traveling for the Black Hills outside of Deadwood, South Dakota in search of gold. However, he returned to Dodge in May of 1877 after James H. "Dog" Kelley, Dodge City's new mayor, wired him, asking him to help with the Texas cowboys who were shooting up the town.

When he returned, Wyatt was made the new town marshal and deputized his brother Morgan. Almost immediately he began to plague the courts for harsher sentences, banned some men from even entering the town, and organized a citizen committee to help the law enforcers to watch the streets.

It wasn't long after Wyatt returned to Dodge that Doc Holliday turned up with "Big Nose" Kate. Doc, after having killed a man in Fort Griffin, Texas, was running from a lynching party. At first Doc hung out his doctor's shingle but soon went back to gambling, frequenting the Alhambra and dealing cards at the Long Branch Saloon. Though Dodge City citizens thought the friendship between Wyatt and Doc was strange, Wyatt ignored them and Doc kept the law while in Dodge City.

One night, while Doc was dealing Faro in the Long Branch Saloon, a number of Texas cowboys arrived with a herd of cattle. After many weeks on the trail, the rowdy cowboys were ready to "let loose."

Leading the cowboy mob was a man named Ed Morrison, whom Wyatt had humiliated in Wichita, Kansas, and a man named Tobe Driskill. The cowboys rushed the town, galloping down Front Street with guns blazing, and blowing out shop windows. Entering the Long Branch Saloon, they began harassing the customers.

When Wyatt came through the front door, he came face to face with several awaiting gun barrels. Stepping forward, Morrison sneered "Pray and jerk your gun! Your time has come Earp!"

Suddenly, a voice sounded behind Morrison. "No, friend, you draw – or throw your hands up!" It was Doc, his revolver to Morrison's temple. Doc had been in the back room, his card game interrupted by the havoc out front.

"Any of you bastards pulls a gun and your leader here loses what's left of his brains!" The cowboys dropped their arms. Wyatt rapped Morrison over the head with his long barrel Colt, then relieving Driskill and Morrison of their arms, he ushered them to the Dodge City Jail. Wyatt never forgot the fact that Doc Holliday saved his life that night in Dodge City. Responding later, Wyatt said, "The only way anyone could have appreciated the feeling I had for Doc after the Driskill-Morrison business would have been to have stood in my boots at the time Doc came through the Long Branch doorway."

While in Dodge City, Wyatt met a saloon girl named Celia Anne Blalock, whom he affectionately called "Mattie." Though the two never married, they lived as husband and wife. At first, the couple was happy, but Mattie had acquired a laudanum dependency due to a prior illness, and this would soon put a strain on their relationship.

Later, Big Nose Kate and Doc Holliday, in their constant love-hate relationship, had one of their frequent, violent quarrels. Holliday soon saddled his horse and headed out to Colorado, leaving Big Nose Kate behind.

An often written about event was the 1878 "showdown" between Wyatt Earp and Clay Allison, the self-proclaimed "shootist" from New Mexico. According to the stories, Allison planned to protest the treatment of his men by the Dodge City marshals and was willing to back his arguments with gun smoke. The Dodge City lawmen had gained a reputation for being hard on visiting cattle herders, with stories circulating that cattlemen had been robbed, shot, and beaten over the head with revolvers. George Hoyt, who had, at one time, worked for Clay Allison, had been shot to death while shooting a pistol in the air in the streets of Dodge City.

There are several versions of the story of the showdown. Some say that Allison and his men terrorized Dodge City, while Wyatt Earp and Bat Masterson fled in fear. Others say that Wyatt Earp pressured Allison into leaving. And yet others say that Allison was talked into leaving by a saloon keeper and another cattleman, with little or no contact with Wyatt Earp at all.

In any case, there is no evidence of any serious altercation ever having happened. Historians basically surmise that Allison might have come to Dodge City looking for trouble, but nothing really happened. While Allison and his men went from saloon to saloon fortifying themselves with whiskey, Earp and his marshals began to assemble their forces. But in the end, Dick McNulty, owner of a large cattle outfit and Chalk Beeson, co-owner of the Long Branch Saloon, intervened on behalf of the town, talking the gang into giving up their guns.

By 1879, Dodge City had been tamed and Wyatt was spending more time at the gaming tables than he was marshalling. So, when brother Virgil wrote him about the new city of Tombstone, Arizona, Wyatt, along with brothers James and Morgan, and common-law wife, Mattie, headed West. Big Nose Kate would follow and when Doc Holliday returned to Dodge City and found everyone gone, he too headed to Arizona.

***Tombstone***

When Wyatt arrived in Tombstone in December of 1879, he planned to establish a stage line but soon discovered there were already two in the town. Instead, he acquired the gambling concession at the Oriental Saloon for a quarter percentage of the proceeds. He also took a side job as a shotgun rider on the stage lines for Wells Fargo shipments. James established a saloon on Allen Street. Virgil was already deputy marshal of Tombstone and Morgan went to work with his brother as a lawman. Doc Holliday met up with Big Nose Kate in Prescott, Arizona, and the pair soon joined the Earps in Tombstone.

Tombstone was the last of the wide-open hellholes, teaming with rustlers, thieves, gunmen, gamblers and prostitutes. The outlaw Clanton Gang had been running roughshod over the territory and immediately resented the Earps arrival. "Old man" Clanton, his sons, Ike, Phin, and Billy; the McLaury brothers, Frank and Tom; Curly Bill Brocius, John Ringo and their followers lost no time in expressing their displeasure.

The Clantons had long been involved in rustling cattle from Old Mexico, moving their plunder northward to their ranch on the San Pedro River. Keeping Cochise County Sheriff John Behan on their payroll, their operation was extremely successful until the arrival of the Earps.

Wyatt wasn't spending all of his time working, as he met Josephine "Josie" Sarah Marcus while in Tombstone. The small 18-year old woman had arrived in Tombstone with a traveling theatre troupe in 1879 prior to Wyatt's arrival. She hooked up with Sheriff John Behan and stayed in Tombstone.

However, shortly after Wyatt appeared on the scene, Sheriff Behan made the mistake of introducing Josie to Wyatt and the two instantly hit it off. The relationship between Wyatt and Mattie had continued to deteriorate as Mattie's laudanum dependency grew worse. Josie thought that Wyatt was the best-looking man in Tombstone and she began to be seen with him almost every night at his faro table while Mattie lingered at home.

Behan refused to accept Josie's apologies and fell in deeper with the Clantons to thwart the Earps at every turn. Now holding a personal grudge, he vowed to help the rustlers rid Tombstone of the bothersome Earp brothers as soon as possible.

So, when in July, 1880, John Behan offered him a job as deputy sheriff under Chief Marshal Fred White, he was suspicious. Wyatt finally came to the conclusion that the offer was designed to keep him too busy to guard the Wells Fargo stage, allowing the Clantons access once again to this lucrative plunder. Wyatt accepted the job, but Behan's plan failed when Wyatt convinced Wells Fargo to hire brother Morgan as the new guard in his place. Their plan having been a "bust", the Clantons were furious.

It was Curly Bill Brocius who first tangled with Wyatt Earp in October, 1880. One day Brocius, along with Billy Clanton, and Frank and Tom McLaury, were riding up and down Allen Street firing their weapons and harassing anyone walking along the boardwalks. When Sheriff White tried to stop the cowboys, Brocius drew his gun, White grabbed it, and in the fracas the gun went off, hitting White in the groin.

Just then Earp arrived on the scene and brought his six gun down on Curly Bill's head, knocking him unconscious. White was taken to the doctor and Brocius was taken to jail.

In the doctor's office, White made a death bed statement that he had been shot by his own carelessness. After White's death, Wyatt confronted the gunmen, stating he would kill any one of them who reached for a weapon, and ordered them out of town. Soon, Curly Bill was released, thanks to White's dying statement.

Meanwhile, one night while Doc Holliday was gambling at the Oriental Saloon, John Behan accused Doc of manipulating a faro game. Doc, never one to back down, quickly challenged Behan, who retreated in haste. Behan's public embarrassment added more fuel to the fire.

Through the early months of 1881, the Clantons continued to rustle cattle from Mexico, a crime that the Earp lawmen could do nothing about. Their hands were tied since cattle rustling was officially a county matter and John Behan was the county sheriff. The gap between the law and the outlaw faction grew wider and the town divided into two camps. While most of Tombstone's citizens supported the Earps, the politically strong outlaw element, with Behan in control, supported the Clantons.

In the meantime Doc and Big Nose Kate continued to live together, but when Kate got drunk, they had serious arguments. Often, her drunkenness would escalate to abuse, and finally Doc had had enough and threw her out. The Clantons used this separation to their advantage.

On March 15, 1881, four masked men attempted a holdup on a stagecoach near Contention and in the attempt, killed the stage driver and a passenger. The Cowboy faction immediately seized upon the opportunity and accused Doc Holliday of being one of the holdup men. Sheriff Behan, who was investigating the hold-up, found Kate on one of her drunken binges, still berating Doc for throwing her out. Feeding her yet even more whiskey, Behan persuaded her to sign an affidavit that Doc had been one of the masked highwaymen and had killed the stage driver.

While Kate was sobering up, the Earps were rounding up witnesses who could verify Doc's whereabouts on the night in question. When Kate realized what she had done, she repudiated her statement and the charges were thrown out. But, for Doc, this was the "last straw" for Kate, and giving her some money, he put her on a stage out of town.

Wyatt and his deputies had gone after the robbers, for that matter, and had arrested a Clanton hanger-on named Luther King who, under pressure, had confessed to taking part in the crime. But, after the arrest, John Behan argued that King was his prisoner, since the crime was territorial, not city. Suspiciously, King escaped from Behan's jail. And it was then apparent to Wyatt that Doc had been shanghaied as an intended sacrificial lamb, and that King was released as to not implicate the real perpetrators of the holdup.

Events, a piece at a time, now moved rapidly toward a final showdown. Old Man Clanton was shot and killed by a band of vaqueros during a rustling attempt below the border; his eldest son, Ike, whose rushed judgments would prove fatal, took the family reins. Also, in the heat of summer, 1881, a fire swept the business district of Tombstone and the citizens blamed Marshall Ben Sippy for not controlling the looting that followed; Virgil Earp, the senior deputy, was appointed marshal, a move that antagonized the already-hostile Clantons. And, of course, there was Josie who continued to see Wyatt. While she made all effort to remain apart from the bad blood churning between the factions, the sight of her riled Behan all over again. Throughout the lazy summer season of 1881, threats against the Earp Brothers increased. Ike Clanton, Johnny Ringo, "Curly Bill" Brocius and others of their ilk would often be heard telling a bar room-full how they were going to send Wyatt Earp to Boot Hill.

***Gunfight at the O.K. Corral***

On Tuesday, October 25th, Ike Clanton spent the day getting drunk, moving from one saloon to the next, and making threats against the Earps and Holliday to any who would listen. That night, he made his way to the Occidental Saloon for a card game with Tom McLaury.

An angry Doc Holliday, who had heard of the boasts, confronted him. "I heard you're going to kill me, Ike," he said. "Get out your gun and commence." Virgil, a U.S. Deputy Marshal, Wyatt, appointed as acting city marshal by Virgil, and Morgan, also a sworn officer, were present during this confrontation. Virgil told Doc and Ike that he would arrest both of them if they continued the argument.

Though boasting violence throughout the day, Clanton was unarmed and finally, Virgil drew Holliday away. But Clanton followed, promising "to kill you tomorrow when the others come to town."

Spotting Wyatt on the streets, the fired-up Clanton continued. "Tell your consumptive friend, your Arizona nightin'gale, he's a dead man tomorrow!" To which, Wyatt just turned and replied "Don't you tangle with Doc Holliday – he'll kill you before you've begun."

Ike's parting shot was "Get ready for a showdown!"

Wednesday, October 26, 1881, was an overcast windy day. The Earps, in anticipation of trouble, woke early. As Virgil watched from his hotel window, he saw Billy Clanton ride into town, accompanied by friend Billy Claiborne. They met the McLaury brothers and Ike Clanton on Allen Street. Ike was looking for Holliday but before he could find him, Virgil and Morgan confronted him. Ike, bracing a shotgun, exchanged words with the two but when Clanton raised his rifle, Virgil subdued him, impounded his rifle, and dragged him before Justice of the Peace Wallace, who fined Ike $27.50 for carrying firearms in the city.

Wyatt and Tom McLaury, both hearing what had happened, met at the judge's door at the same time, literally bumping into each other. Though Wyatt apologized, McLaury insulted him and, in return, Wyatt brought his gun down on McLaury's head.

Later that morning, the cowboys met at Spangenbergs, a gunsmith shop. Then Frank McLaury rode his horse onto the boardwalk, frightening pedestrians off its path outside the gunsmith shop. Wyatt grabbed the reins of the horse, leading it to the streets as McLaury yelled profanities. After this latest confrontation, the outlaws retreated in a group around the corner off Allen Street. With all of the tension, there was bound to be a fight. Several members of the town's Citizens' Committee offered their assistance to the Earp brothers, but thanking them, Wyatt said it was his and his brothers' responsibility as law officers.

Then John Behan, the County Sheriff, appeared pronouncing, "Ike Clanton and his crew are on Fremont Street talking gun-talk." Evidently, Ike Clanton, the two McLaurys, Billy Clanton and Billy Claiborne were meeting in a vacant lot planning to bushwhack Doc Holliday, who passed that way every morning.

Virgil, as Chief Marshal, agreed to go down there to break them up, but contended that Behan should accompany him. Behan only laughed. "Hell, this is your fight, not mine."

However, the cowboys were surprised when the Earps showed up and Doc was with them. As they made their way to the O.K. Corral, witnesses said that the three Earp brothers were all dressed in black with firm, mean grimaces on their faces while Doc was nattily clad in grey and was whistling. Where the two forces finally met was actually 90 yards down an alley from the O.K. Corral. The actual gunfight took place off Fremont Street between Fly's Photo Gallery and Jersey's Livery Stable. The Earps passed by the O.K. Corral, but cut through the alley where they found the troublemakers waiting at the other end.

"You are under arrest for attempting to disturb the peace," Virgil announced. As senior officer, he displayed only a non-threatening walking stick, having given his shotgun to Doc to carry. The rustlers tightened and Morgan and Doc simultaneously braced for action. "Hold on, I don't want that!" cried Virgil.

What happened next was a blur, occurring in about 30 seconds. The shooting started when Billy Clanton and Frank McLaury cocked their pistols. It is not really known who fired the first shot, but Doc's bullet was the first to hit home, tearing through Frank McLaury's belly and sending McLaury's own shot wild through Wyatt's coat-tail. Billy Clanton fired at Virgil, but his shot also went astray when he was hit with Morgan's shot through his rib cage.

Billy Claiborne ran as soon as shots were fired and was already out of sight. Ike Clanton, too, panicked and threw his gun down, pleading for his life. "Fight or get out like Claiborne!" Wyatt yelled and watched Ike desert his brother Billy, as he ran towards the door of the photography shop. But, Ike then withdrew a hidden gun firing one more round towards Wyatt before disappearing. The sound distracted Morgan, enough so that Tom McLaury sent a bullet into Morgan's shoulder. Doc instantly countered, blowing Tom away with blasts from both barrels of his shotgun. Desperately wounded and dying, Billy Clanton fired blindly into the gun smoke encircling him, striking Virgil's leg. Wyatt responded by sending several rounds into Billy.

Then it was silent and the townspeople ran from their homes and shops, wagons were to convey wounded Morgan and Virgil to their respective homes, and doctors followed.

The 30-second shootout left Billy Clanton, Frank McLaury and Tom McLaury dead. Virgil Earp took a shot to the leg and Morgan suffered a shoulder wound. As Wyatt stood, still stunned, Sheriff Behan appeared advising him he was under arrest. The Earps and Doc Holliday were tried for murder but it was determined that the Earps acted within the law. Virgil was later terminated as marshal for his role in the homicides.

On March 18, 1882, the cowboy gang struck again while Morgan Earp was playing pool at Campbell and Hatch's Saloon. A shot was fired from the darkness of the alley striking Morgan in the back. Morgan's body was dressed in one of Doc Holliday's suits and shipped to the parents in Colton, California for burial.

The entire Earp party, including Mattie, accompanied Morgan's body. However, in Tucson, Wyatt, Warren and Doc Holliday hopped off the train in search of Frank Stilwell, who supposedly worked in the railroad yards. The train went on to California without them.

Spotting Stilwell, Wyatt chased him down the track, filling him full of bullet holes. A Coroner's Jury named Wyatt and Warren Earp, Doc Holliday, and two other men named "Texas Jack" Johnson and Sherman McMasters, as those men who had killed Stilwell and warrants were issued for their arrest.

Earp sought vengeance on the men who shot Virgil and killed Morgan. Killing Stilwell was just his first step. Along with Doc Holliday and others, Wyatt began what is known as the Earp Vendetta Ride. Wyatt heard that Pete Spence was at his wood camp in the Dragoons and on March 22, 1882, he and his men quickly headed out, finding not Pete Spence, but Florentino Cruz. The frightened Cruz named all the men who had murdered Morgan, himself included. Earp and his men filled Cruz with bullet holes. The Earp "posse" rode out once again and on March 24, 1882, they ran into Curly Bill Brocius and eight of his men near Iron Springs. A gunfight ensued where Curly Bill was killed and Johnny Barnes received a wound from which he eventually died.

In just over a year, the Earp "posse" along with Doc Holliday, eliminated "Old Man" Clanton, Billy Clanton, Frank McLaury, Tom McLaury, Frank Stilwell, Indian Charlie, Dixie Gray, Florentino Cruz, Johnny Barnes, Jim Crane, Harry Head, Bill Leonard, Joe Hill, Luther King, Charley Snow, Billy Lang, Zwing Hunt, Billy Grounds and Hank Swilling. Pete Spence turned himself in to the authorities where he could "hide" in the penitentiary.

In May, 1882, Wyatt and Doc left Tombstone, swearing they would never return, but still vowing vengeance on Ringo, Clanton, and Spence if they could ever find them. Riding their horses to Silver City, New Mexico, they sold them, rode a stage to Deming, and boarded a train for Colorado. Josie soon joined Wyatt in Denver where they were married.

Though Mattie had traveled with the Earps to California where they joined up with Wyatt's parents, at some point she left them and ended up in Globe, Arizona where she lived a life of prostitution. She told her friends that her husband had destroyed her life when he deserted her. Tragically, she died of a laudanum overdose on July 3, 1888 in Pinal City, Arizona.

While in Colorado, Wyatt initially worked as a private investigator and as a driver for Wells Fargo. He and Josie also occasionally prospected in the mountains. Sometimes Bat Masterson would visit the couple and the pair would see Doc Holliday who had settled down in Leadville, Colorado, when they could.

Wyatt and Josie returned to Dodge City, Kansas in 1883 for a time, then he took his new bride on a tour of Texas and northern Mexico, before they made their way to California.

In the meantime, Doc Holliday's health was badly deteriorating and he soon migrated from Leadville to Denver in the winter of 1885. Though he did not improve in Denver, he was able to see his old friend, Wyatt Earp in the late winter of 1886, where they met in the lobby of the Windsor Hotel. Sadie Marcus described the skeletal Holliday as having a continuous cough and standing on "unsteady legs."

Holliday's health continued to get worse. As a realist, Doc was not one to believe in miraculous cures, but hoping that the Yampah hot springs and sulfur vapors might improve his health, he headed for Glenwood Springs, Colorado in May, 1887. Registering at the fashionable Hotel Glenwood, he grew steadily worse, spending his last fifty-seven days in bed at the hotel and was delirious fourteen of them.

On November 8, 1887, Doc awoke clear-eyed and asked for a glass of whiskey. It was given to him and he drank it down with enjoyment. Then, looking down at his bare feet he said, "This is funny," and died. He always figured he would be killed with his boots on.

Spending several years in California, Wyatt and Josie spent time with the Earps in San Bernardino, and Josie's family in San Francisco. While in California, Wyatt acted as a referee in boxing matches, continued to gamble, and invested in real estate, saloons and a race horse.

In 1897 the gold fever broke in Alaska and the couple headed to Nome where they opened a Saloon during the height of the gold rush. The pair also panned for their own gold throughout the Yukon, and did very well. They returned to California in 1901 with an estimated $80,000. However, their stay was short lived when they heard about the gold strike in Tonopah, Nevada.

Taking up prospecting in earnest, Wyatt staked several claims in the Mojave Desert, where he discovered several veins of gold. Near Vidal, California he discovered copper, where they spent winters in a small cottage.

Spending summers in Los Angeles, he befriended several early Hollywood actors and became an advisor for several Hollywood westerns during the silent movie days.

On January 13, 1929 Wyatt Earp died in Los Angeles at the age of 80 of prostate cancer. Cowboy actors Tom Mix and William S. Hart were among his pallbearers. Wyatt's cremated ashes were buried in Josie's family plot in Colma, California, just south of San Francisco. When Josie died in 1944, she was buried there beside him.

As to the other Earp brothers, Virgil was taken to the family homestead in Colton, California where he recovered from his wounds suffered at the O.K. Corral. Later, he prospected with his wife and, still later, was elected city marshal of Colton. He then returned to prospecting with his wife Allie and died of pneumonia in Goldfield, Nevada in 1905. Virgil is buried in the Riverview Cemetery in Portland, Oregon.

After helping Wyatt in tracking down the Morgan's killers, Warren served as a stage driver and did some prospecting in Globe, Arizona. He then moved to Wilcox, Arizona and in 1900 got into a drunken fight with a cowboy named Johnny Boyet. Boyet shot and killed Warren, who was unarmed at the time. Boyet was acquitted on grounds of self-defense, the jury believing that even an Earp without a gun was more dangerous than most men with a gun in their hand. He is buried in the Wilcox Pioneer Cemetery in Wilcox, Arizona.

When Morgan was killed, James traveled with Virgil and the Earp women to Colton, California for Morgan's burial. Later he lived in Shoshone County, Idaho before settling in permanently in California in 1890. James Earp died on January 25,1926 and is buried in Mountain View Cemetery, in San Bernardino, California.

## Frank Boardman "Pistol Pete" Eaton

*Fastest Draw in Indian Territory*

*"I'd rather have pockets full of rocks than an empty gun."*
Frank B. Eaton

Cowboy, Indian fighter, U.S. Deputy Marshal, scout, and author, Eaton was born on October 26, 1860 in Hartford, Connecticut. When he was eight years old, he moved with his family to a homestead in Twin Mounds, Kansas. That very year, his father, a Union Army veteran, became involved in a dispute with several Confederate men who had ridden with Quantrill's Raiders during the Civil War. A short time later, six of these men appeared at their home and Frank's father was shot in cold blood right in front of the boy. Encouraged by a family friend to avenge the death of his father, the friend began to teach young Eaton to handle a gun.

By the time he was just 15 years-old, he had earned the nickname of "Pistol Pete," for his superior gun handling skills and deadly shots. It was a remarkable feat, as Eaton had been born with a crossed left eye. However, he had overcome this "disability" by figuring out how to aim the gun without sighting down the barrel. He was so good that a friend said he could "Shoot the head off a snake with either hand."

That same year, wanting to learn even more about handling a gun, he visited Fort Gibson, Oklahoma. There, instead of learning anything more, he began to compete with some of the cavalry's best marksmen, beating them every time. His reputation as "packing the truest and fastest guns in Indian Territory" was born.

Frank then began to search for the men who had killed his father years before and legend has it before he was done avenging his father's death, he had tracked down and killed five of the six men who had been involved in the murder in 1868. The last man had been killed in a card game and all had lived lives of crime.

At the age of just 17, he was one of the youngest U.S. Deputy Marshals to have ever been commissioned in the Western District at Fort Smith, Arkansas. Serving under "hanging judge," Isaac Parker, his territory extended from southern Kansas to northern Texas.

He made his home in Bartlesville, Oklahoma and soon had a girlfriend named Jennie who gave him a crucifix to wear around his neck for protection. The girl must have had a premonition as the crucifix actually saved Eaton's life on one occasion when it deflected a bullet that the lawman would have taken in his chest. Frank would later write of this, "I'd rather have the prayers of a good woman in a fight than half a dozen hot guns: she's talking to Headquarters." Unfortunately, Frank never got the opportunity to thank Jennie, as she died of pneumonia. He buried the cross at the head of her grave.

During his career, he was involved in a number of gunfights and was known to always carry a pair of loaded Colt .45 pistols on his hips. In his own words he said his best insurance was: "Throwin' a lot a lead fast and straight."

"Pistol Pete" Eaton

When he was 29, he joined the Oklahoma Land Rush and settled southwest of Perkins, Oklahoma where he served as sheriff and later became a blacksmith. In August, 1893, he married a woman named Orpha Miller of Guthrie, Oklahoma and the couple had two children. Unfortunately, she died of a lung disease seven years into the marriage. He remarried in December, 1902 to a woman named Anna Sillix and the couple would eventually have another eight children.

Frank would continue to serve as a marshal, a sheriff or a deputy sheriff until late in life. By the time his career as a lawman was completed, he reportedly had some 15 notches on his gun belt.

Later, he wrote two books telling the story of the Old West. The first was an autobiography entitled *Veteran of the Old West: Pistol Pete*, which tells of his life as a U.S. Deputy Marshal and cowboy. His second book, entitled *Campfire Stories: Remembrances of a Cowboy Legend* wasn't published until 30 years after his death.

He continued to carry his loaded pistols until his death and was still said to be extremely quick on the draw when he was in his nineties. He died on April 8, 1958 at the age of 97.

During his lifetime, he was married twice, had ten children, 31 grandchildren, and several great-grandchildren.

The phrase "hotter than Pete's pistol," traces back to Eaton's shooting skills and his legendary pursuit of his father's killers.

Frank is honored as the mascot for Oklahoma State University, signifying the Old West and the spirit of Oklahoma. In March, 1997, he posthumously received the prestigious Director's Award at the National Cowboy Hall of Fame.

## Camillus "Buck" Sydney Fly

*Photographer and Lawman*

Though most noted for the many photographs he took during Tombstone, Arizona's wild and wooly days, many may not know that Camillus Sydney Fly was also a lawman.

The Fly's lived in Andrew County, Missouri at the time of Camillus' birth. His parents, Captain Boon and Mary Percival Fly planned to move to California, but Mary was pregnant with her seventh child. Not wanting to deliver her baby on the trail, they waited for him to be born. On May 2, 1849, Camillus Sydney Fly was born and a few weeks later, on May 24th, the family began their trek to California where Fly grew up in Napa County.

He married Mary "Mollie" E. Goodrich on September 29, 1879 in San Francisco. Mary, who was also a photographer, and Camillus soon moved to Arizona Territory, where they settled in Tombstone in December, 1879. Camillus, who preferred to be called "Buck," and his wife immediately set up a photographic studio in a tent before going to work on more permanent quarters.

In July, 1880, they opened up a 12-room boarding house and a studio called the "Fly Gallery" in the back of the building located at 312 Fremont Street in Tombstone.

On October 26, 1881, Fly was in a unique position, as the infamous Gunfight at the O.K. Corral actually took place just off Fremont Street between his studio and Jersey's Livery Stable. During the shootout, Cochise County Sheriff John Behan cowered inside the studio, watching the gunplay, only to be joined by Ike Clanton who fled in terror proclaiming he was unarmed. When the smoke cleared, it was Fly, armed with a Henry rifle, who disarmed a dying Billy Clanton. For some strange reason Fly did not photograph the aftermath of the shootout, but legend has it that he was threatened by one of the Earp's if he did.

Somewhere along the line, Camillus and Mary adopted a little girl they called Kitty, and Mary continued to run the boarding house and studio as Camillus traveled around the area taking photographs. While her husband was out, she acted as one of the few female photographers of the times, taking pictures of anyone who could pay the studio price of 35 cents.

In March, 1886, Camillus accompanied General George Crook to the Canyon de Los Embudos for the negotiations with Geronimo. He became most famous for the photographs of the negotiations, Geronimo and the other wild Apaches he took on March 25 and 26th.

However, at the same time, Fly had become a heavy drinker and the year after these famous photographs were taken, his wife, Mary, took their child and separated from her husband. He then left Tombstone on December 17, 1887 to tour Arizona with his photographs and briefly established a studio in Phoenix in 1893. However, the following year, he returned to the area. In the meantime, Mary continued to run the studio in Tombstone during his absence.

Though his drinking was becoming more and more heavy, he was elected as the Cochise County Sheriff in 1895 and served for two years. Afterwards, he ranched in the Chiricahua Mountains, until his death at Bisbee on October 12, 1901. Though Camillus and his wife had been separated for years, she was at his bedside when he died and made arrangements to have his body returned to Tombstone, where it was buried at the Tombstone Town Cemetery, complete with a stone marker.

Mary continued to run the Tombstone gallery on her own and in 1905, she published a collection of her husband's Indian campaign photographs entitled "Scenes in Geronimo's Camp: The Apache Outlaw and Murderer." In 1912, Mary finally retired, moved to Los Angeles, and donated her husband's negatives to the Smithsonian Institution in Washington, D.C. She died in 1925.

During his lifetime, the Fly Studio created one of the best pictorial records of the early Tombstone area that exists.

## Henry Garfias

*1st Marshal of Phoenix*

Not known in history like many of his more famous counterparts, Enrique "Henry" Garfias, the first marshal of Phoenix, Arizona should be better recognized, as many of his feats of bravery far surpass many of the more famous lawmen of the Old West.

Hailing from what is now Anaheim, California; Enrique was born in 1851, the son of a Mexican Army General. At the age of 20 he headed to Arizona, first settling in Wickenburg. Three years later, in 1874, he moved once again to the fledgling town of Phoenix. At that time, Phoenix had about 1,600 residents, downtown lots were selling for $7 to $11 each, and that same year, the city would get its first telegraph line.

Henry took a job as a county deputy sheriff and quickly honed his shooting skills as he dealt with all manner of riffraff on "Whiskey Row," on the north side of Washington Street. One night in the Capital Saloon, he entered to stop a free-for-all fight that was going on. Pushing his way into the crowd, the 5'9" deputy, who was slender, but well-built, was challenged by a much larger man, who said: "Look who's here. You start dancing and you'd better cut some fancy steps ahead of this lead." The bigger man then moved his hand toward his gun when Henry warned him: "Don't do it."

But the foolish man evidently wasn't aware of Henry's six-gun skills and started to draw. However, before his gun even left his holster, Garfias had drawn and shot him dead.

The town continued to grow quickly and within a year of Henry's coming to Phoenix, there were 16 saloons and four dance halls, most of which were located on hell-raising Whiskey Row. Garfias set his mind to taming the lawless town, quickly responding to disturbances, which were common affairs, especially on Saturday nights.

The only other "law" in the region, filled with rowdy cowboys and miners, was the military garrison stationed at Fort McDowell. More than 30 miles away, they could hardly help matters that often arose quickly and became lethal within minutes. The Latino lawman's reputation began to spread, as one after another, he curtailed the many disturbances.

When Phoenix was officially incorporated into a town in 1881, Garfias was appointed as the town marshal. Later, when a formal municipal election was held he won hands down, becoming the highest elected Mexican American official in the Valley during the 19th century. For the next five years he would serve as the city's first marshal, continuing to subdue the rowdies of Phoenix.

Another tale reports that when he went to arrest an outlaw named Oviedo, who was better known as the "Saber Slasher," Garfias was most definitely not looking forward to the arrest, as the men were personal enemies and Oviedo had threatened to kill Garfias on sight. However, he followed through with the warrant and went after the desperado. When he found him, Garfias fearlessly walked toward the dangerous man. Oviedo wasted no time grabbing his shotgun and firing point blank at the marshal. Again, one of the bad men had underestimated Garfias. By the time that the buckshot from Oviedo's shotgun harmlessly whistled over the marshal's head, Oviedo had two fatal bullets in his body.

On another occasion, several Texas cowboys rode into Phoenix, quickly displaying their habit of shooting up the town. Obviously, they were not familiar with Marshal Garfias. The minute Henry heard the shots, he was headed towards them, watching as the cowboys headed down Washington street, occasionally taking shots at doors, signs, and hanging lamps. Demanding they drop their guns and immediately surrender, the cowpunchers paid no heed and opened fire. When the smoke cleared, Garfias was unharmed, but one cowboy was wounded, and one of them was dead. He then rounded up the others and deposited them in the town jail.

Yet another story tells of a time that the marshal was confronted by four rowdy cowboys who began to take shots at him from horseback, while Garfias was on foot.

This time too, Garfias prevailed, leaving all four of them laying dead in the dusty street. In the meantime, Henry got married to Elena Redondo on April 13, 1883 and the two would eventually have a daughter and a son. He also had a number of other interests in addition to his lawman duties, which paid him $100 a month and a $3 bonus for every conviction he obtained. The marshal also ran a successful cattle ranch in Castle Springs, and established a Spanish newspaper called El Progreso, with his brother-in-law.

For 22 years, Garfias would continue to serve in an official capacity, holding not only the position of town marshal, but later as an assessor, tax collector, constable, pound master, and street superintendent.

Ironically, Henry would not die in one of his many dangerous confrontations, but rather from a fall from a horse. On May 2, 1896, while he was riding one of his favorite horses, the animal spooked and threw him off then rolling on him. Though Garfias initially survived the fall, he was also suffering from tuberculosis and pains from several old wounds. Seven days later he died.

Of the courageous man, the newspapers would say: Garfias was "brave and conscientious and never failed in his duty no matter how much danger menaced him," while the headlines raged: “He was one who knew no fear,” and “Some of his deeds won for him Southwestern renown.”

The Republican also reported, “Arizona has had many brave men, but for cool determined nerve, coupled with a modest unassuming manner, Henry Garfias stood at the head.” The Phoenix Herald praised his bravery and reported what has been stated repeatedly, that Henry Garfias, “had the reputation of never going after a man that did not return with him, dead or alive.”

During his lifetime, Garifas was arguably one of the most honest lawmen and sharpest gunfighters in the American West, on par with more famous names such as Wyatt and Virgil Earp, and Wild Bill Hickok. His deeds were the stuff that legends are made of, but for whatever reasons, his contributions have, sadly, been mostly ignored in history.

Another Latino would not lead Phoenix’s police authority for nearly a century, until Ruben B. Ortega was appointed police chief on February 25, 1980.

## Patrick "Pat" Garret

*An Unlucky Lawman*

Born in Chambers County, Alabama, on June 5, 1850, Patrick Floyd Jarvis Garrett was one of seven children born to John and Elizabeth Garrett. Three years later, Pat's father, John Garrett, purchased a Louisiana plantation in Claiborne Parish, where young Garrett grew up.

Pat Garrett

A tall, thin angular man with prominent cheek bones, Garrett left Louisiana for Dallas County, Texas at the age of 19. There, he worked on the large LS Ranch in west Texas as a cowboy and cattle gunman when rustling was rampant in the area.

From there he joined up with W. Skelton Glenn, as a buffalo hunter. However, he soon got into a disagreement with a fellow hunter over some hides. The altercation soon led to gun play and when the other man drew on Garrett, Pat shot him dead.

By 1878, he had moved on to Fort Sumner, New Mexico just as the Lincoln County War was drawing to an end. The battle between rival gangs spawned a storm of lawlessness and violence which would continue in southeastern New Mexico for the next two decades.

Garrett first went to work on Peter Maxwell's ranch. A year later he quit and worked as a bartender at a saloon called Beaver Smith's. Soon after, he married a woman named Juanita Gutierrez, but she died before the end of the year. A little more than a year later, on January 14, 1880, he married Juanita's sister Apolinaria. The two would have nine children over the years.

It was at the saloon that Pat Garrett met and often gambled with William Bonney, better known as Billy the Kid. The two were seen together so often they soon took on the nicknames of "Big Casino" and "Little Casino."

On November 7, 1880, Garrett was appointed as the Lincoln County Sheriff. Friends or not, his first vow was to bring the current reign of lawlessness to an end with the primary goal of apprehending Billy the Kid.

On December 15, 1880, Governor Wallace put a $500 reward on Billy's head and Pat Garrett began the relentless pursuit of the outlaw. Garrett set-up many traps and ambushes in an attempt to apprehend Billy, but the Kid seemed to have an animal instinct that warned him of danger. However, that was not to last.

On December 19, 1880 Garrett confronted Billy and his gang when they rode into Fort Sumner, New Mexico. Killing Tom O'Folliard, the rest of the gang escaped. Soon, the determined Garrett and his posse tracked the outlaws down to Stinking Springs and surrounded the hideout. After a several day siege, the posse killed Charlie Bowdre and captured Billy the Kid, Dirty Dave Rudabaugh, Tom Pickett and Billy Wilson on December 23, 1880.

Billy the Kid was tried and sentenced to hang in Lincoln, New Mexico on May 13, 1881. However, he escaped from jail on April 18, 1881, killing two guards in the process.

Garrett went after the Kid once again and arrived at Peter Maxwell's ranch on July 14, 1881 to question him about Billy's whereabouts. As Maxwell and Garrett sat in Peter's darkened bedroom in Old Fort Sumner, Billy unexpectedly entered the room. The Kid didn't recognize Garrett in the poor lighting conditions and asked "¿Quien es? ¿Quien es?" (Spanish for "Who is it? Who is it?), to which Garrett responded with two shots from his revolver, the first striking Billy's heart.

Billy the Kid was buried in a plot in-between his dead friends Tom O'Folliard and Charlie Bowdre the next day at Fort Sumner's cemetery.

Though the New Mexican newspaper said, "...Sheriff Garrett is the hero of the hour," most people in the area saw him as a villain for having killed a favorite son. Although he had put his life on the line for his community, he lost the next election for sheriff of Lincoln County.

Garrett then turned to ranching and began to write a book about Billy the Kid. Published in 1882, *The Authentic Life of Billy the Kid, the Noted Desperado of the Southwest*, didn't sell well as eight books had already beat him to the press.

In 1884, Garrett ran for New Mexico state senator where he again lost the election. Fed up, Garrett moved his family to Tascosa, Texas where he became captain of the LS Texas Rangers. However, this role would not last long, as Garrett quit within just a few weeks and returned to southeastern New Mexico, this time to Roswell.

In 1890 he ran for sheriff of the newly created Chaves County. However, when he lost, he bitterly left New Mexico once again, living in Uvalde, Texas, where he raised and raced horses for several years.

In 1899, Garrett purchased a ranch in the San Andres Mountains of New Mexico and in October, he was appointed sheriff of Dona Ana County, New Mexico. His family stayed on the ranch while Pat worked in Las Cruces, Mesilla and Dona Ana.

On December 16, 1901, President Theodore Roosevelt, infatuated by gunfighters in the West, appointed Pat Garrett as a United States Customs Collector at El Paso, Texas. However, it was a controversial appointment and when his term was over in 1905, Roosevelt refused to reappoint him. Garrett and his family returned to the ranch only to find Garrett in the midst of financial difficulties due to back taxes and liability for a loan he had co-signed for a friend.

Becoming increasingly morose over the situation, he began to drink and gamble too much. However, still trying to make a living, he started a new horse breeding operation.

To help with his financial problems, Garrett leased part of his land to a man named Wayne Brazel who was to graze cattle upon the land. However, he soon found that Brazel had brought in several thousand goats, which were considered to be even worse than sheep, as far as cattlemen were concerned.

Owing money to many people in the Roswell area, Garrett desperately approached another rancher named Carl Adamson in January, 1908 to see if he might be interested in buying his ranch. However, when he neared Adamson's home, Carl's wife, Amanda, ordered him from the property at gunpoint.

However, Adamson and Garrett met later and agreed on the sale. But, Wayne Brazel refused to break his five year lease unless Garrett bought his goats. Brazel and Garrett made the deal, but soon Brazel wanted even more money. Though angry, Garrett finally agreed to Brazel's terms.

On February 29, 1908, Garrett and Adamson were in a buckboard bound for Las Cruces, where they would meet Brazel to close the deal. On the way, Brazel caught up with them and as words grew heated, Adamson threatened to back out of the purchase. Afterwards, Brazel rode on while Garrett and Adamson continued in the buckboard.

Just miles outside of Las Cruces, they stopped the wagon and while Adamson was relieving himself off the back of the buckboard, three shots rang out. Pat Garrett lay dead. Adamson left his body in the desert and continued on to Las Cruces. Once there,

Adamson swore he never saw who shot Garrett and Brazel confessed to the shooting, claiming it was self-defense.

When the body was retrieved, numerous cigarette butts were found off the trail, indicating that someone had been waiting for them. This led to the belief that the shooting was an obvious conspiracy, involving two more people. Allegedly, Brazel took the "fall" for the murder because he was single. Also implicated in the killing was hired assassin, Killin' Jim Miller, because Carl Adamson was married to a cousin of Jim Miller's wife, Sallie. However, most historians deem this unlikely.

While Garrett's remains lay in the undertaker's parlor, dozens of gawkers came to see the man who had killed Billy the Kid. On March 5, 1908, he was buried in Las Cruces, New Mexico.

Brazel was later tried; however, he was acquitted of the crime.

Controversy still exists over whether Garrett's murder was a conspiracy in order to gain his land or if it was just simply the dispute with an irate Brazel.

## James Butler "Wild Bill" Hickok

*Wild Bill Hickok & The Dead Man's Hand*

Wild Bill Hickok was born James Butler Hickok in Troy Grove, Illinois on May 27, 1837 to William Alonzo Hickok and Polly Butler Hickok. Bill had four brothers and two sisters and his parents were God-fearing Baptists who expected Bill to keep up his chores on the farm and to attend church every Sunday. Bill's parents also operated a station along the Underground Railroad, where they smuggled slaves out of the South. It was during this time that the lean and wiry young man got his first taste of hostile gunfire when he and his father were chased by law officers who suspected them of carrying more than just hay in their wagon. Bill became enamored with guns and began target practice on the small wildlife around the farm. His romantic notions of the Wild West never sat very well with his father, but despite the protests, Bill became locally recognized as an outstanding marksman even in his youth. At the age of 14, Bill's father was killed because of his stand on abolition. Three years later, when Bill was 17, he went to work as a towpath driver on the Illinois and Michigan Canal. However, a year later he headed to Kansas getting a job in Monticello driving a stagecoach on the Santa Fe and Oregon Trails. One of the first people he was to meet in Kansas was Bill Cody, who would later claim fame with his Buffalo Bill Wild West Show.

Wild Bill Hickok

In 1855, stagecoaches were often subject to the threats of bandits and Indians along the trail and Bill quickly put his marksmanship to work, as well as developing a ready belligerence to the frequent attacks. On one such overland trip, the stage broke down near Wetmore, Colorado. As Wild Bill slept under some bushes outside, the customers stayed within the coach until they were awakened by a disturbance. One of the travelers lit a kerosene lantern to find Bill being attacked by a cinnamon bear. When the struggle between man and bear was over, Bill was severely wounded, but the bear lay dead on the ground from Hickok's six inch knife.

After recovering from the almost lethal attack, Wild Bill headed back to Monticello, Kansas where he accepted a position as a peace officer on March 22, 1858. Sometime after that he worked for the Pony Express and Overland Express station in Rock Creek, Nebraska, where he met David McCanles. McCanles teased Hickok unmercifully about his girlish build and feminine features. Perhaps in retaliation, Hickok began courting a woman by the name of Sarah Shull who McCanles had his eye on.

On July 12, 1861, McCanles, along with his young son and two friends by the names of James Woods and James Gordon came to the station, supposedly to collect a debt. However, profanities were exchanged which resulted in gunfire. McCanles was killed and both James Woods and James Gordon, who were seriously wounded, later died of their wounds. No charges were made against Hickok on the grounds of self-defense. Later, when Hickok's fame began to spread, writers looked back and began to call this gunfight the "McCanles Massacre", embellishing the story to the point that Wild Bill had polished off a dozen of the West's most dangerous desperados.

Wild Bill Hickok in 1869

Hickok moved on again, landing in Sedalia, Missouri where he signed on with the Union Army as a wagon master and scout on October 30, 1861. The military records of his service give very little information regarding his services, but we do know that Hickok received the nickname "Wild Bill" while he was serving in the Union Army. As the story goes, he was in Independence, Missouri when he encountered a drunken mob with intentions of hanging a bartender who had shot a hoodlum in a brawl. Hickok fired two shots over the heads of the men, staring them down with an angry glare until the mob dispersed. A grateful woman was allegedly heard to shout from the sidelines, "Good for you, Wild Bill!" She may have mistaken Hickok for someone else, but the name stuck.

In July of 1865 Hickok met up with a twenty-six-year-old gambler in Springfield, Missouri, to whom Hickok lost at the gaming table. When Bill couldn't pay up, Dave Tutt took his pocket watch for security. Hickok growled that if Tutt so much as used the timepiece, he would kill him.

On July 21, 1865, the two met in the public square, Tutt proudly wearing the watch for all to see. Moments later, Tutt lay on the ground dead. Hickok was acquitted of any wrong doing.

During his time in the Army, Hickok became good friends with General George Custer, working as one of his principal scouts. Custer was said to have admired Hickok, played poker with him, and would have known him better had it not been for the disaster at Little Big Horn.

Shortly after the war, in 1867, Hickok was tracked down by Henry M. Stanley, correspondent for the New York Herald who later went to Africa and "found" Dr. Livingstone. Hickok blithely told the gullible Stanley that he had personally slain over 100 men. Stanley immediately reported this claim as gospel fact and Wild Bill became a national legend.

On November 5, 1867, Wild Bill ran for sheriff of Ellsworth County, Kansas, but lost. He returned to the army where he was lanced in the foot during a skirmish with an Indian in eastern Colorado. Returning to Kansas, he became the sheriff of Hays City, Kansas in 1869. On August 24, 1869, he shot and killed a man named Bill Mulrey. Just a month later on September 27, 1869, he killed a ruffian named Strawhan when he and several others were causing a disturbance in a local saloon.

On July 17, 1870, real trouble started for Hickok when several members of the 7th U.S. Cavalry caught him off guard in Drum's Saloon, knocked him to the floor and began kicking him. Hickok drew his pistols, killing one private and seriously wounding another. After this skirmish, Bill resigned his position in Hays City, landing back in Ellsworth, Kansas for a time, then on to Abilene, Kansas.

On April 15, 1871, Hickok was appointed city marshal in Abilene, for $150 per month, plus one fourth of all fines assessed against the persons he arrested. At first Wild Bill tended to routine business.

When John Wesley Hardin, purportedly the worst killer in the Wild West, arrived in Abilene, Wild Bill took an indulgent and parent-like attitude toward the nasty little murderer. They drank together, visited the brothels together, and Hickok often gave Hardin advice. Hardin enjoyed being seen with the celebrated gunfighter, but he was also cautious around the city marshal, sure in the knowledge that if he got seriously out of line, Wild Bill would add him to his reputation.

However, it didn't take long before Hardin crossed the line. Sleeping at the American House Hotel, he was awakened by the sound of snoring coming from the next room. Angry at having been awakened, Hardin fired two shots through the wall. In the deathly silence, Hardin knew that Marshal Hickok would waste no time in chasing him down.

Crawling out a window onto the roof dressed only in his undershirt, Hardin spotted Wild Bill approaching and dove from the roof into a hay stack, where he hid for the rest of the night. With the dawn, Hardin merged, stole a horse and high-tailed it out of town dressed only in his underclothes.

Hickok gradually spent more time at the gaming tables and with the ladies of the evening than he did taking care of his sheriff duties. One young man in Abilene, by the name of Samuel Henry, described Hickok's gambling habits as:

> His whole bearing was like that of a hunted tiger – restless eyes, which nervously looked about him in all directions closely scrutinizing every stranger. When he played cards, which he did most of the time in the saloons, he sat in the corner of the room to prevent an enemy from stealing up behind him.

A local newspaper complained that Hickok allowed Abilene to be overrun with gamblers, con men, prostitutes and pimps.

However, Wild Bill did have some marshalling to do and the Bull's Head Saloon gave him the most trouble. Phil Coe and Ben Thompson, gamblers and gunmen, were the owners of the saloon and what brought matters to a head was an oversize painting of a Texas Longhorn painted in full masculinity. Most Abilene townspeople were offended by the sign and demanding the animal's anatomy be altered, Hickok stood by with a shotgun as the necessary deletions were made to the painting. Later, Thompson left town and Coe sold his interest in the saloon, although he remained on as a gambler. When Hickok and Coe began to court the same woman, rumors started to circulate that each planned to kill the other.

On October 5, 1871, the trouble finally came to a head. Many cowboys were in town, fighting, drinking, carousing, and only Deputy Mike Williams offered Hickok his assistance. Coe was celebrating the end of the cattle season and when he and his friends neared the Alamo Saloon, a vicious dog tried to bite him, prompting Coe to take a shot at the dog.

Though he missed the dog, Hickok appeared just minutes later to investigate the shots. Upon Coe's explanation, Wild Bill explained to Coe that firearms were not allowed in the city, but for whatever reason, all hell broke loose and Coe sent a bullet Hickok's way. Bill returned the fire and shot Coe twice in the stomach. Suddenly, Hickok heard footsteps coming up behind him and turning swiftly; he fired again and killed Deputy Mike Williams. Coe died three days later.

Abilene had had enough. The city fathers told the Texans there could be no more cattle drives through their town and dismissed Hickok as city marshal.

At about this time the east coast was thriving on the Wild West stories in the dime novels that were being turned out and the exaggerated articles displayed in the press.

Having had some luck at the gaming tables, Hickok decided to join the foray and put together a show called "The Daring Buffalo Chase of the Plains" in the early 1870's. Making a thousand dollar investment, he packed up six buffalos, four Comanches, three cowboys, a bear and a monkey, and headed on a train to Niagara Falls. But the show was a disaster. The once frisky buffalo acted like Jersey cows, until Wild Bill fired a shot. Suddenly the buffalo ran circles with the Comanches screaming in pursuit, some stray dogs mixed into the fray, as well as several children chased by their parents, and all hell broke loose. Suddenly, the buffalo broke through a wire fence and stampeded the audience. Wild Bill made only a little over $100 for his show and had to sell the buffalos to a butcher shop to pay the expenses home for everybody.

However, his old friend Buffalo Bill Cody came to his rescue. Inviting Hickok to join his dramatic play entitled "Scouts of the Prairies," Wild Bill made a decent income and was able to indulge in his love for women and gambling, but an actor he was not. Nor was he happy, beginning to drink a lot, his acting became even worse, and finally in March of 1874 he said goodbye to Cody and headed back out West.

On March 5, 1876, Hickok married an older woman by the name of Agnes Lake Thatcher, who had been chasing him around the country for years and patiently waiting for him to tire of his long string of female companions.

By this time he was almost 39, going bald, wearing glasses, and was said to have sensed his oncoming death. Marrying in Cheyenne, Wyoming, the two traveled to Cincinnati for their honeymoon. Just a month later, Bill explained to her that he was headed to the western goldfields to make a grubstake and would send for her later. She would never see him again.

By the time Hickok accompanied Charlie Utter's wagon train to Deadwood, South Dakota, his reputation as a gunfighter had preceded him. Initially, he attempted to lead a quiet, reasonably respectable life in the wild mining camp, but his two greatest failings – gambling and liquor, led him into the rough saloons lining the main street of the narrow gulch.

Along the wagon train to Deadwood, Hickok met Calamity Jane in Laramie, Wyoming. Being very much alike with their outrageous tales and heavy drinking habits, the two hit if off immediately. Later, Calamity Jane would tell everyone that they were a "couple," but this has been much disputed.

Seemingly uninterested in a grubstake, Wild Bill tried vainly to resume a career as a gambler, but no longer possessed the requisite skills. In fact, he was just barely able to keep himself properly suited and situated so as to hold on to the reputation and the illusion. He was seldom sober and was repeatedly arrested for vagrancy.

On the evening of August 1, 1876, Hickok was playing poker in a Deadwood saloon with several men, including a man by the name of Jack McCall, who lost heavily. Wild Bill generously gave him back enough money to buy something to eat, but advised him not to play again until he could cover his losses.

The next afternoon when Wild Bill entered Nuttall & Mann's Saloon he found Charlie Rich sitting in his preferred seat. After some hesitation, Wild Bill joined the game, reluctantly seating himself with his back to the door and the bar – a fatal mistake. Jack McCall, drinking heavily at the bar, saw Hickok enter the saloon, taking a seat at his regular table in the corner near the door.

McCall slowly walked around to the corner of the saloon where Hickok was playing his game. From under his coat, McCall pulled a double-action .45 pistol, shouted "Take that!" and shot Wild Bill Hickok in the back of the head, killing him instantly. Hickok had been holding a pair of eights, and a pair of Aces, which has ever since been known as the "dead man's hand."

Hickok's good friend, Charlie Utter, claimed the body, made the funeral arrangements, and bought the burial plot. He was buried in the cemetery outside Deadwood on August 3, 1876. Calamity Jane insisted that a proper grave be built in honor of the man she loved, and a 10'x10' enclosure was built around his burial plot encircled by a 3' fence with fancy cast iron filigree on top. A small American flag was stuck into the ground in front of the tombstone in honor of his service in the War.

The entire population of the gulch, prospectors to prostitutes, followed his funeral procession to "boot hill." Charlie Utter placed a wooden marker on the grave inscribed:

Wild Bill<br>
J. B. Hickok<br>
Killed by the assassin Jack McCall<br>
Deadwood, Black Hills<br>
August 2, 1876<br>
Pard we will meet again in the<br>
Happy Hunting Grounds to part no more<br>
Good bye<br>
Colorado Charlie, C. H. Utter

Soon, his new bride would receive a letter that Bill had penned just one day before his death. Seemingly, it appears that he had a premonition of his rapidly approaching demise:

Agnes Darling, if such should be we never meet again, while firing my last shot, I will gently breathe the name of my wife – Agnes – and with wishes even for my enemies I will make the plunge and try to swim to the other shore.

The day after Hickok was killed, a jury panel was selected to try Jack McCall. McCall claimed he had shot Wild Bill in revenge for killing his brother back in Abilene, Kansas and maintained that he would do it all over again given the chance. In less than two hours the jury returned a "not guilty" verdict that evoked this comment in the local newspaper: "Should it ever be our misfortune to kill a man ... we would simply ask that our trial may take place in some of the mining camps of these hills."

McCall hung about Deadwood for several days, until a man called California Joe strongly suggested the air might be bad for McCall's health. McCall got the message and believing he'd escaped punishment for his crime, headed to Wyoming bragging to anyone who would listen that he had killed the famous Wild Bill Hickok.

Less than a month later, the trial held in Deadwood was found to have had no legal basis, Deadwood being located in Indian Territory. McCall was arrested in Laramie, Wyoming on August 29, 1876, charged with the murder, and taken to Yankton, South Dakota to stand trial.

Deadwood, South Dakota in 1876

Lorenzo Butler Hickok traveled from Illinois to attend the trial of his brother's murderer and was gratified by the guilty verdict. On March 1, 1877, Jack McCall was put to death by hanging. As to McCall's earlier claim of having shot Hickok out of revenge for his brother, it was later discovered that Jack McCall never had a brother.

Fourteen years after Hickok's death, in 1900, an aging Calamity Jane arranged to be photographed next to his overgrown burial site. Elderly, thin and poor, her clothes were ragged and held together with safety pins. Holding a flower in her hand, she said that when she died she wanted to be buried next to the man she loved. Three years later, she was.

# John B. Jones

*Commanding the Texas Rangers*

Confederate officer and Major in the Texas Rangers, John B. Jones was born in Fairfield District South Carolina, on December 22, 1834 to Henry and Nancy (Robertson) Jones. He moved with his family to Texas when he was just four years old, first settling in Travis County. He attended Rutersville College near La Grange, Texas before moving back to South Carolina, where he attended Mt. Zion College at Winnsboro.

John B. Jones

After he graduated, he returned to Texas and began farming and stock-raising. When the Civil War broke out, he volunteered in the Confederate Army as a private in Colonel Benjamin Terry's Texas Rangers. However, only after a month, he was appointed Adjutant of the Fifteenth Texas Infantry and remained in the Trans-Mississippi Department throughout the war. He saw service in Texas, Arkansas, Louisiana and Indian Territory. In 1863, he was appointed Adjutant-General of a brigade.

At wars end, Jones took the defeat of the Confederacy hard, and after the war, he spent some time traveling in Mexico and Brazil trying to establish a colony for other disgruntled former Confederates. However, never finding a suitable location, he returned to Texas and in 1868 was elected to the Texas State Legislature, but did not take the seat.

In May, 1874, he was appointed by Governor Richard Coke, Major of the Frontier Battalion of Texas Rangers, and took command of six companies. While in command, he participated in a number of Indian skirmishes with the Comanche, Kiowa and Apache. In 1877, he was sent to El Paso in an attempt to restore order among the citizens. That same year, he was sent to Lampasas, Texas to negotiate a truce in the notorious Horrell-Higgins Feud. He was also involved in capturing or killing a number of outlaws including Sam Bass in 1878.

In 1879, he was appointed as the Adjutant-General of the State of Texas. While serving as adjutant general and still commanding the Frontier Battalion, he died of natural causes in Austin on July 19, 1881. He is buried in Oakwood Cemetery.

John B. Jones is a member of the Texas Ranger Hall of Fame.

## Charles Frederick "Kid" Lambert

*Lawman & Artist of Cimarron, New Mexico*

Fred Lambert, sworn in at the age of 16, was the youngest Territorial Marshal from New Mexico.

In 1887 Charles Fred "Cyclone" Lambert was born to Henri and Mary Lambert in Room #31 of the famous St. James Hotel in Cimarron, New Mexico.

It was a blustery winter night with a blizzard blowing outside and at the time of his birth one of the hotel guests, and good friend of the Lambert family, laughingly commented that he should be named "Cyclone Dick," much to Mary's chagrin. However, she went along with it and the couple soon asked the guest to be Fred's godfather, which he gladly accepted. The guest and Fred's godfather was none other than Buffalo Bill Cody. Buffalo Bill would later give Fred instruction in the use of guns when he got older.

Fred Lambert in this 1968 photo depicting all of the various law enforcement badges he wore during his career.

Fred's father, Henri Lambert, started Lambert's Inn which later became the St. James Hotel. Henri was the one time personal chef of President Abraham Lincoln and Lambert's Inn, which he built in 1872, became a notorious place during the wild and bawdy days of the Old West.

The Inn hosted all manner of famous and infamous people including Wyatt Earp, Bat Masterson, Jesse James, Black Jack Ketchum, Clay Allison and many more. Fred grew up knowing some of these people and was a bit of a showman himself. During the saloon's early heyday 27 men were shot and killed. In fact the saloon was so notorious that during the 1870's the favorite expressions in Cimarron were: "Who was killed at Lambert's last night?" and "It appears Lambert had himself another man for breakfast."

In 1902, the dining area was remodeled by the Lambert sons and they counted over four hundred bullet holes in the ceiling, many of which can still be seen today. A double layer of heavy wood prevented anyone sleeping upstairs from being killed. Today, the ceiling of the dining room still holds 22 bullet holes.

At 15, Fred was a freight wagon driver on the run between Cimarron and Taos. About the same time he took a job with the Indian Police. On one of his first assignments, staking out Picuris Peak near the Taos Pueblo, Fred and two other deputies got into a brawl with some outlaws. Suspecting moonshine traffic, the trio watched as a train of mules and six men came down the trail loaded with whiskey. When Fred approached them, the leader, a man by the name of Juan Gallegos, drew his gun. But Fred was too quick for him and grabbed the gun around the cylinder at the same time that the hammer came down smashing the web of his hand. With his other hand, Fred pulled his own gun and struck Gallegos between the eyes. Gaining the upper hand the deputies arrested the entire gang, but Fred would live with a scar on his hand for the rest of his life.

At the age of 16, Fred would become the youngest Territorial Marshal from New Mexico and would continue to serve as a tough lawman in many capacities for his entire life.

When Fred was still learning the tricks of the Sheriff trade, he was befriended by a man named Frank Harrington, the man who shot Black Jack Ketchum, which ultimately resulted in his arrest. Frank took him out behind the stone walls of the Cimarron Jail, and taught him to shoot.

By the time Fred became the Sheriff of Cimarron, the wild days of Cimarron were over. As Fred walked the streets of Cimarron the worst thing that usually happened was taking care of a drunken "Bunny" Alpers.

Alpers, who also happened to be the mayor, had a habit for Saturday night binges. Whenever "Bunny" passed out or there was trouble at the tavern, the bar keeper would hang an old red railroad lantern on the porch, a signal for Fred to come and help. When Bunny passed out in chair, Fred would load him in a wheelbarrow and haul him home, where he would dump him in front of his house.

Fred was also many things other than a lawman. Somewhere along the line he married a woman named Katie Hoover and they adopted a young Navajo boy named Manuel Cruz. When not serving for the law, he was also an active rancher. Fred also took on the restoration of the Aztec Mill, which was built in 1864 by Lucien B. Maxwell, of the Maxwell Land Grant. For many years, Fred operated the century-old Maxwell grist mill as a museum and a tourist attraction. The Aztec Mill Museum is now operated by the Cimarron Historical Society. Due to his efforts, many other historic landmarks in Cimarron were made sites of markers which tell their story.

Mr. Lambert was also caring, thoughtful and a well-read man. During his life he wrote poetry, published and contributed to several books, and made many pen and ink drawings and paintings. He published a book of his poems and pen and ink drawings titled, *Bygone Days Of The Old West* and contributed to other books including, *A Cowboy Detective,* and *New Mexico, A Guide to the Colorful State*. He assisted in the preparation of a book on the history of the New Mexico Mounted Police, *The Thin Gray Line*, and wrote a brief introduction entitled, "A Few Words From an Old Mountie". He also served as a consultant for other publications such as, *Satan's Paradise: From Lucien Maxwell to Fred Lambert and Haunted Highways.*

Fred Lambert passed away on February 3, 1971.

## John M. Larn

*Vigilante, Outlaw & Lawman*

So respected as a vigilante in the lawless settlement of Fort Griffin, Texas, John M. Larn was elected sheriff, a mistake the town's population would not soon forget.

Born in Mobile, Alabama on March 1, 1849, Larn traveled to Colorado as a teenager where he found work as a ranch hand. However, after an argument with his boss over a horse around 1869, he shot and killed him. Soon he fled to New Mexico, where he killed a local sheriff who he thought was trailing him. Continuing on into Texas, he settled in Fort Griffin, where in 1871 he worked as a trail boss for a local rancher named Bill Hays. While on a cattle drive to Trinidad, Colorado, he allegedly killed two Mexicans and a sheep herder. Somewhere along the line, Larn married Mary Jane Matthews from the noted Matthews family and became a well known citizen of Shackelford County.

John M. Larn

However, by 1873, allegations began to surface that Larn was involved in cattle rustling. Ironically, that same year, he got a warrant for the arrest of every member of Bill Hays' cattle outfit for rustling.

As he accompanied a posse of thirteen soldiers from Fort Griffin, the men ambushed and killed every member of the outfit near Bush Knob, Texas. In 1874 he joined the Tin Hat Brigade in Fort Griffin, a vigilante group that worked swiftly bringing "justice" to many a horse thief who was left hanging from a tree near the river. As a member of the Tin Hat Brigade, he gained so much respect, he was elected sheriff of Fort Griffin in April, 1876. That same month, the Tin Hat Brigade caught a man in the act of stealing a horse and promptly hanged him to a pecan tree. Leaving his body hanging there for all to see, they also left a pick and shovel below his gruesome remains for anyone who might have wished to remove the thief and bury him. In the next three months the Fort Griffin vigilantes shot two more horse thieves and hanged six others.

Shortly after taking the sheriff's position, Larn entered into a private contract with the local territorial garrison to deliver three steers of cattle per day. However, Larn had different ideas and began to plan with longtime friend and recently deputized John Selman, to simply rustle the cattle from neighboring ranchers rather than having to provide his own. Before long, he and Selman, instead of controlling the area crime, were controlling the vigilantes, rustling even more cattle and otherwise terrorizing the county. However, suspicions were soon raised as a number of ranchers noticed that while their herds were slowly shrinking, Larn's remained unaffected. Obviously profitable, Larn soon built a house at Camp Cooper Ranch on the Cedar Fork in Lambshead, Texas.

After serving less than a year as sheriff, Larn resigned as sheriff on March 7, 1877 and was replaced by his deputy, William Cruger, a month later. Moving on to outright cattle rustling, he and Selman continued to profit and in March, 1877 were appointed as deputy hide inspectors for Shackelford County. Opportune positions for the cattle thieves, they were to inspect all cattle herds entering and leaving the county, as well as supervising the butchers. Larn also continued to supply Fort Griffin with its beef and as more and more cattle went missing, the complaints grew louder and louder. A number of violent acts were also being reported as a band of men, allegedly led by Larn and Selman, were bushwhacking area ranchers, driving off their cattle, shooting horses, and firing potshots at the homes of terrified citizens.

Finally, in February, 1878, a group of civilians secured a warrant to search the river behind Larn's house. Looking for hides that didn't belong to him, six were recovered from the river with brands other than Larn's own. Though Larn was arrested, he was later released and violence continued.

However, in June, 1878 a local rancher named Treadwell, who had reportedly uncovered the cattle rustling, was wounded by Larn and the Albany court issued a warrant for his arrest. Sheriff William Cruger was then tasked with arresting his former boss, which he did on June 22, 1878. After placing him in the jail, Cruger had the local blacksmith shackle Larn to the floor of the cell to prevent a breakout by Larn's supporters.

Instead, the next night, the Tin Hat Brigade, stormed the jail intending to hang Larn. When they found they couldn't lynch the shackled man, they shot him in his cell. Afterwards, his body was returned to Camp Cooper Ranch where he was buried beside his infant son.

After Larn was captured and killed, Selman took off for lawless Lincoln County, New Mexico, where he started a vicious gang called Selman's Scouts. For two months these outlaws terrorized the area, stealing horses and cattle, murdering innocent men and boys, and pillaging businesses and homes.

They were finally stopped when Governor Lew Wallace issued a proclamation threatening martial law. Selman returned to Texas where he was captured by Texas Rangers in 1880 and taken to Shackelford County to stand trial for his previous crimes. However, he soon escaped and made his way to Chihuahua, Mexico where he lived until 1888. The Texas charges were then dropped and he moved to El Paso where he remarried and made his living primarily as a gambler and sometimes as a City Constable. On April 5, 1894, he killed former Texas Ranger Baz (Bass) Outlaw during a fight in Tillie Howard's brothel.

The following year, on August 19, 1895, he killed the famous gunman John Wesley Hardin in the Acme Saloon. Though charged with murder, his trial resulted in a hung jury. While out on bond, he ran into Marshal George Scarborough and when talk elevated into a dispute, then to gunplay, Scarborough shot Selman four times. Selman died on April 6, 1896 and Scarborough was acquitted of murder.

## William Sidney "Cap" Light

*Texas Marshal and Soapy Smith Man*

William Sidney "Cap" Light served as an exemplary lawman in Belton, Texas until his brother-in-law, Soapy Smith, convinced him to join his criminal empire.

Light was born around 1864 near Belton, Texas to merchants W.R. and Eliza Hyatt Light, who originally hailed from Tennessee. He started out his working life as a barber, but at the age of 20 accepted the position of deputy marshal in Belton. He had barely begun the job when he was a member of the posse that tracked down and killed a local outlaw by the name of William Northcott on March 24, 1884.

Three years later, he married Eva Katherine Smith of Temple, Texas in June 1887. Eva was the sister of Randolph Jefferson "Soapy" Smith, who Light would later be involved with in criminal affairs.

But, for the time being, Light remained faithful to the law. He and Eva had two children, William Jeff Light in 1890 and a daughter, Emma Ruby Light in 1892.

In August, while Light was helping out the marshal of nearby Temple, Texas, "Cap" was trying to take a captured prisoner by the name of Ed Cooley to jail. When Cooley tried to escape, Deputy Light shot him.

A short time later, in the fall, a man named Sam Hasley, was carrying on drunk and disorderly in Belton. Hasley, who had been involved in the Early-Hasley feud decades earlier following the Civil War, had continued to maintain a rowdy reputation as a trouble maker. When Light ordered him to go home, Hasley ignored him and began to ride his horse on the sidewalk, daring Light to do something about it. Light responded by attempting to arrest the wayward Hasley. But when Sam pulled out his gun, Light had little choice to respond and shot Hasley dead.

Light killed another man the following year in March. When Felix Morales was drunk and creating a ruckus in Temple's Cotton Exchange Saloon, Light confronted him. The drunken Morales made the mistake of pulling his gun, but Light was quicker on the draw and Morales was soon dead on the floor. According to a local newspaper article of the time, Morales died with "his pistol in one hand and a beer glass in the other."

Up until 1891, William Light had served law enforcement in an exemplary capacity. However, it was in this year that his brother-in-law, the notorious Randolph Jefferson "Soapy" Smith, convinced him to join him in Denver, Colorado. Soapy, known as the "King of the Frontier Con Men," was by then firmly in control of the Denver underworld crime faction. Light was with Soapy when the gang "attacked" the Glasson Detective

Agency. Allegedly the agency had attempted to force a confession from a pretty young girl and upon hearing about it, Smith and his men raided their offices with pistols in hand. This further led to Soapy's reputation as a hero with many of the locals.

The next year, when Soapy moved his operations to the booming silver rush camp of Creede, Colorado, he convinced Light to go with him. "Cap" soon became a deputy marshal in the camp and helped Soapy to become the "boss" of the quickly growing settlement. On March 31, 1892 he showed his gunfighting skills once again when he encountered a drunken William "Reddy" McCann. "Reddy," a Creede faro dealer, who had a long gunfighting history of his own, had been drinking heavily all night. By 4:15 a.m. he was showing his shooting skills by blasting the streets lights in the camp. By the time Deputy Light confronted him, McCann was back drinking in the Branch Saloon.

When Light tried to arrest McCann, the drunken man became argumentative and resisted. Light tried to talk sense into him, but McCann continued to resist until finally the deputy slapped him in the face, knocking a cigar out of his mouth.

McCann pulled his gun, but Light was faster, once again. As McCann lay dying on the floor his last words were reportedly, "I'm killed." The coroner's jury found that Light had acted in self-defense. But, Light had had enough of killing. He soon quit his deputy job as well as the Soapy Smith Gang and returned to Texas.

Settling in Temple, Light applied for a job as a detective for the Gulf, Colorado & Santa Fe Railroad in June, 1892. When he didn't get the position, he blamed the railroad's chief detective, T.J. Coggins. Sometime later when Light was drinking heavily he ran into Coggins and began to beat him with both his fists and his pistol barrel. He soon found himself in jail for assault.

At his hearing, Coggins pulled his revolver, firing several shots at Light's head. Hit just below the jaw, in the neck, and near his right ear, the wounds were so severe that most thought he would die. Amazingly, Light recovered from the shots. In the meantime, Coggins was arrested for attempted murder, but for whatever reason, he never faced a trial.

Ironically, a year later on December 24, 1893, when Light was traveling on a train, he accidentally pulled the trigger of the revolver in his pocket. Severing his femoral artery, he bled to death within minutes. He was 30 years old.

## Steve Long, aka: Big Steve

*Outlaw Lawman*

"Big Steve" Long allegedly served on the Confederate side of the Civil War before becoming a professional gunfighter. He landed in Wyoming in 1866, where he joined with half-brothers Ace and Con Moyer, in establishing a saloon in Laramie City, Wyoming. The Moyer brothers founded the town, appointing themselves as justice of the peace and marshal, respectively. Steve Long was made the deputy marshal in 1867.

Long quickly earned a reputation as an extremely violent lawman, killing eight men in gunfights within two months. Ruling with an iron hand, the trio meted out "justice" in the backroom of the saloon, ordering ranchers to sign over deeds to their lands and miners to hand over their claims. Those who refused were shot to death by Long on the pretense that the victim reached for a weapon.

Numerous others were killed when they objected to crooked card games run at the saloon. By October, 1868, Long had killed thirteen men and was suspected of killing another seven who died under suspicious circumstances. The violence became so prevalent that the townsfolk began to refer to the saloon as "The Bucket of Blood".

Meanwhile, a local rancher by the name of N.K. Broswell began talk of forming a vigilante group to put the trio out of business.

Long also was in the habit of moonlighting as a thief and on October 18, 1868 he attempted to ambush and rob prospector Rollie "Hard Luck" Harrison. In the ensuing gunfight, Harrison was killed and Long was shot. Though wounded, he was able to make it home. While Long's fiancée treated the wound, he confessed to her what had happened and incensed, she told N.K. Broswell. Wasting no time, Broswell gathered up several men in the town and they stormed into The Bucket of Blood on October 28, 1868.

Seizing Long and the Moyer brothers, the mob dragged them to a partially finished cabin, where they began to string them up to the rafters. But before he could be strung up Long asked the vigilantes to remove his boots. His last words were "my mother always said that I would die with my shoes on." He was hanged with his bare feet dangling.

## George Maledon, aka: Prince of Hangmen

*Prince of Hangmen*

George Maledon earned the moniker of the Prince of Hangmen while serving as Judge Isaac Parker's chief executioner during the lawless days when Parker served as judge of the Federal Court for the Western District of Arkansas.

Born in Germany on June 10, 1830, Maledon migrated with his parents to Detroit, Michigan when he was still a child. When he grew up, he headed westward where he worked as a Fort Smith, Arkansas police officer. When the Civil War broke out, he enlisted in the Arkansas Light Artillery, serving in its 1st Battalion.

Maledon, a diminutive man standing at just about five and a half feet, was described as a "whispy" little fellow, with dark eyes and hair, a fair complexion and a long beard. Quiet in nature, he rarely smiled and was almost always dressed in black, an "appearance" that would soon seem appropriate to his new profession.

George Maledon

After the war, Maledon returned to Fort Smith where he worked as a deputy sheriff before being hired as a turnkey at the federal jail in May, 1871. The next year, he was appointed as a "special deputy" in charge of execution of the condemned prisoners.

For the next 22 years, he would execute more than sixty criminals and was forced to shoot five prisoners during escape attempts, two of which were killed. In no time, he was given the title of the "Prince of the Hangmen" by the local newspaper - the Fort Smith Elevator, who was only too happy to publish each and every morbid detail of Maledon's handiwork for the "entertainment" of its readers.

For three years, between 1873 and 1876, these executions upon the gallows were made public, drawing thousands of people from not only the surrounding areas, but sometimes from across the nation. During this time, a total of 22 men were hanged in seven different public displays. As the morbid gawkers gathered around the twenty foot wide scaffold, where as many as twelve men could be hanged at one time, the question was not "who was going to be hanged first," but rather, "would they be executed at the same time?"

On September 3, 1875, the largest group ever to be executed at once occurred when Maledon hanged six men. The scheduled event had been widely publicized in the media and a week before the execution was to occur, the city began to fill up with strangers from all over the country. Reporters from Little Rock, St. Louis and Kansas City flocked to Fort Smith, as well as newspapermen who traveled far from eastern and northern cities to catch the "scoop." By the time the event was to take place, more than 5,000 people watched as the six men were marched from the jail to the gallows.

Of the six felons, three were white, two were Native American and one was black. Seated along the back of the gallows, their death warrants were read to them and each was asked if they had any last words. When the preliminaries were over, the six were lined up on the scaffold while executioner George Maledon adjusted the nooses around their necks. The trap was sprung, all six died at once at the end of their ropes.

The Fort Smith Independent was the first newspaper to report the event on September 3, 1875 with the large column heading reading: "Execution Day!!"

Other newspapers around the country reported the event a day later. These press reports shocked people throughout the nation. "Cool Destruction of Six Human Lives by Legal Process" screamed the headlines.

This event earned Judge Isaac Parker the nickname of "The Hanging Judge" and called his court the "Court of the Damned."

Ironically, though the public flocked to watch these gruesome displays, Maledon was shunned by the community, as the town folk were afraid to associate with the "Prince of Hangmen."

However, there was one man who was morbidly attracted to Maledon's occupation - Heck Thomas. On one occasion while Thomas was at Fort Smith, he was asking Maledon for all the particulars when the executioner proudly displayed a collection of leg irons, straps, and ropes that were actually utilized in some of the hangings.

When showing Thomas one rope that had been used in eleven hangings, Maledon commented, "It is made of the finest hemp fiber, hand made in St. Louis and treated to keep it from slipping".

When Thomas questioned him about the type of knot that Maledon used for the executions, George, seemingly pleased to show off his expertise, said:

"You see, a big knot is necessary to have a humane hanging. If it doesn't break the man's neck when he drops, he strangles. That isn't a pretty sight. He just kicks and twists a lot."

But for the curious onlookers, these public events would be short-lived. In 1878, a 16 foot tall fence was built around the gallows and the executions became "private affairs," usually having less than 50 spectators.

The only execution that Maledon refused to carry out was that of Sheppard Busby, a U.S. Deputy Marshal, who had been convicted of killing another marshal by the name of Barney Conneley, when Busby tried to arrest Conneley for adultery. Maledon, who had had many associations with Busby in the past, refused to carry out his duty in this one instance, and the execution was performed by Deputy G. S. White.

After more than two decades carrying out these gruesome tasks, Maledon retired from the federal court in 1894 and opened a grocery business in Fort Smith. But he was yet to face one of his most difficult life situations, when the next year his eighteen year old daughter, Annie, was murdered by Frank Carver. Annie met Carver in Fort Smith while he was in Fort Smith being tried on whiskey charges. The two soon began a short love affair which led to her following him to Muskogee, Oklahoma where the young girl was surprised to find that Carver was already married to an Indian woman. When the two entered into a heated argument on March 25, 1895, a drunken Carver shot the girl. Seriously wounded, she was taken back to Fort Smith, where she died three weeks later, on May 17th.

Finding himself before Judge Isaac Parker, Carver was found guilty of murder and sentenced to hang. However, Carver hired a fancy lawyer, who soon appealed the case to the Supreme Court, and the sentence was changed to life in prison.

George Maledon was so disgusted by the decision that he left Fort Smith and took a "show" on the road where he displayed relics from hangings, including ropes, pieces of the gallows' beam, and photographs of some of the nation's most notorious outlaws. Setting up a tent in various cities, hundreds of people flocked to the show to hear Maledon speak and view the gruesome displays.

Just before he left Fort Smith, Maledon was asked if his conscience ever bothered him about the hangings or if he feared the spirits of the departed. To this he replied, "No, I have never hanged a man who came back to have the job done over."

By 1905, Maledon's health was seriously failing and he entered an old soldiers home in Humboldt, Tennessee, where he spent the remainder of his days. Though some sources say he died June 5, 1911, just shy of his 81st birthday, according to government records and other reliable sources, Maledon died on May 6, 1911, and was buried at the Johnson City Cemetery.

Maledon has the dubious honor of having executed more men than any other executioner in U.S. history.

The final execution in Fort Smith occurred on July 30, 1896. Eleven and a half months later, the original gallows was demolished and the debris completely burned. However, a new gallows was reconstructed at the original site in 1981, as part of the Fort Smith National Historic Site. The site also includes the barracks, courthouse, commissary, jail building, and a visitor's center that focuses both on Fort Smith's military history, as well as the years that it served as the federal court.

## William Bartholomew "Bat" Masterson

By Alfred Henry Lewis in 1907. ***Note***: Though widely acclaimed during his time, we found this article somewhat difficult to read as it included a number of words not (or no longer) used in everyday language, plus assumed that the reader would know such things as "on the Medicine Lodge" refers to the Medicine Lodge River, and other such assumptions. Additionally, the article included a number of misspellings and grammatical errors. Therefore, the story on these pages is not verbatim, as it has been edited for corrections, clarification, and ease of the modern reader.

### *King of the Gun Players*

William Barclay Masterson was born in Iroquois County, Illinois, in 1856. His father was a farmer and came originally from St. Lawrence County, New York. His mother and father lived and counted themselves among the Sedgwick County pioneers of Kansas, with a sunflower residence that reaches rearward half a century.

First a Kansas farm boy, Mr. Masterson was early abroad upon the plains. What is farmland now was savage wilderness then, and those who invaded it did so with a knowledge that their hands must keep their heads. For twenty years, beginning when he was thirteen, Mr. Masterson lived by his own personal powers of offense and defense, and was in more or less daily peril of death from Indians, or from outlaw spirits common enough.

**Has Wasted Least Lead of any Man**

Just as some folk are born poets, so others are born shots, and Mr. Masterson, from the first, evinced a genius for firearms. With either rifle or pistol he proved himself infallible, and of all who ever plied trigger he has wasted the least lead.

It was as a hunter he won his name of "Bat," which descended to him, as it were, from Baptiste Brown, or "Old Bat," whose fame as a mighty Nimrod was flung all across, from the Missouri River to the Spanish Peaks, and filled with admiration, that generation of plainsmen which immediately preceded Mr. Masterson upon the Western stage.

For his deadly accuracy with the rifle, Mr. Masterson was early employed to "do the killing"' for great hunting outfits, which in the '70's ransacked the country between the Arkansas and Canadian [Rivers] for buffalos, in the name of robes and leather. Mr. Masterson would "kill" for a dozen men to skin and cure; and the majestic character of that commerce, wherein he bore his powder-burning part, may be guessed at from the fact that in such years as 1872, more than three hundred thousand buffalo hides, to say naught of one-fourth as many robes, were shipped eastward from the single town of Dodge [City].

Crossing and re-crossing the buffalo ranges, Mr. Masterson came naturally by a close knowledge of the country, and, in a region not overstocked of water, could locate every spring and stream, as surely as astronomers locate stars. Thus it befell that General Miles was quick to enlist him as scout, in his campaign against the Cheyennes in '74. In truth, there were more than the Cheyennes engaged in that trouble; for those copper-colored Richards drew with them to the field the flower of the Kiowa, Comanche and Arapaho tribes.

Bat Masterson

It is to be thought that Mr. Masterson himself was, in half fashion, the partial first victim of that war. The cunning Indians were apparently steeping themselves in peace, with never a notion of warpaths and paleface scalps. They were none the less sedulously, and not always quietly, about the collection of what rifles and pistols and cartridges they could lay red hands upon. Mr. Masterson was one day skinning a buffalo he had killed, when a quintette of Cheyenne bucks rode amiably up. They belonged with old Bear Shield's band, whose home-camp was on the Medicine Lodge [River.] Mr. Masterson thought little or nothing of the five Cheyennes. They were everyday sights in his life, and the last thing he looked for was trouble. He kept on with his skinning, merely ejaculating "How!" to clear himself of any imputation of impoliteness.

Mr. Masterson's rifle was lying on the grass – a 50-caliber Sharp's buffalo gun, for which he had paid eighty dollars. One of the Cheyennes carelessly picked up the rifle, as though to examine it. As he did so, another reached across – Mr. Masterson was bending over the dead buffalo bull, skinning knife in hand – and whipped the six-shooter from the Masterson belt.

At these maneuvers, Mr. Masterson straightened up, and was just in time to receive a confusing blow over the head from his own rifle. The 8-square barrel cut a handsome gash and covered his face with blood. As the Cheyenne struck the blow, he broke into excellent agency English, through which flowed a dominating element of profanity, and commanded Mr. Masterson to "dig out."

Since the Cheyenne had the muzzle of the rifle not two feet from his stomach, and those four fellow Cheyennes evinced an eagerness to bear a helping hand, Mr. Masterson decided to "dig out." That is to say, with blood covering his face, he backed away from the rifle-pointing profane Cheyenne, towards a ravine which yawned conveniently in his rear. Arriving at the brink, Mr. Masterson with hasty strategy fell into that saving canyon, and was out of range in a moment.

Running along the bottom of the ravine for half a mile, Mr. Masterson reached his own buffalo camp. After a consultation with his two camp mates, the whole party packed their burros, and pointed their noses for Dodge, sixty miles to the north. Mr. Masterson, sore of head from the blow and sore of heart from the loss of his new rifle, was all for following the five Cheyennes and giving them battle. But his comrades, whose unvisited heads were still intact, and whose hearts had been wrung by no rifle losses, overruled him.

They said, "Let's pull our freight," and they pulled it.

Mr. Masterson, however, was not to be consoled. That night – Christmas night it was – he rode back, and ran off forty of old Bear Shield's ponies. These brought him twelve hundred dollars in Dodge, and repaired what monetary losses he had suffered, to say the least. The wounds to his head, and to his honor, videlicet (permitted) his boyish vanity, which those five Cheyennes had inflicted, he cured later at the battle of the 'Dobe Walls.

It was in the last days of June that the fight at the 'Dobe Walls occurred. The "Dobe Walls" consisted of two buildings, one a great outfitting store belonging to Mr. Wright, present head of the Kansas State Historical Society, and the other, Mr. Hanrahan's saloon. The latter gentleman is now, I think, a member of the Idaho legislature; but, at the time whereof I write, he cheerfully conducted a bar and restaurant, for the comfort of buffalo hunters who worked along the Canadian [River,] two hundred miles south of the last sign of civilization.

There were fourteen buffalo hunters at the 'Dobe Walls that night in June. Nine – among them Mr. Masterson – slept in Mr. Hanrahan's saloon, and five in Mr. Wright's store. Not one anticipated attack.

Luckily, about three o'clock in the morning, the roof – a dirt roof – of Mr. Hanrahan's saloon fell in. The sleeping buffalo hunters were forced to turn out. This was all that saved them; otherwise, the prophecy of the Comanche medicine man would have been fulfilled, and the buffalo hunters knocked on the head as they slumbered.

Morning came streaking the east, and found the buffalo hunters still engaged in aiding Mr. Hanrahan about the restoration of his roof. It was at this moment of morning that a full five hundred Indians, the picked warriors of the Kiowas, Comanches, Arapahos, and Cheyennes, swung out from the shadow of a fringe of cottonwoods that ranked the Canadian River.

In a moment, every buffalo-hunting man jack of them, abandoning roof for rifle, clawed up his gun and took to a window. Mr. Masterson's window mate was Mr. Dixon, who has since – for the sentiment of the thing, perhaps – homesteaded the one hundred and sixty acres which include the 'Dobe Walls, and makes the same his residence.

**The Famous 'Dobe Walls Battle**

The firing instantly began, and the charging Indians had the tremendous worst of it. The Indian is in several respects defective. He is a bad shot; he won't dismount and fight on foot; and he is so much the Parthian that it's against his religion to fight in the night. Mr. Masterson and his fellow buffalo killers were, in these three particulars, the precise opposite of their enemies.

They were dead shots; they preferred to fight on foot; and, as for night and day, when it came to bloodshed, the two were synonymous. Daylight or dark, they transacted their wars the moment the foe was found, holding – as held a famous jurist concerning the law – fighting to be a so sacred matter that "for it all places are palaces, all seasons summer."

Wherefore, when those hopeful five hundred savages charged, the fourteen hunters tore into them blithely with their big buffalo guns, and began emptying redskin saddles at a most disheartening rate. The Indians charged fiercely three times, and the unerring Mr. Masterson and his friends corded up over twenty of them. The siege, before all was over, lasted two weeks; but the fighting, so far as the Indians were concerned, after those first three furious charges – which broke the aboriginal teeth – was but half-hearted and desultory.

To tell the whole of the battle at the 'Dobe Walls would go beyond the limits of an article such as this. The excited comments of a tame crow which, while the fight raged, flew chatteringly to and fro from Hanrahan's to Wright's and back again; would of themselves make a story; while how Mr. Masterson crossed to Wright's store in quest of cartridges for a pet rifle he possessed, and was deeply bombarded in transit by a wounded Kiowa hiding in a clump of weeds; how a boy in Wright's died from a bullet in his lungs; how Old Man Richards walked through a hail of lead to a pump ten rods away in the open, and, while a dog was killed at his feet, and his hat shot from his gray head, and bullets plowed and spattered the pump platform and ground about him, drew a bucket of cool water for the dying boy; how a wild tenderfoot, one Thompson – killed afterward by Billy the Kid – persisted, in the teeth of command and the very face of slaughter, in rushing forth to rob dead Indians of their war bonnets and guns; how the lookout on Hanrahan's roof blew out his own brains instead of an Indian's; how Mr. Masterson, in the plenitude of his young conceit, leaped from a window and scalped a Comanche – he owned an unusually alluring top-knot, black and glossy-under the very noses of his scandalized tribesmen; how each night the beleaguered ones, to save their own noses, must bury the dead Indians and ponies; how throughout the long two weeks, when not at the windows fighting, the said beleaguered ones beguiled the tedium of their lives by profound games of draw poker; how the Comanche medicine man was luckily killed by Mr. Masterson on the first charge; how that same faultless rifle shot afterward brought down a negro bugler, who had deserted the standards of Uncle Sam for those of the Cheyennes, and was then sounding charge and rally as war music cheering to the aboriginal heart; and how finally, after two weeks, the cavalry came down from Dodge and raised the siege, must one and all, as battle elements, wait for their relation upon occasion more comprehensive than this. Suffice it that the Indians were beaten, with a whole battle-loss – by their own story told later at the agencies – of over eighty killed, to the meager count of one slain by savage lead on the side of the buffalo hunters.

**His First Gun Trouble**

Once, so runs the tale, a gentleman of extensive pistol practice was testifying as a witness. "How many men have you killed?" asked the cross-examining lawyer:

The witness seemed for the moment posed, almost puzzled. At last, as one seeking exact light, he enquired:

"You don't mean Mexicans and Indians?"

The cross-examining lawyer explained that he intended only white men, Mexicans and Indians to be excluded. The witness then took up the count.

Excluding Mexicans and Indians, Mr. Masterson's first gun trouble was at Mobeetie in the Texas Panhandle, the theatre thereof being a dance hall called the Lady Gay. Sergeant King, a soldier and a gambler, found fault with Mr. Masterson, and lay in prudent wait to take his life at a side door of the Lady Gay.

The evening was dark. A girl named Anna Brennan came up. The lurking King, giving some excuse, asked her to rap at the door, conjecturing that Mr. Masterson, who was just inside, would open it. The King conjecture was justified; Mr. Masterson did open it, and asked the girl what was wanted. At the sound of his voice, King stepped forward and, placing the muzzle of his pistol against the Masterson groin, fired. King fired a second shot, and accidentally killed the girl. Coincident with that second shot, however, Mr. Masterson's pistol exploded, and King fell shot through the heart. The girl, King, and Mr. Masterson went down in a bleeding heap; the two first were buried, while to the amazement of the surgeons at Fort Elliot, Mr. Masterson was back in the saddle by the end of eight weeks. So much for the recuperative powers of one who had lived healthfully and close to the ground.

Mr. Masterson's hat measures seven and three-eighths. Wise, cool, wary, he is the born captain of men. Generous to a final dollar, the poor and needy make for him like night birds for a lighthouse. To a courage that is proof, he adds a genius for justice, and carries honesty to the pitch of romanticism. To these virtues of mind and heart, add the thews (muscular power or strength) of a grizzly bear, and you will have a picture of Mr. Masterson. Such he is; such he was when, at the age of twenty-two, the public elected him sheriff for Ford County, whereof the seat of justice was the stormy little city of Dodge.

**Smothering Ebullient Cowboys**

As sheriff, Mr. Masterson's duties carried him over sixteen unorganized counties, besides the county of Ford. His more immediate responsibility; however, was the good order of Dodge, and to prevent ebullient cowboys, when the Autumn herds came up, from "standing" that baby hamlet "on its head." It took judgment and nerve and forbearance and military skill; but Mr. Masterson accomplished the miracle, and did it, too, at a minimum of bloodshed. In the words of a satisfied citizen and taxpayer:

"He never downed a man who didn't need it, and kept Dodge as steady as a church."

Scores of lurid spirits, whose lives were forfeit by every Western rule, have been spared to live a quieter life by the forbearing Mr. Masterson. Mr. Sutton, a lawyer and a present resident of Dodge, was out recently in the papers with a story in illustrative point. Three cowboys, moved of whisky and a taste for violence, dashed down the single street of Dodge, their six-shooters blazing like roman candles. Most peace officers would have harvested these boys; Mr. Masterson was more leniently inclined, since thus far the young merrymakers had not succeeded in hitting anybody. Sure of its aim, Mr. Masterson's pistol barked three times. Two of the ponies fell, and Mr. Masterson dragged their riders – sprawled all abroad in the dust of the street – off to the calaboose.

The third pony lasted until he reached the south side of the Arkansas [River,] and then dropped dead. Thereupon, its rider stripped off saddle and bridle, "stuck up" the incoming buckboard, and compelled the driver to turn nose-about, and land him at a nearest ranch more than forty miles away.

There was a lady aboard the buckboard who sang in the theatres. She was coming north from Mobeetie to fill a Dodge engagement. As shortening those tiresome forty miles, the dismounted cowboy – pistol in hand, eye on the buckboard driver, who might at any moment rebel – told the cantatrice that he thought she ought to sing. With that, she thought so too; and so, for forty miles she warbled "Silver Threads Among the Gold," and kindred melodies of concert hall vogue at the time. This boy got clear away, while the ravens and the coyotes, at their feast over his dead pony, gloried in the fatal accuracy of the Masterson guns.

As demonstrating his huge strength, Mr. Masterson once seized a recalcitrant cow puncher who, seated in his saddle, was making ready to "shake up the village." The cowboy was himself as strong as whalebone, and gripped his pony with legs of iron. Throwing his soul into the business, Mr. Masterson gave that adhesive cowboy such a wrench – the boy meanwhile clinging to his mount like grim death – that both pony and boy were thrown heavily to the ground.

It was not always convenient, nor even feasible, to spare the blood of the wrong doer. The following might furnish an example in line. Mr. Kennedy rode up to the Alhambra, kept by Mr. Kelly, the then Mayor, and took a shot at that publican and magistrate with his Ballard. Mr. Kennedy missed Mr. Kelly, and killed a lady who had come to the Alhambra to have part in the nightly ball. Mr. Kennedy – it was eight o'clock in the evening – on the heels of the homicide, dug spurs into his pony's flanks, and flew southward through the darkness. He was heading for the Canadian [River] two hundred miles away.

Mr. Masterson saddled a fleetest horse, and started 'cross country for the ford where the flying Mr. Kennedy must cross the Medicine Lodge [River.] There were three or four trails, and direct pursuit in the dark was out of the question. Mr. Masterson reached the ford in the gray of the morning, bettering Mr. Kennedy's time by an hour. He hobbled his horse, and threw himself in behind a convenient knoll, to wait the coming of the murderous flying one. At last, the latter drew near, eye scanning the ribbon of trail to the rear, pony worn and panting. No wonder, this last seventy miles, at a swinging hand gallop, is no mere canter.

"Hold up your hands!" cried Mr. Masterson.

Mr. Kennedy almost leaped from the saddle with the surprise of it; he wasn't looking for an enemy in front. The next moment, however, he pulled himself together, and drove a bullet at Mr. Masterson from the Ballard. Mr. Masterson was quite as brisk. The retort of his big buffalo gun made one report with the Ballard; Mr. Kennedy's shot went wide, while the 50-caliber bullet from the buffalo gun tore its fearful way into his side. As he fell, an accidental yank on the Spanish bits brought the tired, broken pony with him.

Mr. Kennedy rolled a dying eye upon Mr. Masterson.

"You blankety-blank-blank!" said Mr. Kennedy; "you'd ought to have made a better shot than that!"

"Well, you blankety-blank murderer!" quoth Mr. Masterson, "I did the best I could."

Mr. Masterson's brother Ed was made Marshal of Dodge, somewhat against the wish of Mr. Masterson. The latter feared that the "bad men," who came and went in Dodge, would "out manage" his brother, whose suspicions were too easily set at rest.

**The Killing of Mr. Masterson's Brother**

It fell out as Mr. Masterson had feared. Mr. Wagner, drunk and warlike, sought to enter Mr. Peacock's dance hall, questing trouble. Marshal Ed Masterson, instead of pulling his own gun, as prudence would have dictated, and stopping the violent Mr. Wagner with the cold muzzle thereof, seized that truculent person by the shoulders. Instantly, Mr. Wagner's six-shooter was brought to the fore. With that, Marshal Ed Masterson shifted his left hand to Mr. Wagner's wrist, and for the moment put that drunkard's weapon out of commission. There the two stood, the situation dead-locked.

From across the street, Mr. Masterson saw events and started to his brother's aid. He was still sixty feet away when Mr. Walker, who, like Mr. Wagner was a person of cows, ran from the dance hall, and snapped his six-shooter in Marshal Ed Masterson's face.

The cartridge failed to explode. Mr. Walker was never given the chance of trying a second; for Mr. Masterson put three bullets from his Colt's 45 through him before he could hit the ground. As the dead Mr. Walker went down, Mr. Wagner, still in a grapple with Marshal Ed Masterson, got his gun to bear, and shot Marshal Ed Masterson in the body.

The latter fell wounded to the death, coat afire from the other's powder. Mr. Wagner fell across him, a bullet from Mr. Masterson's pistol through his brain.

And after this fashion did Mr. Masterson maintain law and order in Dodge. Many were his battles, many the wounds he wrought; and it was said that the local doctor traced half his practice to the untiring efforts of Mr. Masterson in behalf of communal peace.

Once upon a time in Dodge a general war was missed by the narrowest margin. Those dead worthies, Messrs. King, Kennedy, Wagner and Walker, had come one and all from Texas in their day, and Lone Star feeling, always clannish, seldom nicely critical, resented their taking off. It is not too much to say that ten thousand dollars might have been borrowed on Mr. Masterson's scalp in a dozen Texas towns. Scores of stark souls came north with the herds, avowing no other intention than to wipe out the hated Mr. Masterson.

Among these was Mr. Driscoll – big, violent, formidable. Mr. Driscoll was not in Dodge ten minutes before Mr. Masterson introduced himself.

"I'll give you half an hour," said Mr. Masterson, "to put yourself on the other side of the Arkansas; and if you ever jingle a spur in Dodge again, I'll shoot you in two."

Mr. Driscoll crossed the "Arkansas;" and later – his laurels somewhat tarnished, and not caring to return to Texas under such diminished circumstances – he journeyed down to Springer, [New Mexico] and went to work for Senator Dorsey's "Triangle-dot." Mr. Burlison was Sheriff of Colfax County, New Mexico, where the Dorsey ranches were, and Mr. Masterson wrote his brother officer a letter.

"Dear Burlison," said Mr. Masterson, "this man Driscoll, who has migrated to your neck of woods, will bear watching. He's a four-flush and a bully. If he tries to start anything down your way, go right at him and he'll quit." Mr. Driscoll "started" something. Mr. Burlison went "right at him," and Mr. Driscoll "quit." Also when he "quit" he was dead.

Mr. [Clay] Allison was a Texan by adoption, and a friend of Mr. Driscoll. Likewise, he was lame with a club-foot, limped when off his horse, and used a Winchester for a crutch. He had slain many men, and took a quiet pride in the fact that, in the teeth of local ordinances to the contrary, he never took his guns off when he visited any town.

### "Kill Every Man with a Big Hat"

Mr. Allison was in Dodge when Mr. Masterson introduced himself to the offensive Mr. Driscoll. Being coldly advised, however, by Mr. Masterson, Mr. Allison was not wearing his hardware. In the day that followed the banishment of Mr. Driscoll, the whisper went Dogian rounds that the Texas cow people, then and there in large numbers, were making war medicine, and would presently "turn loose" under the leadership of Mr. Allison. With that, the careful Mr. Masterson made preparations; and such berserks as Mr. Earp, Mr. Brown, Mr. Kelly, Mr. Holliday, Mr. Bassett, Mr. Short, and others whose names were high and famous in the annals of that hour, began cleaning responsive shotguns to be in readiness for the Masterson call to arms. The word was, if war broke out, to "kill every man with a big cow hat on." The Dodgians, be it known, wore hats of moderate and exemplary rim.

Mr. Masterson believed that if carnage descended it would come in the night. Which perhaps was the reason why Mr. Allison chose the afternoon. Of a sudden, the latter gentleman rode into the middle of that single thoroughfare – so often a battlefield –

armed to the teeth. Halting his horse in front of Mr. Webster's Alamo, Mr. Allison spake loud and fiercely, but he was heedful to leave Winchester and pistols in their scabbards, and, while his oratory was terrible, his hands continued as harmlessly empty as a child's.

Mr. Masterson, at the time, was sitting in his office. With the earliest note of war from Mr. Allison, he snatched up a shotgun and "covered" that Texas chieftain. Since Mr. Masterson was to the rear of Mr. Allison, the latter enthusiast did not notice his "covered" condition.

Having Mr. Allison "covered," Mr. Masterson turned to Judge Colborn, now of Salt Lake City, then District Attorney of Dodge.

"Skip out the back door, Judge," observed Mr. Masterson, "and tell Wyatt and the rest that I've got Allison dead to rights. Tell them not to close in on him; if he reaches for a gun, I'll hive him. When they hear me shoot, let them get busy right and left; tell them to bump off every Texan they find in the town."

The warning word went down the line, and Mr. Allison was left unmolested in his eloquence. But that very fact made him uneasy. He was not without a working knowledge of homicide as a science; and the sight of the several heads of Messrs. Earp, Holliday, Bassett, Short, and a score besides, protruded in an expectant fringe from doors and windows all along the street, as though a common idea obtained that something interesting was about to happen, chilled him and bid him pause. Mr. Allison looked excessively bothered. Finally he shut down his oratory in mid flow, got off his horse, limped dubiously into Mr. Webster's Alamo saloon, and took a thoughtful drink. Mr. Masterson put away the shotgun and joined him. Observing Mr. Masterson enter, Mr. Allison pretended great joy.

"Where were you, Bat?" he asked. "I've been looking all over town for you."

"I've been see-sawing on you with a shotgun for ten minutes," returned Mr. Masterson grimly, "What's the matter, Clay?"

Mr. Allison appeared a bit confused, but explained that he had been aroused by the insults of a red-headed hardware clerk who didn't know who he, Mr. Allison, was. Being calmer now, he would again disarm in deference to the prevailing local taste as to shooting irons.

Thus the business passed without actual hostilities and Mr. Allison confessed later that his reason for "simmering" was he had had a "premonition."

It's just possible he did. In any event, and whatever the cause, his change of offensive front that afternoon saved many a life. Also, it saved Dodge from what would else have proved the ruddiest chapter in all her crimson history.

### "Had It In" for "Bat"

When the new liquor law took effect in Kansas in '81, Mr. Masterson laid down his office. He was not sumptuary, and, while he himself never drank liquor, refused to be drawn into deadly collision with gentlemen whose only offense had been a too vehement thirst. Besides, he urged, considering the many strenuous years he had gone through, he felt he had earned a rest.

There was at least one gentleman in Dodge who didn't share this vacation view. The hour was evening, and Mr. Masterson, no longer sheriff, was sitting in the rear room of Mr. Kelly's Alhambra, in talk with Judge Colburn. Mr. Bell appeared abruptly in the door, a six-shooter in his right hand, another in his belt. Mr. Bell is the sober, quiet sheriff now of that same county of Ford; but in these, his younger years, he was a sturdy customer, and had "shot up" several of his acquaintances. Per incident, he "had it in" for Mr. Masterson.

"I think," remarked Mr. Bell, as he stood thus triumphantly in the door, "there's a horned toad here I want to kill."

Like a flash, the sensitive Mr. Masterson – who, had he been either slow or dull would never have lived till now – was on his feet, the muzzle that never missed pointing squarely between the eyes of Mr. Bell. Naturally, the latter warrior froze up; he stood as though planet-struck.

There was a darkling pause; then Mr. Masterson, gun still unwaveringly upon Mr. Bell, began slowly to advance. Mr. Bell never moved. Coming within reach, Mr. Masterson suddenly let down the hammer of his pistol and smote Mr. Bell such a jealous blow upon the head that he went to the floor, and from the floor to his bed for two weeks.

Years later, I asked Mr. Masterson why he withheld his fire. "I didn't think I had to shoot," he said. "I once saw Bell jump over a bar-counter to get at a man, when he might just as well have gone around, and it struck me all at once that he was much too dramatic. If it had been Wyatt Earp now, or Doc Holliday, or Luke Short, or Ben Thompson, I'd have begun to bombard him out of hand. But I didn't think such extreme measures were demanded in the case of Bell," and here Mr. Masterson smiled peacefully at the retrospect. "My size-up of Bell may have been wrong," he concluded, "and if it was, I hope he'll pardon me. He ought to; for, between us, it was all that saved him from death that day."

**Some of his Other Adventures**

This chronicle of Mr. Masterson might be extended to one hundred thousand words, and only the half be glanced at, not told. I might relate how he rescued from a mob the State's Attorney General, and the Chief of the Prohibition Leagues of Kansas, when those reforming functionaries led a temperance crusade against Dodge. Or how, when Mr. Webster of the Alamo and incidentally Mayor of Dodge, exiled Mr. Short of the Long Branch – the rival shop – Mr. Masterson, then a citizen of Leadville, returned to Dodge at the militant head of such choice fighting men as Wyatt Earp, Doc Holliday, Henry Brown, Shotgun Collins, and Shoot-your-eye-out Jack, to say naught of the redoubtable Mr. Short himself, and restored that persecuted one to all his property right, as well as what elevated station, as owner of the Long Branch, he should occupy in the social life of the place.

Or how – this was a case of mistaken identity – Mr. Masterson smote the Pueblo railway policeman so grievously upon his skull with a six-shooter, that the latter officer, who had wrongfully assailed Mr. Masterson with a bludgeon, must be furloughed to a hospital for a month. Or how Mr. Masterson took a man from a mob of lynchers at Buena Vista, and carried him before a magistrate; and how, when the magistrate, in sympathetic league with the lynchers, would have committed the man to the local jail, where the mob could get at him, he, Mr. Masterson, tore up the commitment papers in the face of the court, and carried the man off to the Denver jail, where subsequently he was sufficiently yet lawfully hanged.

Or, how Mr. Masterson protected Mr. Holliday from the requisition of Arizona's Governor for killing Mr. Stillwell in Tucson, by the simple stratagem of having that consumptive gun player put under arrest on a charge of highway robbery – a fiction – in Colorado. Or how, when Mr. O'Neal, with a six-shooter in each overcoat pocket, and a hand on each six-shooter, sent forward a drunken ruffian to attack Mr. Masterson, with full and fell intent on Mr. O'Neal's part of "bumping off' Mr. Masterson when once entangled with the drunken one he, Mr. Masterson, knocked the drunken one senseless with his left fist, while with his right hand he abruptly acquired the draw on the designing Mr. O'Neal. With that never-erring six-shooter upon him, Mr. O'Neal's empty hands came out of his pockets, and went into the air, like winking.

"Don't kill me!" he faltered.

Mr. Masterson's finger was itching upon the trigger. In an instant he shifted. Letting down the hammer, he repeated the maneuver which had worked so well in the days of Mr. Bell. Later, the wounded Mr. O'Neal, head in bandages, sent from his bed a message of peace, asking Mr. Masterson to see him, and give him an opportunity to "explain."

"Well," said Mr. Masterson to the messenger. "I'll come. But tell O'Neal to be careful and keep his hands outside the blankets while he's doing his 'explaining.' "

Or, I might set forth how a dear but intoxicated friend, forgetting for the moment – an election moment wherein the "dear friend" resented the indomitable republicanism of Mr. Masterson – those close social ties which subsisted between them, pulled his pistol, intending the destruction of Mr. Masterson; and how Mr. Masterson shot the weapon from his dear friend's hand, and let him live to apologize for his murderous rudeness. That apologetic one is sober now, and a Denver detective of much good repute.

Or, I could tell how Mr. Gallagher of Denver imported a desperate character, one Smith. for the wiping out of Mr. Masterson; and how Mr. Masterson, when he heard, sent a 100-dollar bill to Mr. Gallagher, with word that the money was his if he would but walk down the street "as far as Murphy's," with his importation. Also, how Mr. Gallagher refused the money, and how Mr. Smith made haste to explain that his purpose in coming to Denver was wholly innocuous.

Or, how – if these be not enough – Mr. Masterson journeyed, in the name of friendship, to far-off Ogallala, and surreptitiously bore away Mr. Thompson – then under arrest, but stiff and sore from buckshot wounds, and held captive in a hotel instead of the jail, because of them. Mr. Masterson, having advantage of a drunken sentinel, rolled the injured Mr. Thompson in a blanket, and packed him to the station on his shoulder, Mr. Thompson aiding his rescue by conveniently fainting away. It was two o'clock of a dark morning, every Ogallalan was at a dance in the far end of camp, and no one beheld the feat. Which was just as well, since there were more buckshot in Ogallala than had been stopped by Mr. Thompson. Mr. Masterson carried Mr. Thompson aboard train as far as North Platt; and there the excellent "Buffalo Bill" Cody presented the fugitive with his wife's phaeton, and a horse of a temper like Satan's and a hideous hammer head, with which double donation they made their safe way cross-country three hundred miles to Dodge.

Or, I might give the story of how, when Mr. Short killed Mr. Courtright in Fort Worth, Mr. Masterson took his six-shooters and begged the privilege of sitting in Mr. Short's cell all night, fearing mob violence. Friendship such as Jonathan's would have hesitated at so desperate a step! It turned out well, however, for the would-be lynchers, told by the Sheriff that Mr. Masterson and Mr. Short were together in the jail, and each with a brace of guns, virtuously resolved that the law should take its course, and went heedfully home to bed.

These and many more have been the adventures of Mr. Masterson, who, coming up through all this perilous trail of smoke and blood, is now peacefully amassing ten thousand dollars a year, as a writer on a New York City paper and a contributor to

Human Life. I asked him if he never yearned for the West. He shook his head.

“I’m out of that zone of fire;” said he, “and I never want to go back. I hope never to see those dreary plains again.”

But the plains come to Mr. Masterson on Broadway, or rather the men of the plains. One day he introduced me to a wiry, eagle-eyed gentleman, dressed as though just out of a bandbox.

“Mr. Tilghman,” said the introductory Mr. Masterson.

Mr. Tilghman, it appeared, was East as the democratic representative of Oklahoma, to notify Mr. Parker that he had been nominated for the Presidency.

“Do you remember,” Mr. Masterson asked – “my telling how, one Christmas Eve, I ran off forty of old Bear Shield’s ponies? And how I saw a party riding about among the herd that I took to be an Indian herder? It was Billy here; he got away with something like fifty good head himself that night.”

Mr. Tilghman – now a sheriff in Oklahoma – beamed at the rich suggestion of those afore time ponies, and then he and Mr. Masterson fell to remembering how Mr. Masterson had one day given Mr. Tilghman warning at Leota to “look out for Ed Prather” and how the next afternoon Mr. Tilghman “looked out” so earnestly that Mr. Prather departed headlong into the misty beyond.

“Billy kept the tail of his eye on him,” explained Mr. Masterson, “and when Ed reached for his gun, he beat him to it.”

One last adventure, and I am through. Mr. Masterson had not seen Dodge for a handful of years. He was in Deming when a telegram was put into his hands. It related to his younger brother, who was still in Dodge. It read:

> “Come at once. Updegraffe and Peacock are going to kill Jim.”

Mr. Masterson was thirty hours reaching Dodge. Unable to sleep, his fancy roved feverishly ahead and drew dark pictures of the probable. Mr. Updegraffe was as game a man as ever buckled a belt, and Mr. Peacock would fight a little. By the time Mr. Masterson reached Albuquerque, he knew that Jim was dead; and when he got as far as Las Vegas, [ New Mexico ] he felt sure that the funeral was over. In this frame he stepped off the cars at Dodge the next day. There they were; Mr. Updegraffe and Mr. Peacock, waiting for him in the little public square.

Mr. Masterson cut short the suspense.

"You murderers," he cried to the waiting Updegraffe and Peacock, "might better begin to fight right now!"

"For Shooting Inside of City Limits."

Mr. Updegraffe's bullet buried itself in the side of a Pullman. Mr. Masterson's bullet drove a five-inch splinter of rib through Mr. Updegraffe's lungs, Mr. Peacock took refuge behind the calaboose, from which coign he fired wild and high, breaking four-story windows in a far-away block. Mr. Masterson shot twice at Mr. Peacock, and missed him by a breath. The scars of those two bullets still show on the side of Dodge's calaboose. Mr. Masterson, aiming to dislodge him, charged the entrenched Mr. Peacock. When he arrived at the corner of the calaboose, Mr. Peacock had vanished. Mr. Masterson caught a disappointing glimpse of him as he disappeared into Mr. Gallon's hotel.

At this pinch, Mr. Webster – Mayor, proprietor of the Alamo and no friend of Mr. Masterson – came panting up, a 10-gauge shotgun in his shaking hands. Mr. Masterson who never forgot his strategy, went instantly and close to Mr. Webster. Mr. Webster was visibly shaken, and as white as paper. Mr. Masterson surveyed him – eye keen as that of a lynx, six-shooter in ready hand.

"What's the matter with you, Web?" asked Mr. Masterson.

"It's just this, Bat," stammered Mr. Webster. "I'm Mayor of this outfit; and this shooting's got to stop."

"Well," returned Mr. Masterson, as steady as a tree, "I think it has stopped, unless you choose to start it again."

"I'll not start it," ejaculated the fervent Mr. Webster.

"Then let me take the 10-gauge," said Mr. Masterson, soothingly, at the same time claiming that weapon. "It doesn't look well for the Mayor of Dodge to be running about the streets with a shotgun in his hands."

Then the unexpected happened. Jim Masterson, not at all dead and buried, but clothed and in his right mind, came running up. Mr. Masterson stared as though he beheld a ghost.

"Where have you been?" he gasped.

"Over in the Wright House, asleep." returned Jim, "until your cannonading woke me up."

There had been trouble with Messrs. Updegraffe and Peacock on one end of it and Jim on the other. Some shooting had taken place, but no one scored. While the brothers stood talking, Mr. Peacock as closing the incident, sent forth an ambassador who paid Jim six hundred dollars – the casus belli (justification.)

"Get your blankets," Mr. Masterson said to Jim. "Out of town you go by the next train! I've had to come twelve hundred miles on your account, to kill one of my friends, and now I won't even let you stay in the state. Get your blankets; you and I take the next train west!"

"But, Bat," expostulated Mr. Webster tremulously, "I've got to have you arrested."

"Be careful, Web!" warned Mr. Masterson. "I won't submit to an arrest. Your people here took to shooting at me the moment I got off the cars; I only defended myself. I give you warning that anyone who attempts to arrest me will have to arrest me in the smoke."

"Not for downing Updegraffe," protested Mr. Webster hastily; "that, as you say, was self-defense. But, Bat, we've passed some ordinances since you were here – ordinances against shootin' inside the town." This last tentatively.

Mr. Masterson smiled: "To ease your official mind, Web," he said at last, "so it's nothing more than a money fine, and you don't over-size my pile, I'll stand it."

Thereupon. Mr. Webster, Mayor, cheered up mightily and fined Mr. Masterson five dollars for "Shooting inside the city limits," which sum Mr. Masterson tossed to Mr. Webster, who as Mayor, gratefully collected it off the grass.

## David A. Mather, aka: Mysterious Dave

*Lawman or Outlaw?*

David Allen Mather, better known as Mysterious Dave, was born August 10, 1851 to Ulysses and Lycia Mather. Dave had come from a family of seafaring lawmen in Massachusetts and his ancestors had been rugged English sailormen of the Seven Seas. Mather was proud of his English heritage and it was common to see him dressed in royal blue and red, even when he got older. Some of his immediate family members were also lawmen in Massachusetts, from whom Mather acquired the desire to become a lawman himself.

David A. Mather

A smallish man with square but frail shoulders, dark eyes and a mustache, Mather was a man of few words, which gained him the nickname of "Mysterious Dave."

Though Mather had aspirations to be a lawman, he like so many other officers of the Old West, rode both sides of the fence, sometimes on the side of the law, and just as often, riding with outlaws.

By the time that Mather was 16, both of his parents were dead so he and his brother, Josiah, headed west. Around 1873, Mather became involved in cattle rustling in Sharp County, Arkansas. A year later, in 1874, Mather had made his first appearance in Dodge City, where he would return frequently both as a lawman and an outlaw.

About this same time, Mather was often seen about the saloons of Denver, Colorado, always with twin Colts bulging under his coat. He was known to keenly watch the players at the faro, blackjack and poker tables, but he never gambled himself.

By 1878, Mather had found his way to Mobeetie, Texas, and into the company of Wyatt Earp, where, one suspicious account related, the two ran a con game peddling "gold" bricks to the naïve citizens of Mobeetie.

In 1879, Mather hooked up with outlaw Dutch Henry Born, who was the leader of a horse-stealing ring operating in a vast area from Kansas, to eastern Colorado and New Mexico, and the Texas Panhandle. Mather was arrested with Henry Born, but was later released. He was soon picked up for complicity in a train robbery near Las Vegas, New Mexico, but was acquitted. Afterwards, Mather was appointed as a Deputy Las Vegas Marshal, becoming part of the notorious Dodge City Gang that was terrorizing the city of Las Vegas.

On January 22, 1880, T.J. House, James West, John Dorsey, and William Randall were parading about town sneering, laughing, and looking for trouble. When they entered the Close & Patterson Variety Hall, Marshal Joe Carson asked them to check their guns but they refused. A wild gunfight ensued and Carson was killed immediately, while Deputy "Mysterious" Dave Mather killed Randall and dropped West. John Dorsey, though wounded, and T.J. House, managed to escape. On February 5, the whereabouts of Dorsey and House was learned; they were at the house of Juan Antonio Dominguez in Buena Vista, thirty miles north of Las Vegas. A posse comprised of J.J. Webb, Dave Rudabaugh, and five other men, surrounded the house and called for the men to surrender. Dorsey and House complied after assurance of protection from the citizens of Las Vegas was given. However, this assurance would mean very little, as within hours of the men being placed in the Old Town Jail, vigilantes relieved the jailers of the prisoners. Taking them to the windmill on the Plaza to hang, Mrs. Carson opened fire on the men, depriving the lynchers their opportunity.

After Marshal Joe Carson's death, Mather was appointed as the Las Vegas Marshal. However, Mather soon moved on again after being accused of "promiscuous shooting" in his capacity as marshal. Next he was known to have served for a short time as Assistant Marshal in El Paso, Texas. However, after an altercation in a brothel in which Mather was slightly wounded, he returned to Dodge City where he was hired as Assistant City Marshal.

By the time Mather returned to Dodge City, the existence of gambling, drinking, prostitution, and dance halls, often in open violation of the law, had heated up as a major town issue. The "Dodge City War" in the spring of 1883 was followed by pressure from the Santa Fe Railroad to clean up "their" town. The reform-minded and status quo factions were still feuding when David Mather accepted the position of Dodge City Assistant Marshal. Before long, Mather also became the co-owner of the Opera House Saloon on Front Street.

Because of its prominent downtown location, the city council objected to Mather's decision to turn the Opera House Saloon into a dance hall and soon passed an ordinance banning all dance houses. However, the council took no action whatsoever against another dance hall owned by Thomas Nixon, allegedly because of its remote location.

For several months, Nixon and Mather battled to put each other out of business. In 1884, the city government replaced Mysterious Dave with Nixon as the Assistant Marshal, and the feud that had been brewing for several months came to a head. On the evening of July 18, 1884, Nixon drew a gun and fired at Mather, but only sprayed him with a few splinters. Three days later, Mather approached Nixon from behind and fired four bullets into his back, killing him instantly. Later, Mather was heard to say, "I ought to have killed him six months ago."

Although Mather was acquitted of Nixon's murder, he killed another man the following year and was run out of town by Marshal Bill Tilghman. After serving as city marshal in a couple small towns in Kansas and Nebraska, Mysterious Dave moved on to San Francisco, where he took a ship to Vancouver.

He soon enlisted in the Royal Canadian Mounted Police, proving his prowess by showing what he could do with a pair of six guns and a horse. He was still seen in the royal blue and red as late as 1920.

## Daniel Boone May

*Protecting the Deadwood Stage*

Said to have been the fastest gun in the Dakotas, Daniel Boone May, began his life in Missouri in 1852. Going by the name of "Boone," he was the son of Samuel and Nancy May, the seventh of nine children. Later, he moved with his family to Bourbon County, Kansas, where his father worked as a farmer. In 1876, he and an older brother moved to Cheyenne, Wyoming, where they worked in the freight business. During this time, the Black Hills were crawling with road agents and hostile Sioux Indians – a dangerous time to be working along the roadways. May did so well, that he bought a ranch between the Platte River and Deadwood by the end of the year.

Daniel Boone May

Hearing of Boone's bravery and work ethic, he was soon recruited as a shotgun messenger for the Cheyenne and Black Hills Stage & Express Company. He also served as the station keeper at Robbers' Roost in Wyoming Territory.

Within just a few years, May was thought to have been in at least eight shooting incidents with outlaws.

One of the first hold-ups he was involved in was in August, 1877, when a Deadwood Coach was held-up at Robber's Roost. On this occasion, though May wanted to fight it out, he lay down his arms, as a woman and child were in the coach, and the robbers made away with the passenger's money, weapons and personal goods. A short time later, he ran into one of the bandits, a man named Prescott Webb, in Deadwood and within no time, gunfire erupted between the pair. Though May was hit in the left wrist, he returned fire as Webb jumped on a horse to flee. May's shots hit Webb in the shoulder, and the horse several times, bringing it down. Webb was quickly arrested by Sheriff Seth Bullock and later that day, Webb's companions who had aided in the robbery, were also arrested.

In 1878, "treasure coaches" were running regularly between Deadwood and Cheyenne, carrying strong boxes laden with gold, as well as the U.S. Mail. These gold-rich stages became the often target of bandits and after one of these coaches was held up on July 2, 1878, the U.S. Postal Service appointed a number of special agents to bring the outlaws to justice. May and ten other men were soon appointed as U.S. Deputy Marshals and equipped with good horses and ammunition.

One of May's first run-in with bandits as a U.S. Deputy Marshal occurred on the night of September 13, 1878 when he and another messenger were trailing a Cheyenne bound coach which was approached by bandits near Old Woman's Creek in Wyoming Territory. May and Zimmerman surprised the outlaws and shooting erupted. May wounded one bandit named Frank Towle and the others fled without any booty. Leaving the wounded man on the ground, the two messengers went after the other bandits but were unable to capture them. When they returned to the robbery site, Towle was gone.

On September 26, 1878, when May and other messengers were waiting to escort a coach at Beaver Station on the Wyoming-Dakota border, the stage failed to show up. They headed down the road in search of the coach when they met another messenger who told them it had been robbed and a passenger killed. May quickly joined a posse to go after the outlaws, but unfortunately they escaped.

The following month, May learned of the hiding place of a road agent named Archie McLaughlin and quickly went after him and his companions. Capturing them north of Cheyenne, the outlaws were sent under guard to Deadwood on the northbound coach. However, the stage would never make it, as on November 3, 1878, it was stopped by vigilantes who hanged Archie McLaughlin and another man named Billy Mansfield.

The next month, May was in another posse that brought in a road agent named Tom Price. The bandit, who resisted arrest, was wounded, before he was brought in.

Late in 1879, May was sent to assist Special Agent William H. Llewellyn in the capture of a mail robber named Curley Grimes.

They tracked the outlaw to Elk Creek, a location about halfway between Rapid City and Fort Meade and arrested him. That evening as the two lawmen and their prisoner neared Fort Meade, Grimes attempted to escape and was shot and killed by May and Llewellyn.

By this time, May had made such a reputation for himself that he became a target for many of the road agents who repeatedly tried to assassinate him, unsuccessfully.

May also worked as a messenger for the Black Hills Placer Mining Company in the summer of 1880, and was said to have killed at least one road agent during this time.

Shortly afterwards, May resigned from the company in September and disappeared from the Black Hills. Next, he was known to have been in Santiago, Chile in 1883, but after shooting an army officer in 1891, he fled to Brazil. He died of yellow fever in Rio de Janeiro in 1910.

## Sherman W. McMasters

*Outlaw or Lawman?*

Sherman W. McMasters was an outlaw, Texas Ranger, and lawman best known for his participation in the Earp Vendetta Ride. Born in 1853 in Illinois, McMasters headed west where he gained a reputation as a gunfighter. He was in Dodge City, Kansas at the same time as were Wyatt Earp and Doc Holliday, where he made friends with the pair. There, he also reportedly killed a man in self-defense after a gambling dispute in a saloon.

By September, 1878, McMasters was working with the Texas Rangers in El Paso County, a position that he held until the following spring. It was in the Lone Star State that he met Curly Bill Brocius, and by some accounts, helped him to escape from jail.

In 1879, he hooked up with other illustrious characters of the Dodge City Gang in Las Vegas, New Mexico. He was known to have associated with the likes of such characters as Hoodoo Brown, who ran the gang that for a time, was firmly in control of a criminal cartel which participated in several stage coach and train robberies, organized cattle rustling, and were said to have been responsible for multiple murders and lynchings.

Later, McMasters drifted to Tombstone, Arizona, where he was friendly with not only the likes of Curly Bill Brocius, Johnny Barnes and Pony Deal, who supported the outlaw Clanton faction; but, was also friendly with the Earp brothers, who were at obvious odds with the Clantons.

During this time, McMasters was a suspect in the stealing of Army mules in July, 1880, and the next year, the theft of two valuable horses from the Contention Mine, and a Globe, Arizona stagecoach robbery. However, by 1882, he was allegedly employed by Wyatt Earp to help track down "Curly Bill" Brocious and Pony Deal following a January, 1882 robbery of the Bisbee, Arizona stagecoach. Whether McMasters was truly an outlaw or was working undercover to break up the Cowboy faction remains a mystery.

McMasters was in the saloon in which Morgan Earp was assassinated in March, 1882. After Morgan's death and an attempt on Virgil Earp's life, McMasters was clearly in allegiance with the Earps, when he joined Wyatt and Warren Earp, when they began their Vendetta Ride. He took part in the murder of Frank Stilwell at Tucson, Arizona, and of

Florentino Cruz, who was also called Indian Charlie, two days later. However, he was not present at Earp's alleged confrontation with Curly Bill Brocius. Following the two week revenge ride of the Earps, McMasters left Arizona with Wyatt and disappeared from history.

Later, Will McLaury, in a letter written to his father, stated that McMasters had been killed in a shootout with the Cowboy faction in 1884. However, Wyatt would say that McMasters died in the Phillipines in 1898, while serving as a soldier in the Spanish American War, though there are no documents to support this. The most reasonable account was by McMasters siblings, who indicated that he died in Colorado in 1892.

## Evett Dumas "E.D." Nix

*Bringing Down the Doolin-Dalton Gang*

E.D. Nix took the oath of office as U.S. Marshal for the Oklahoma Territory on July 1, 1893 and served until 1896. He led the posse that fought in the Ingalls, Oklahoma Shoot-out and was primarily responsible for the capture and killing of the members of the Doolin-Dalton Gang.

Evett Dumas "E.D." Nix

Born in Kentucky on September 19, 1861, he would come by his lawman experience honestly, as his father served as a deputy sheriff and his uncle, a county sheriff. As a young man, he worked in his father's factory and later operated a grocery, hardware, and furniture business in Coldwater, Kentucky. He became a traveling sales representative and moved to Paducah, Kentucky in 1885, where he married Ellen Felts.

He and his wife moved to Guthrie, Oklahoma in October, 1889, where he became a prosperous businessman and formed a number of influential friendships.

At the age of 32, he was appointed as U.S. Marshal of Oklahoma Territory on July 1, 1893, the youngest man assigned to such a position. At the time of his appointment, the Guthrie Daily News said of him:

"He has, right now, all the sturdy characteristics of a veteran. A forceful independence, a clear, cool head, a quiet, unostentatious confidence in himself that is the best equipment it is possible for a man to have who would fill successfully the high office to which his merits, and his merits alone, were the signal cause of his call."

During these last years of Judge Isaac Parker's tenure, the territory was still a lawless frontier, filled with desperadoes. Recognizing the tough job ahead, he quickly appointed a formidable force of deputies, including Henry Andrew "Heck" Thomas, William Matthew "Bill" Tilghman, Chris Madsen, Frank M. Canton, Charles Colcord, John Hixon, and others, most of whom were already veteran peace officers.

At the time he took office, the Doolin-Dalton Gang was terrorizing the territory and Nix made it one of his first responsibilities, to take them down. Just a few months later, on September 1, 1893, he led a posse of some 27 deputy marshals and Indian Police and headed towards Ingalls, Oklahoma, a known hideout of the gang. In what would become known as the Battle of Ingalls, three of his deputy marshals – Thomas Hueston, Richard Speed, and Lafeyette Shadley were killed and Doolin-Dalton Gang members, "Bittercreek" Newcomb, Charley Pierce, and "Dynamite Dan" Clifton were wounded, but escaped. Only gang member "Arkansas Tom" Jones was captured. Though the battle was won by the outlaws, the "war" was not yet over. Nix then organized an elite group of about 100 U.S. Deputy Marshals to bring down the infamous Doolin-Dalton Gang. By 1898, the entire gang had either been captured or killed.

He was dismissed from his position on January 24, 1896, when an audit alleged that he had misused funds. However, it was later found that the "misuse" was probably the result of an inadequate fee system used at that time for payment of U.S. Marshals Service officers.

Nix returned to life as a Guthrie businessman and in 1929 co-authored a book titled *Oklahombres: Particularly the Wilder Ones* with Gordon Hines, which detailed the demise of the Doolin-Dalton Gang.

Nix died on February 4, 1946 in Riverside, California and was buried in Paducah, Kentucky.

## Thomas Clayton Nixon

*Buffalo Hunter & Lawman*

Earning a reputation for one of the most prolific buffalo hunters in the American West, Nixon once shot 120 buffalo in just 40 minutes in 1873, an event that was witnessed by a crowd he brought from town and positioned on a hill to watch. That same year, he set a record for having killed over 3,200 buffalo in just 35 days.

Thomas Clayton Nixon was born about 1837 in Georgia but somewhere along the line moved westward, landing in Kansas. He was one of the first pioneers of Dodge City and by the 1870's he was a successful buffalo hunter, as well as a ranch owner. With the likes of Bat Masterson, Bill Tilghman, and Levi Richardson, Nixon honed his skills as a buffalo hunter, besting all but Buffalo Bill Cody. He married Cornelia Caroline Houston about 1870 and the two would have a son they named Howard Tracy Nixon.

By 1880, the buffalo were not as prevalent and Nixon turned to freighting, in charge of Charles Rath's bull trains. Often loaded down with thousands of pounds of buffalo bones, Rath's hide yards in Dodge were now filled with huge piles of bleached bones rather than buffalo hides.

In the spring of 1883, Dodge City was embroiled in the so-called Dodge City War, a dispute between saloon owners who were friends of Dodge City's former Mayor, Alonzo B. Webster, and Luke Short, owner of the Long Branch Saloon. In the midst of this dispute was Tom Nixon, who was one of Webster's supporters and by that time owned his own saloon called the Lady Gay. While he was mayor, Webster passed ordinances that protected his own two saloons and those of his friends, while establishing rules restricting competing saloons and levying taxes upon them. Nixon led a vigilante group to "force" Webster's rules and to run competing saloon owners out of town.

Into this mix came "Mysterious Dave" Mather, who had frequently made Dodge City his home in previous years. He soon became Dodge City's Assistant Marshal.

When Luke Short pulled in several of his friends to support him in the Dodge City War, including Bat Masterson and Wyatt Earp, the show of force caused Short's enemies to back down and violence was avoided. Though the Dodge City War had ended without gunfire and the city breathed a sigh of relief, the saloon dispute had not ended. Ironically, after having won his battle, Luke Short moved on to Texas. But, in his wake, the disputes continued.

Mather, in the meantime, had established his own saloon called the Opera House Saloon and planned to make it a dance hall. However, because of its prominent downtown location, the city council objected to Mather's decision and soon passed an ordinance banning all dance houses. Ironically, the ordinance restricted all the saloons in town except for Tom Nixon's Lady Gay. For months, Nixon and Mather battled to put each other out of business. In 1884, the city government replaced Mysterious Dave with Tom Nixon as the Assistant Marshal, and the feud that had been brewing for several months came to a head. Mather's resentment toward Nixon obviously grew.

In the meantime, Nixon was collecting $100 per month as the assistant marshal under Bill Tilghman. The lawmens' wages were paid by collecting license fees from the city's gamblers, prostitutes, madams and pimps. The Lady Gay was the only dance hall left in town and Webster was profiting from his own saloons, while controlling the action and profits in the city.

Though it was Mather who was most resentful, tension for Tom Nixon evidently came to a boil on the night of July 18, 1884. As Mather was standing on the front steps of the Opera House Saloon, Nixon took a shot at him. Although Mather's face was powder burned and his left hand injured by flying splinters, he did not return the fire and refused to press charges. Evidently, he had his own plans for handling the affair.

Three nights later, on July 21st, Tom Nixon was standing at the corner of First Avenue and Front Street in front of the Opera House about 10 p.m. When Nixon heard a voice calling out to him from behind, he turned to see Mather pointing a Colt .45 at him. Within seconds, Nixon took four bullets, one piercing his heart, and he was dead before he hit the ground.

Mather then surrendered himself to authorities and though witnesses said that Nixon never drew his pistol, Mather was acquitted for self-defense. Later, Mather was heard to say, "I ought to have killed him six months ago."

After the trial, Mather remained in Dodge until the following year. On May 10, 1885, however; he and his brother Josiah were involved in a gunfight at the Junction Saloon. One man was killed and several were wounded, including Mather, whose head was grazed by a bullet. Both Dave and his brother Josiah were arrested but soon made bail and left town.

## Robert "Bob" Ollinger

*Killer With a Badge*

Though Robert "Bob" Ollinger was a lawman, he was actually better known as a killer with a penchant in fighting in range wars.

Ollinger was born about 1841 and when he was just a boy he moved with his family from Ohio to Oklahoma. When he grew up, he made his way to New Mexico.

In 1876 he was named marshal of Seven Rivers in Lincoln County, New Mexico. However, the job was short lived as he was soon fired when he was suspected of consorting with an outlaw band. This would be the "norm" for Ollinger, as his love of gambling and drinking often placed him in bad company.

The first man known to have been killed by Ollinger was a Mexican named Juan Chavez. The two, who were friends and had no history of violence between them, were playing poker in the Royal Saloon in Seven Rivers. However, when Chavez accused Ollinger of cheating, Bob stood up and leveled his six-shooter at his friend's head. Another player then tossed the unarmed Chavez a gun and the two exchanged shots. When the smoke cleared, Chavez lay dead on the floor with a bullet in his throat. Without remorse, Ollinger simply looked at him stating, "All's well that end's well," before he strode out the door.

The second man Ollinger killed also involved gambling. When he and a man named John Hill were playing poker at Diamond Lil's casino and dance hall, Ollinger quickly won Hill's money. Afterwards, Hill loudly stated that he had been "hornswoggled," implying that Ollinger had tricked or cheated him. Though initially Ollinger did nothing, when Hill left the saloon later that night, Ollinger shot him dead.

In February, 1878, when the Lincoln County War erupted, Ollinger was right in the midst of it. When the Dolan-Murphy faction obtained a court order to seize some of John Tunstall's horses as payment for an outstanding debt, and Tunstall refused, Lincoln County Sheriff, William Brady, formed a posse to go after Tunstall. In this group was Bob Ollinger, as a Dolan-Murphy "hired gun." Rather than arresting Tunstall; however, the unarmed man was killed on February 18, 1878. Although several riders participated in the murder, only James Dolan and Jacob "Billy" Matthews were charged with being accessories to the murder.

In the end, Ollinger's participation in the Lincoln County War would be a fatal mistake, as a Tunstall supporter, Billy the Kid avowed: "I'll get every son-of-a-bitch who helped kill John if it's the last thing I do."

Seemingly, as time went on, each of Ollinger's killings got a little worse. The next year, when Ollinger was playing poker with a man named Bob Jones, yet another gambling dispute arose. Jones, who had heard of Ollinger's reputation wisely avoided the killer.

However, Ollinger saw a chance to even the score when he found that Deputy Pierce Jones had a misdemeanor warrant to serve on Bob Jones. Ollinger decided to tag along and when they arrived at Bob Jones home, Jones was working in the yard while his three children played and his wife was in the kitchen.

Offering no resistance, Bob asked the deputy if he could explain to his wife that he would return as soon as he paid his fine. The deputy agreed and Bob made his way into the house passing by his hunting gun, which was lying on the porch. Though Bob Jones made no attempt to pick up the rifle, Ollinger drew a pistol and fired three shots into Bob's back. As Jones' wife and children stood by screaming and Deputy Jones was shocked, Ollinger was smug in his belief that he could claim self-defense for the outright murder.

Deputy Jones quickly brought murder charges against Ollinger, and Lincoln County authorities issued a warrant for his arrest. Sheriff George Kimball arrested him and brought him to Lincoln for trial in October, 1879. However, for unknown reasons, the case was dismissed without going to court.

That very same month, Pat Garrett was elected Sheriff of Lincoln County. Amazingly, Ollinger was appointed his deputy, much to Garrett's chagrin. Aware of Ollinger's violent tendencies, he would begin to see them first-hand. On one occasion when the pair went to arrest an armed Mexican, Garrett promised the fugitive, who had taken cover in a ditch, that he would not be harmed if he came in. However, as the man came forward with his hands in the air, Ollinger drew his pistol as if to shoot him. The man was saved by Garrett, who placed himself in between, saying to Ollinger: "Put it away, Bob. Unless you want to try me."

When a price was put on Billy the Kid's head and Pat Garrett determined to track him down, the swaggering Ollinger hoped he would be the one that might kill the famous outlaw. In December, 1880 Billy the Kid, along with Dave Rudabaugh, Tom Pickett, and Bill Wilson, were tracked down by Pat Garrett and taken to Santa Fe, New Mexico.

After Billy was convicted, he was then sent to Lincoln to await his execution, scheduled for May 13, 1881. Ollinger, along with several other men, were assigned the task of escorting the Kid back to Lincoln. Along the way, Ollinger constantly tormented Billy, so much so, that even the other guards had some sympathy for the outlaw. To this, Billy said to the deputy, "Be careful, Bob, I'm not hung yet." Though Ollinger, no doubt, looked for opportunities to kill the Kid on the way to Lincoln, the party arrived without incident.

Placed in the county jail, Ollinger continued to taunt Billy to the point that Garrett told him to "lay off the Kid." On one occasion, the shifty lawman even went so far as to place a pistol on a table within Billy's reach, but the Kid was too smart to take the bait.

On April 28th, Garrett was out of town on business and Billy was left in the hands of Deputies James Bell and Ollinger. While Ollinger took several other prisoners to the Worthy Hotel, a block away for their daily meal, Bell remained with Billy the Kid. Somehow, Billy had obtained a pistol and shot Bell. He then stole Ollinger's 10-gauge double barrel shotgun and waited for the deputy by the window in the room he was being held in. Ollinger obliged by running immediately from the hotel upon hearing the shots.

When he was directly under the window of the courthouse, he heard his prisoner say, "Hello, Bob." Ollinger then looked up and saw the Kid, gun in hand. It was the last thing he ever saw as Billy blasted him with his own shotgun killing him instantly.

The bodies of deputies Ollinger and Bell were placed in a room in the corral behind the courthouse and remained there until Garrett's return. Garrett swore to make Billy pay, and he did when he killed the infamous outlaw on July 14, 1881.

Hiding behind a badge for much of his life, Ollinger was a killer worse than the likes of most outlaws. Even his own mother would remember him by saying:

"Bob was a murderer from the cradle, and if there is a hell hereafter, then he is there."

## Judge Issac C. Parker

*Hanging Judge of Indian Territory*

"I have ever had the single aim of justice in view... 'Do equal and exact justice,' is my motto, and I have often said to the grand jury, 'Permit no innocent man to be punished, but let no guilty man escape.'"
-Judge Isaac C. Parker, 1896

Judge Isaac Parker often called the "Hanging Judge," from Fort Smith, Arkansas ruled over the lawless land of Indian Territory in the late 1800s. In 1875, Indian Territory (now Oklahoma) was populated by cattle and horse thieves, whiskey peddlers, and bandits who sought refuge in the untamed territory that was free of a "White Man's Court." The only court with jurisdiction over Indian Territory was the U.S. Court for the Western District of Arkansas located in Fort Smith, Arkansas, which was situated on the border of Western Arkansas and Indian Territory.

Judge Isaac Parker

Judge Isaac Parker was born in a log cabin outside Barnesville, Belmont County, Ohio on October 15, 1838. The youngest son of Joseph and Jane Parker, Isaac helped out on the farm, but never really cared for working out of doors. He attended the Breeze Hill primary school and then the Barnesville Classical Institute.

At the age of 21, he was admitted to the Ohio bar in 1859. He soon met and married Mary O'Toole and the couple had two sons, Charles and James. Over the years, Parker built a reputation for being an honest lawyer and a leader of the community. To help pay for his higher education, he taught students in a country primary school. When he was 17, he decided to study law, his legal training consisting of a combination of apprenticeship and self study. Reading law with a Barnesville attorney, he passed the bar exam in 1859 at the age of 21.

After passing the bar he traveled west to St. Joseph, Missouri, a bustling Missouri River port town. He soon went to work for his uncle, D.E. Shannon, a partner in the Shannon and Branch legal firm. By 1861, he was working on his own in both the municipal and county criminal courts, and in April he won the election as City Attorney. He was re-elected to the post for the next two years.

In 1864, Isaac Parker ran for county prosecutor of the Ninth Missouri Judicial District and in the fall of that same year, he served as a member of the Electoral College, casting his vote for Abraham Lincoln.

In 1868, Parker sought and won a six-year term as judge of the Twelfth Missouri Circuit. A new judge, Parker would soon gain the experience that he would later use as the ruling Judge over the Indian Territory.

On September 13, 1870, Parker was nominated on the Republican ticket for the Seventh Congressional District. To pursue his political ambitions and devote all his energy to the campaign, Parker resigned his judgeship. The heated campaign ended with Parker's opponent withdrawing from the race two weeks prior to the election and Parker easily defeated the replacement candidate in the November 8, 1870 election.

As a freshman representative, Parker took his seat in the first session of the Forty-second Congress, convened on Saturday, March 4, 1871. In November, 1872, he easily won a second national attention for speeches delivered in support of the Bureau of Indian Affairs.

By the fall of 1874, the political tide had shifted in Missouri, and as a Republican, Isaac Parker had no chance of re-election to Congress. Instead, he sought a presidential appointment to public office and submitted a request for appointment as the judge of the federal district court for the Western District of Arkansas, in Fort Smith. On March 18, 1875, President Grant nominated Parker as judge for the Western District of Arkansas.

After the Civil War, the number of outlaws had grown, wrecking the relative peace of the five civilized tribes that lived in Indian Territory. By the time Parker arrived at Fort Smith, Indian Territory had become known as a very bad place, where outlaws thought the laws did not apply to them and terror reigned.

Replacing Judge William Story, whose tenure had been marred by corruption, Parker arrived in Fort Smith on May 4, 1875. At the age of 36, Judge Parker was the youngest Federal judge in the West. Holding court for the first time on May 10, 1875, eight men were found guilty of murder and sentenced to death. Judge Parker held court six days a week, often up to ten hours each day, and tried 91 defendants in his first eight weeks on the bench. In that first summer, 18 persons came before him charged with murder and 15 were convicted. Eight of them were sentenced to die on the gallows on September 3, 1875. However, only six would be executed as one was killed trying to escape and a second had his sentence commuted to life in prison because of his youth.

When the fateful day of September 3, 1875 arrived, the hanging became an extraordinary media event when reporters from Little Rock, St. Louis, and Kansas City, flocked to the city. Other newspapermen traveled far from eastern and northern cities to catch the "scoop." Beginning a week before the hanging, the city began to fill with strangers from all over the country, anxious to view the hangings. On the day they were to be condemned, more than 5,000 people watched as the six men were marched from the jail to the gallows.

Of the six felons, three were white, two were Native American, and one was black. Seated along the back of the gallows, their death warrants were read to them and each was asked if they had any last words.

When the preliminaries were over, the six were lined up on the scaffold while executioner, George Maledon, adjusted the nooses around their necks. The trap was sprung, all six died at once at the end of the ropes.

Though the hangings were an indication that the once corrupt court was functioning again, it earned Isaac Parker the nickname of "The Hanging Judge."

The Fort Smith Independent was the first newspaper to report the event on September 3, 1875 with the large column heading reading: "Execution Day!!" Other newspapers around the country reported the event a day later. These press reports shocked people throughout the nation. "Cool Destruction of Six Human Lives by Legal Process" screamed the headlines.

Soon Parker's critics dubbed him the "Hanging Judge" and called his court the "Court of the Damned." However, most of Parker's critics didn't live in the frontier and did not understand the ethics (or lack thereof) of the untamed Indian Territory. Most of the local people approved of Parker's judgments, feeling like the utter viciousness of the crimes merited the sentences imposed. From these first six hangings in 1875, there would be 73 more until his death in 1896.

Though Parker was hard on killers and rapists, he was also a fair man. He occasionally granted retrials that sometimes resulted in acquittals or reduced sentences. Though Parker actually favored the abolition of the death penalty, he strictly adhered to the letter of the law. At one time he said, "in the uncertainty of punishment following crime, lies the weakness of our halting justice." However, Parker reserved most of his sympathy for the crime victims and is now seen as one of first advocates of victim's rights.

Parker's jurisdiction began to shrink as more courts were given authority over parts of Indian Territory. The restrictions of the court's once vast jurisdiction were sometimes a source of frustration to Parker, but what bothered him the most were the Supreme Court reversals of capital crimes tried in Fort Smith. Fully two-thirds of the cases appealed to the higher court were reversed and sent back to Fort Smith for new trials. In 1894, the judge gained national attention in a dispute with the Supreme Court over the case of Lafayette Hudson.

In 1895, a new Courts Act was passed which would remove the last remaining Indian Territory jurisdiction effective September 1, 1896. Following the escape attempt of Cherokee Bill in the summer of 1895, which resulted in the death of a jail guard, Judge Parker again came into conflict with his superior when he blamed the Justice Department and the Supreme Court for the incident. Cherokee Bill was eventually hanged in Fort Smith on March 17, 1896. But the debate was not yet over and a very public argument was carried on between Judge Parker and the Assistant Attorney General.

When the August term in 1896 began, Judge Parker was at home, too sick to preside over the court. Twenty years of overwork had contributed to a variety of ailments, including Bright's Disease. When the jurisdiction of the court over lands in the Indian Territory came to an end on September 1, 1896, the Judge had to be interviewed by reporters at his bedside. Scarcely two months after the jurisdictional change took effect, the Judge died on November 17, 1896.

In 21 years on the bench, Judge Parker tried 13,490 cases, 344 of which were capital crimes. 9,454 cases resulted in guilty pleas or convictions. Over the years, Judge Parker sentenced 160 men to death by hanging, though only 79 of them were actually hanged. The rest died in jail, appealed, or were pardoned.

Fort Smith Hanging

## Henry Plummer

*Sheriff Meets a Noose*

One of the most colorful characters of the Wild West, Henry Plummer, allegedly played both sides of the law during his short twenty-seven years. Though for more than a century he was thought to have been guilty of numerous crimes and rightly hanged in Bannack, Montana, today's historians question whether or not he was truly guilty of the crimes he was accused of.

Henry Plummer

Born in Addison, Maine in 1832, to William Jeremiah and Elizabeth (Handy) Plummer, he was the youngest of seven children. His father, older brother and brother-in-law, were all sea captains and Henry was expected to follow in their footsteps. However, the young man was slight of build and consumptive, making the rigors of the sea trade too much for him to handle.

When Henry was a teenager, his father died and the family began to struggle financially. Just two years after the California Gold Rush began; Henry promised his widowed mother that he could help the family by making his fortune in the West.

In April, 1852, nineteen-year-old Henry sailed from New York on a mail ship to Aspinwall, Panama, traveled by mule train to Panama City, then boarded another ship for the rest of his journey to California. Twenty-four days after his departure, he arrived in San Francisco. Gaining a job at a bakery, Plummer soon earned enough money to move on to the mining camps of Nevada County, about 150 miles north of San Francisco.

About a year after his arrival in California, documents show that he owned a ranch and a mine outside Nevada City, California. Some twelve months later, he traded some of his mining shares for the Empire Bakery in Nevada City. By 1856, the local residents, so impressed by the young man, persuaded him to run for sheriff. At the age of 24, he became marshal of the third largest settlement in California.

The young marshal was well liked by the Nevada City citizens and respected for his promptness and boldness in handling his duties. He easily won the re-election in 1857.

But, shortly after the election, he killed his first man. At the time, Henry was said to be having an affair with the wife of a miner by the name of John Vedder, and when he was confronted by the angry husband, the two competed in a dual, for which, Henry obviously won.

Plummer was arrested and tried in a sensational, emotionally-charged case that went twice to the California Supreme Court before he was finally convicted of second degree murder and sentenced to ten years in California's infamous San Quentin Prison. He began to serve his sentence on February 22, 1859 and local residents quickly petitioned the Governor for a pardon, claiming that Henry had acted in self-defense.

Among his comrades behind bars was Cyrus Skinner, serving time for grand larceny, who would later be connected with Plummer again. Plummer served time only until August 16, 1859 when he was released due to his tuberculosis and pressure on the Governor by the petition.

After his release, Henry returned to Nevada City, to the bakery, and became an avid customer to the many brothels of the settlement.

Before long, he was penniless and soon joined a group of bandits intent upon robbing area stage coaches. In one such incident, the stage driver got away with his passengers and cargo, but Plummer was arrested. Standing trial for the attempted robbery, the former sheriff caught a reprieve when he was acquitted due to lack of evidence.

But trouble had begun to follow Plummer around and soon he was caught up in a brawl over a "painted lady" with a man by the name of William Riley. When Henry shot the man on October 27, 1861, he was once again arrested. This time he escaped prison by bribing a jailer before he could be tried and fled for Oregon.

Along the way, he met another bandit by the name of Jim Mayfield, who had allegedly killed the sheriff of a neighboring town.

Both were obviously wanted men, and the ex-sheriff sent word to California newspapers that both he and Mayfield had been hanged in Washington. It had the desired effect, curtailing the need for the desperadoes to constantly look over their shoulders for the pursuing posse.

In January, 1862, Plummer landed in Lewiston, Idaho with a woman companion and registered at the Luna House. Working in a casino, he soon ran into his old cellmate, Cyrus Skinner, and other individuals destined for the gallows in Montana, such as Club Foot George Lane and Bill Bunton.

Forming a gang, the like-minded men began to rob the local families of the area mining camps, and especially targeted the gold shipments traveling the roads from the mines.

Somewhere along the line, Plummer abandoned his mistress, a woman with three children who had to resort to prostitution to feed herself and family, and finally died an alcoholic, in one of the seedier brothels in town.

Plummer began to roam the area between Elk City, Florence, and Lewiston. In Orofino, Idaho, he killed a saloon keeper by the name of Patrick Ford. When the saloonkeeper kicked Plummer and some of his friends out of the saloon, Ford then followed them to the stable where he fired upon them. Plummer returned fire and killed Ford. When some of Ford's friends began to form a lynch mob, Plummer hightailed it out of there and headed east to Montana.

By September, 1862, Plummer was beginning to feel the effects of his tuberculosis and wanted to return home. Heading from Idaho across the Bitterroot Mountains, he traveled to Fort Benton with the intention of going back east. Unfortunately, the upper Missouri River at Fort Benton was frozen and closed to Riverboat traffic. Planning to hold over for the winter, Henry went to work as a ranch hand at the Sun River Farm, a government ranch and Indian Agency, in October.

Plummer soon became enamored with Indian Agent James Vail's beautiful sister-in-law, Electa Bryan. Henry and Electa spent about two months together and were quickly engaged to be married.

A former cohort of Plummer's by the name of Jack Cleveland was also vying for Electa's attention, which incensed Henry. Nevertheless, both men headed to Bannack, Montana, the most recent site of gold rush fever, in January 1863.

Hastily built to accommodate the many miners flooding to the area, Bannack was called home to all manner of transient men, including Civil War deserters from both sides, river pirates, professional gamblers, outlaws, and villains. Lawlessness ran rampant as holdups occurred daily, and killings were just as frequent.

Henry soon rounded up another gang, calling themselves the Innocents, and began to relieve the gold-laden travelers from the Montana camps of their valuables. The Innocents grew quickly and became so large that secret handshakes and code words were instituted so one "Innocent" could recognize another.

One night while Henry was drinking in Bannack's Goodrich Saloon, Jack Cleveland, his old nemesis, began to taunt him by making numerous references to Plummer's outlaw activities. When Henry warned him to stop, Cleveland continued to spout his accusations and Plummer fired a warning shot. Cleveland then pulled his own six-gun, but Henry was faster and soon Cleveland lay on the floor, mortally wounded.

Not yet dead, Cleveland was taken to the home of a butcher named Hank Crawford, two doors down from the saloon. Crawford heard Cleveland's last words as he continued to extol the tale of Plummer's deceit and corruption. Three hours later, Cleveland was dead and Plummer was arrested. However, Plummer received yet another reprieve when he was acquitted based on witness testimony that Cleveland had threatened him.

By late spring 1863, there were more than 10,000 men hunting for gold along Grasshopper Creek and the lawlessness in Bannack had reached epidemic proportions. The frightened citizens of the settlement decided that the outlaws had to be stopped and advertised for a sheriff. Two men, vowing to corral the outlaws, stepped up to the plate – Plummer and a butcher named Hank Crawford.

Plummer lost the election to the popular butcher, an event that fired his reckless temper and he went after the new sheriff with a shotgun. However, a friend warned Crawford, who shot Plummer in his right arm, temporarily ruining his gunfighting abilities. Undaunted, Plummer immediately began to practice shooting with his left hand until his accuracy was just as deadly. When Hank Crawford caught wind of this, he turned in his badge and left Bannack, never to return.

In the new election for sheriff, Plummer was made the leading lawman on May 24, 1863. Plummer was quick to appoint two of his henchmen, Buck Stinson and Ned Ray, as deputies. Unknown to the people of Bannack, Plummer's group of Innocents had now reached over 100. Having the opposite desired effect for the citizens of Bannack, crime in the town increased dramatically after Plummer was elected. In the next few months, more than 100 citizens were murdered.

One of Plummer's first tasks was to build a jail for the growing community. It still stands today.

On June 20, 1863, Henry and Electa were married and soon settled into their log home in Bannack. However, Electa did not stay long. Less than three months later, she left for her parents home in Cedar Rapids, Iowa. She would never see Henry again.

The Innocents stepped up their efforts at robbing the gold-laden travelers from the Montana camps and helped the Sheriff to punish the "villains" of the community on a gallows that Plummer had erected. However, the few that were hanged on it by Plummer and his men were not members of the Innocents. The Innocents were well organized and said to have killed anyone that might be a witness to their crimes, most of which were easily covered up. Blatant killings went unpunished. Local residents who suspected anything feared for their lives and kept their mouths closed. The ambitious sheriff soon extended his operations to Virginia City when he was appointed Deputy U.S. Marshal for the region of Idaho Territory east of the mountains in August of 1863.

By December, 1863, the citizens of Bannack and Virginia City had had enough. Men from Bannack, Virginia City, and nearby Nevada City, met secretly and organized the Montana Vigilantes. Masked men began to visit suspected outlaws in the middle of the night issuing warnings and tacking up posters featuring a skull-and-crossbones or the "mystic" numbers "3-7-77." While the meaning of these numbers remains elusive, the Montana State Highway patrolmen wear the emblem "3-7-77" on their shoulder patches today. Interesting.

Sheriff Henry Plummer was hanged from the very gallows that he, himself had built earlier in the year.

The vigilantes dispensed rough justice by hanging about twenty-four men. When one such man, by the name of Erastus "Red" Yager, who was about to be hanged, pointed a finger at Henry Plummer as the leader of the gang, all hell broke loose.

The residents were divided on whether or not Henry was part of the murderous gang. But one night after heavy drinking in a local saloon, the vigilantes decided that Henry was guilty and tracked him down. On January 10, 1864, fifty to seventy-five men gathered up Plummer and his two main deputies, Buck Stinson and Ned Ray.

The three were marched to those very same gallows that Plummer, himself, had built. Ned Ray was the first hanged, followed by Buck Stinson–both men spewing epithets every step of the way. According to one legend, Plummer promised to tell the vigilantes where $100,000 of gold was buried, if they would let him live. However, the vigilantes ignored this as they gradually hoisted him up by the neck.

After the execution, armed guards stood by the gallows for about an hour. The three bodies were left hanging until the next morning. Plummer's was the only body placed in a wooden coffin and none were buried in the cemetery, but instead all three were buried in shallow graves in Hangman's Gulch about a hundred yards up from the gallows.

The Vigilantes went on to hang the rest of the Road Agents that they could locate, in such locations as Hellgate (Missoula), Cottonwood (Deer Lodge), Fort Owen, and Virginia City.

Vulnerable to vandalism, legend has it that the grave was broken into on two occasions. The first time, allegedly by the local doctor, who out of curiosity, severed the right arm from the body to search for the bullet that had hit Plummer when he went after Hank Crawford. Reportedly, the doctor found the bullet "worn smooth and polished by the bones turning upon it." The second time it was broken into, it was reportedly by two men around the turn of the century who, after spending several hours in a local bar, decided to dig up the grave. To prove they had done it, they severed the head and carried it back to the Bank Exchange Saloon, where it remained on the back bar for several years, until the building burned, along with all its contents. Yet, another legend states that the skull found its way into the hands of an unnamed doctor who sent the specimen back east to a scientific institution to try to figure out why Plummer was so evil.

Electa learned of her husband's death in a letter and she always maintained that he was innocent. In fact, in the past several decades, many historians, researchers, and authors have also questioned whether the tale of Henry Plummer was rightfully told.

Many believe that the whole thing is all a fraud, a story fabricated to cover up the real lawlessness in the Montana Territory - the vigilantes themselves. Many of the early stories, on which the outlaw tale is based, were written by the editor of the Virginia City Newspaper, who was a member of the vigilantes, himself.

Further testimony to support the theory is that the robberies did not cease after the twenty-one men were hanged in January and February of 1864. In fact, after the "Plummer Gang" hangings, the stage robberies showed more evidence of organized criminal activity, more robbers involved in the holdups, and more intelligence passed to the actual robbers.

Having taken control, the vigilantes were ruthless. On one such occasion, in attempting to get the names of the road agents, they looped a noose around the neck of a suspect named "Long John" Franck and repeatedly hoisted him until the poor man gasped out the answers the vigilantes wanted to hear. They did the same to Erastus "Red" Yager who pointed the finger at Henry Plummer as the gang's leader.

Further, the vigilantes brooked no criticism of their methods. When a preacher's son named Bill Hunter expressed his outrage by shouting on a mining camp street that pro-vigilantes were "stranglers," his frozen corpse was found three weeks later dangling from the limb of a cottonwood tree.

There is really little evidence connecting Plummer with any crime committed in the Bannack area, other than the "confession" of a criminal attempting to save his own life. Plummer's activities as an outlaw band leader in Lewiston have also been disputed; when evidence was found that he was actually living in California at the time.

Three years after Plummer was killed, the Vigilantes virtually ruled the mining districts. Finally, leading citizens of Montana including Territorial Governor Thomas Meagher, began to speak out against the ruthless group.

In March, 1867, the miners issued their own warning that if the Vigilantes hanged any more people, the "law abiding citizens" would retaliate "five for one." Though a few more lynchings occurred, it was clear that the era of the Vigilantes was past.

As to what happened to Electa – she ultimately moved to Vermillion, South Dakota, where she married James Maxwell, a widower with two daughters. Electa and James had two sons of their own, Vernon and Clarence. Electa lived until May 5, 1912 and was buried at Wakonda, South Dakota.

The historical town of Bannack, Montana was placed under the protection of Montana's Department of Fish, Wildlife, and Parks in 1954 and is now called the Bannack State Park.

## Bass Reeves

*Black Hero Marshal*

Born to slave parents in 1838 in Paris, Texas, Bass Reeves would become the first black U.S. Deputy Marshal west of the Mississippi River and one of the greatest frontier heroes in our nation's history.

Owned by a man named George Reeves, a farmer and politician, Bass took the surname of his owner, like other slaves of the time. Working alongside his parents, Reeves started out as a water boy until he was old enough to become a field hand.

A tall young man, at 6'2", with good manners and a sense of humor, George Reeves later made him his personal companion and body servant when Bass was older. When the Civil War broke out, Texas sided with the Confederacy and George Reeves went into battle, taking Bass with him.

It was during these years of the Civil War that Bass parted company from his "master," some say because Bass beat up George after a dispute in a card game. Others believe that Bass heard too much about the "freeing of slaves" and simply ran away. In any event, Bass fled to Indian Territory where he took refuge with the Seminole and Creek Indians. While in Indian Territory, Reeves honed his firearm skills, becoming very quick and accurate with a pistol. Though Reeves claimed to be "only fair" with a rifle, he was barred on a regular basis from competitive turkey shoots.

"Freed" by the Emancipation Proclamation in 1863 and no longer a fugitive, Reeves left Indian Territory and bought land near Van Buren, Arkansas, becoming a successful farmer and rancher. A year later, he married Nellie Jennie from Texas, and immediately began to have a family. Raising ten children on their homestead – five girls and five boys, the family lived happily on the farm.

However, Reeve's life as a contented farmer was about to change when Isaac C. Parker was appointed judge for the Federal Western District Court at Fort Smith, Arkansas on May 10, 1875. At the time Parker was appointed, Indian Territory had become extremely lawless as thieves, murderers, and anyone else wishing to hide from the law, took refuge in the territory that previously had no federal or state jurisdiction.

One of Parker's first official acts was to appoint U.S. Marshal James F. Fagan as head of the some 200 deputies he was then told to hire. Fagan heard of Bass Reeves' significant knowledge of the area, as well as his ability to speak several tribal languages, and soon recruited him as a U.S. Deputy.

The deputies were tasked with “cleaning up” Indian Territory and on Judge Parker’s orders, “Bring them in alive – or dead!”

Working among other lawmen that would also become legendary, such as Heck Thomas, Bud Ledbetter, and Bill Tilghman, Reeves began to ride the Oklahoma range in search of outlaws. Covering some 75,000 square miles, the United States Court at Fort Smith, was the largest in the nation.

Depending on the outlaws for whom he was searching, a deputy would generally take with him from Fort Smith, a wagon, a cook and a posse man. Often they rode to Fort Reno, Fort Sill, and Anadarko, a round trip of more than 800 miles.

Though Reeves could not read or write, it did not curb his effectiveness in bringing back the criminals. Before he headed out, he would have someone read him the warrants and memorize which was which. When asked to produce the warrant, he never failed to pick out the correct one.

An imposing figure, always riding on a large stallion, Reeves began to earn a reputation for his courage and success at bringing in or killing many desperadoes of the territory. Always wearing a large black hat, Reeves was usually a spiffy dresser, with his boots polished to a gleaming shine. He was known for his politeness and courteous manner. However, when the purpose served him, he was a master of disguises and often utilized aliases. Sometimes appearing as a cowboy, farmer, gunslinger, or outlaw, himself, he always wore two Colt pistols, butt forward for a fast draw. Ambidextrous, he rarely missed his mark.

Leaving Fort Smith, often with a pocketful of warrants, Reeves would often return months later herding a number of outlaws charged with crimes ranging from bootlegging to murder. Paid in fees and rewards, he would make a handsome profit, before spending a little time with his family and returning to the range once again.

The tales of his captures are legendary – filled with intrigue, imagination and courage. On one such occasion, Reeves was pursuing two outlaws in the Red River Valley near the Texas border. Gathering a posse, Reeves and the other men set up camp some 28 miles from where the two were thought to be hiding at their mother’s home. After studying the terrain and making a plan, he soon disguised himself as a tramp, hiding the tools of his trade – handcuffs, pistol and badge, under his clothes. Setting out on foot, he arrived at the house wearing an old pair of shoes, dirty clothes, carrying a cane, and wearing a floppy hat complete with three bullet holes.

Upon arriving at the home, he told a tale to a woman who answered the door that his feet were aching after having been pursued by a posse who had put the three bullet holes in his hat. After asking for a bite to eat, she invited him in and while he was eating she began to tell him of her two young outlaw sons, suggesting that the three of them should join forces.

Feigning weariness, she consented to let him stay a while longer. As the sun was setting, Reeves heard a sharp whistle coming from beyond the house. Shortly after the woman went outside and responded with an answering whistle, two riders rode up to the house, talking at length with her outside. Shortly, the three of them came inside and she introduced her sons to Reeves. After discussing their various crimes, the trio agreed that it would be a good idea to join up.

Bunking down in the same room, Reeves watched the pair carefully as they drifted off to sleep and when they were snoring deeply, handcuffed the pair without waking them. When early morning approached, he kicked the boys awake and marched them out the door. Followed for the first three miles by their mother, who cursed Reeves the entire time, he marched the pair the full 28 miles to the camp where the posse men waited. Within days, the outlaws were delivered to the authorities and a $5,000 reward collected.

One of the high points of Reeves' career was apprehending a notorious outlaw named Bob Dozier. Dozier was known as a jack-of-all-trades when it came to committing crimes, as they covered a wide range from cattle and horse rustling, to holding up banks, stores, and stagecoaches; to murder, and land swindles. Because Dozier was unpredictable, he was also hard to catch and though many lawmen had tried to apprehend the outlaw, none were successful until it came to Reeves. Dozier eluded Reeves for several years until the lawman tracked him down in the Cherokee Hills. After refusing to surrender, Reeves killed Dozier in an accompanying gunfight on December 20, 1878.

Though the tales of Reeves' heroics are many and varied, the toughest manhunt for the lawman was that of hunting down his own son. After having delivered two prisoners to U.S. Marshal Leo Bennett in Muskogee, Oklahoma, he arrived to bad news. His own son had been charged with the murder of his wife. Though the warrant had been lying on Bennett's desk for two days, the other deputies were reluctant to take it and though Reeves was shaken, he demanded to accept the responsibility for finding his son. Two weeks later, Reeves returned to Muskogee with his son in tow and turned him over to Marshal Bennett. His son was tried and sent to Kansas' Leavenworth Prison. However, sometime later, with a citizen's petition and an exemplary prison record, his son was pardoned and lived the rest of his life as a model citizen.

In 1907, law enforcement was assumed by state agencies and Reeves' duties as a deputy marshal came to an end. Next, Bass took a job as a patrolman with the Muskogee Oklahoma Police Department. During the two years that he served in this capacity, there were reportedly no crimes on his beat. Reeves' diagnosis with Bright's disease finally ended his career when he took to his sickbed in 1909. He died January 12, 1910 and though he was buried in Muskogee, Oklahoma, the exact location of his grave is unknown.

Over the 35 years that Bass Reeves served as a Deputy United States Marshal, Reeves earned his place in history by being one of the most effective lawmen in Indian Territory, bringing in more than 3,000 outlaws and helping to tame the lawless territory. Killing some 14 men during his service, Reeves always said that he "never shot a man when it was not necessary for him to do so in the discharge of his duty to save his own life."

## Andrew Jackson Royal

*One Bad Pecos County Sheriff*

Though Sheriff A. J. Royal only served one term as Pecos County Sheriff; he made an unfortunate impact on Fort Stockton, Texas.

He was born on November 25, 1855 to Ethel Joseph and Mary Frances Ousley Royal, in Lee County, Alabama, the only son in a family of five daughters. While still a young man, he headed west, landing in Fort Worth, where he went to work for the railroad.

Andrew Jackson Royal

On January 19, 1879 he married Naomi Obedience Christmus in Coryell County, Texas and the couple would eventually have six daughters and one son. Shortly after his marriage, the couple moved to Junction, Texas, were Royal operated a ranch and a saloon. Several years later, after he was reportedly indicted for murder, he took his family to Pecos County in 1889.

He soon established another ranch near Fort Stockton as well as a saloon located at Callaghan and Main Street. Called the Gray Mule Saloon, the building still stands in Fort Stockton today.

A quarrelsome and intimidating man, Royal killed one of his employees after the two got into a dispute. Despite the killing and his personality, Royal was elected Pecos County Sheriff in 1892. A controversial figure from the start, area citizens were initially split in their opinions. While some thought he was a tough lawman who worked hard to establish law and order, others thought he abused his power as sheriff, often terrorizing those who disagreed with him.

During his short two-year term as sheriff, his time in the position was certainly not uneventful. One story tells of how he won the Koehler Saloon in a card game, but the owner died before signing it over.

Another tale, which occurred in 1893, relates a story of a man who was accused of stealing a watermelon. As Royal was taking the man to jail, he tried to escape, but was quickly recaptured. After the thief spent three days in jail and was released, the sheriff and another man, most likely his infamous deputy, Barney Riggs, were said to have taken him outside of town where Royal horsewhipped him and told the man never to return to Pecos County.

Royal got more aggressive and intimidating the longer he was in his sheriff's role. He began to make threats toward several leading citizens in the community including County Judge O.W. Williams; merchants, Frank and James Rooney; and County Clerk, W.P. Matthews. All these men had backed his opponent R.B. Neighbors in the 1892 election and were planning to back him again in the upcoming election to be held in October, 1894.

On August 4, 1894, while drinking in his saloon, he sent word to the two Rooney brothers and Matthews, who were in Koeler's Store that he was going to "wipe them out." The sheriff would later deny sending the message, but, it was confirmed that the threat was delivered.

Later, the sheriff went to Koeler's Store looking for the Rooney brothers. However, as he walked in with a cocked pistol, he was spied by James Rooney, who was in a small room adjoining the saloon. After Royal found no one in the store and turned to go back out, Rooney confronted him with a shotgun. The sheriff began to shoot and Rooney also fired, but, no one was hit and Royal fled.

Royal then gathered up his deputies and some friends, who surrounded the store, threatening to burn it. The Rooney brothers and W.P. Matthews, who was also in the saloon, soon surrendered to Sheriff Royal, who arrested them and marched them to the Justice of the Peace for preliminary examination. However, the three arrested men, sure they would not be guaranteed safety in the city court, waved the examination, stating they wished to appear before the grand jury.

When the Grand Jury was formed the next month, most of its members were Royal's friends. The jury issued numerous indictments on several people opposed to A.J. Royal including Judge O.W. Williams for not paying an occupation tax. They also indicted another man for "fornication," but did not cite his partner, as she was also intimate with one of Royal's hired men. They indicted the Rooneys, for charges that we were unable to determine. Obviously, all those indicted felt that there was no protection of the law in Pecos County.

Sheriff Royal and his deputies wasted no time arresting those who had been indicted and once they were behind bars, refused to accept bail. However, County Judge O.W. Williams issued a writ of Habeas Corpus and they were released.

When Royal's opponents continued to receive threats, it began to look as if the political dispute could erupt into an all out "range feud." Five men of Texas Rangers' Company D were sent to town at the request of citizens because of the volatile, feuding atmosphere. Extremely unimpressed with Sheriff Royal, they soon advised Royal's enemies to arm themselves.

Of the sheriff's character, Texas Ranger Sergeant Carl Kirchner stated that Royal was "a very overbearing and dangerous man when under the influence of liquor. Almost the entire county seems to be against him."

Judge Walter Gills of the 41st Judicial District Court would echo Kirchner's appraisal, saying: "You may think it strange that a sheriff would be charged with creating the necessity of Rangers by his own lawless acts but, unfortunately, we sometimes have the worst men in the county to fill that office in this end of the state."

In the meantime, Royal and his deputies were using other tactics to secure his re-election. One such scheme was to allow a Mexican-American prisoner named Victor Ochoa to escape in exchange for making campaign speeches for Royal to Hispanic voters.

However, before the election even occurred, Royal, along with his deputies, Barney Riggs, Camilio Terrazas, and John P. Meadows, were arrested by the Texas Rangers for conspiring to let Ochoa escape from the jailhouse. Complaints were also lodged directly against the sheriff for assault. Furious, the sheriff screamed that the arrest was a conspiracy by his political enemies. Royal retaliated by signing a complaint that charged Judge O.W. Williams, Jim and Morgan Livingston, and Shipton Parke with being involved in smuggling horses and mules from Mexico. The Texas Rangers then arrested these men as well, adding further fire to the already boiling political feud.

But, all his tactics would all be for naught. When the election rolled around in October, Royal lost to R.B. Neighbors. However, before he could finish his term of office, he would become a target.

After adjourning court on November 21, 1894, Judge O.W. Williams went to the clerk's office. While he was there, he heard a voice call "Royal" and then the muffled sounds of gunshots that came from the east door of the courthouse. Thinking that the sheriff had shot someone, he went into the hall, where he found a number of men loitering. Entering the sheriff's office, he then found the soon to be ex-sheriff, A.J. Royal sitting at his desk with blood coming from his mouth and streaming onto the floor. There were six or seven buckshot holes in his left shoulder and neck area.

Another man, who was in Royal's office during the shooting, reported that he heard Royal's name being called out but, could not identify the voice. He also stated that all that he had seen was the barrel of a shotgun thrust through the door and a glimpse of someone in dark clothes when the shot was fired.

No one was ever arrested for the crime, which continues to be one of the biggest historic mysteries of the city. However, according to local lore, several prominent Fort Stockton businessmen drew straws to determine who would kill the controversial sheriff.

Andrew Jackson Royal was buried in the old fort cemetery, where his grave remains today. His tombstone bears the inscription "assassinated," a testament to this violent period in Fort Stockton's history.

The desk where he was murdered is now housed in the Annie Riggs Memorial Museum and his bloodstains still remain in a drawer. The Gray Mule Saloon that the corrupt sheriff once operated continues to stand, now serving as a coffee shop and art gallery. Koehler's old store and saloon later became a bank, and now serves as a small community hall.

In the meantime, R. B. Neighbors would go on to fill the office of sheriff, and would be re-elected for four additional terms.

James Rooney, one of the men that Royal had tried to kill in Koehler's old store and saloon, ended up buying the store, naming it the Rooney Mercantile Company, and becoming quite successful. He later also served as a vice president of the Fort Stockton State Bank.

Royal's deputy, the infamous gunfighter, Barney Riggs, would continue to create chaos in the area for several years. In 1896, he killed William Earheart and John Denson at R.S. Johnson's Saloon in Pecos, Texas. Today, the saloon is part of the West of the Pecos Museum and has a plaque on the floor designating the spot where William Earheart was killed. Later, however, karma would come back on Riggs when he was killed by his step-son-in-law in 1902. Riggs is buried in the same cemetery with his old partner, A.J. Royal.

## John Selman

*Wicked Lawman and Vicious Outlaw*

Though by far, not the most well-known of the Old West's infamous characters, John Henry Selman's life was certainly one of the most notorious. Sometimes referred to as "Old John," or "Uncle John," he would variously operate in a number of roles, including soldier, lawman, vigilante and vicious outlaw.

Born in Madison County, Arkansas on November 16, 1839, the family later moved to Grayson County, Texas in 1858. A few years later, on December 16, 1861, Selman's father died and the young man joined the 22nd Texas Cavalry, fighting as a private in the Civil War. However, just 15 months later, he deserted from Fort Washita, Oklahoma in April, 1863.

He then moved to Stephens County, where in 1864, he enlisted in the Texas State Militia. He must have done a better job in this regiment, as the following year, he was promoted to the rank of lieutenant in April, 1865.

John Selman

Just a few months later, on August 17th, he married Edna Degrafenreid, who would soon be pregnant with his first son. Over the years, the couple would have four children. Selman moved his family to Colfax County, New Mexico briefly before returning to Texas and settling in Fort Griffin.

He soon began to work as a deputy sheriff under Shackelford County Sheriff John M. Larn. Fort Griffin during these days was a very lawless place, filled with a number of notable characters that Selman, no doubt, came in contact with. In the decadent settlement that was called the "Babylon on the Brazos" were the likes of Doc Holliday, Wyatt Earp, Big Nose Kate, Dave Rudabaugh, Lottie Deno, Pat Garrett, and John Wesley Hardin.

Sheriff John Larn, however, was not what he appeared to be. Shortly after taking the sheriff's position, Larn had entered into a private contract with the local territorial garrison to deliver three steers of cattle per day. However, Larn had no intentions on filling these contracts legally. When Selman came on board, the pair rustled the cattle from neighboring ranchers. Before long, Larn and Selman, instead of controlling the area crime, were controlling the vigilantes, rustling even more cattle and otherwise terrorizing the county.

However, suspicions were soon raised as a number of ranchers noticed that while their herds were slowly shrinking, Larn's remained unaffected. Larn then resigned as sheriff on March 7, 1877, and was replaced by William Cruger. He and Selman then moved to outright cattle rustling, as the complaints grew louder and a number of violent acts were perpetuated by the pair as they drove off cattle, shot horses, and fired potshots at the homes of terrified citizens.

Finally, a warrant was issued for Larn's arrest in June, 1878, and William Cruger was tasked with arresting his former boss. On June 22nd, Larn was taken to the Fort Griffin jail where Cruger had the local blacksmith shackle Larn to the floor of the cell to prevent a breakout by Larn's supporters. Instead, the next night, the Tin Hat Brigade, stormed the jail intending to hang Larn. When they found they couldn't lynch the shackled man, they shot him in his cell.

Selman wisely disappeared, next landing in lawless Lincoln County, New Mexico. There, he formed a gang of vicious outlaws called Selman's Scouts. For two months in September and October, 1878, the Scouts rustled horses and cattle, murdered innocent men and boys, and pillaged businesses and homes. They were finally stopped when Governor Lew Wallace issued a proclamation threatening martial law.

Selman returned to Texas and his wife died in 1879. The following year, he was captured by Texas Rangers and taken to Shackelford County to stand trial for his previous crimes. However, he soon escaped and made his way to Chihuahua, Mexico where he lived until 1888, when the Texas charges were dropped.

He then moved to El Paso where he remarried and made his living primarily as a gambler and sometimes as a City Constable.

On April 5, 1894, John Selman met Texas Ranger, Bass Outlaw. Outlaw, who was in a drunken stupor, made his way to Tillie Howard's brothel and Selman followed. As Selman sat in the parlor, Outlaw made his way to the back. A short time later, Bass dropped his gun and it accidentally went off. All hell broke loose. Selman, as well as Texas Ranger, Joe McKidrict who was in the neighborhood, ran to see about the commotion.

As both tried to calm down the drunken gunman, Outlaw pointed his gun at McKidrict and shot him in the head and back, killing him instantly. Outlaw then fired at Selman, nearly striking him in the face and causing deep powder burns. Selman returned fire, hitting Outlaw just above the heart. As Bass staggered back he fired two more shots, hitting Selman above the right knee and in the thigh. He then staggered into the street where he surrendered to Texas Ranger, Frank McMahon. He died four hours later. John Selman was then put on trial for killing Outlaw, but the judge instructed the jury to find him not guilty.

The following year, on August 19, 1895, Selman arrested John Wesley Hardin's prostitute girlfriend. Unhappy, Hardin soon confronted Selman and the two argued. Hardin then went to the Acme Saloon, where he began playing dice. Just a short time later, Selman followed him into the saloon and without notice shot Hardin three times from behind, killing him.

While out on bond, he ran into U.S. Deputy Marshal George Scarborough who had been close friends with another man Selman had killed. In no time, their talk elevated into a dispute, then to gunplay. In the end, Scarborough shot Selman four times. Selman died on April 6, 1896 and Scarborough was acquitted of murder.

Selman was buried in El Paso's Concordia Cemetery in the Catholic section, but his grave was unmarked, and all attempts to locate it have been unsuccessful.

Scarborough, himself, was mortally wounded in a gunfight with two robbers and died on April 5, 1900, exactly four years after he shot John Selman.

## Charles Angelo Siringo

*Cowboy Detective*

One of the most famous detectives of the Pinkerton National Detective Agency, Charles Angelo Siringo, also served as a lawman for many years and became an author. Born in Matagorda County, Texas to an Irish immigrant mother and an Italian immigrant father, he attended public school until he was 15 years-old, at which time he started working as a cowboy at area ranches.

Charles Siringo

Working for a number of Texas ranches over the next several years, he became a trail driver in 1876, accompanying a herd of 2,500 longhorns over the Chisholm Trail from Austin to Kansas. He made a second trip in the spring of 1877, following the trail's western branch. Siringo was in Dodge City, Kansas when an altercation almost erupted between gunfighter, Clay Allison and Dodge City Assistant Marshal, Wyatt Earp. After Allison's death in 1887, Earp would claim that he and Bat Masterson had forced Allison to back down from an impending confrontation. Siringo, however, later gave a written account of the incident which contradicted Earp's claim, stating that Earp never came into contact with Allison, and that two businessmen in Dodge City actually defused the situation. Siringo's account was also verified by other witnesses of the time.

In Dodge City he signed on with David T. Beals and W. H. "Deacon" Bates to drive a herd into the Panhandle, where they establish the LX Ranch. For the next several years he worked as a LX cowboy, where he met a young man named Henry McCarty, aka: Billy the Kid, later he would lead a posse in New Mexico in an attempt to capture the Kid and his gang.

In 1884 Siringo married Mamie Lloyd and after having been a cowboy for more than two decades, changed careers, opening a store in Caldwell, Kansas. That same year, he also began writing a book, entitled *A Texas Cowboy; Or Fifteen Years on the Hurricane Deck of a Spanish Pony*. It was published a year later to wide acclaim and became one of the first true accounts of the cowboy life during the days of the Old West.

Bored with being a merchant, Siringo moved to Chicago in 1886, applying for a job with the Pinkerton Detective Agency. Using Pat Garrett's name as a reference, he got the position and for the next 22 years worked all over the West as a successful cowboy detective. Traveling as far north as Alaska and as far south as Mexico City, he often worked undercover, infiltrating gangs of robbers and rustlers, and making hundreds of arrests.

Charles Siringo helped to romanticize both the myths and realities of the Old West

By the early 1890's Siringo was working out of Pinkerton's Denver office, where he worked with noted Pinkerton agent, gunman, and later assassin, Tom Horn. Though he greatly admired Horn's talents and skills in tracking down suspects, he would later reflect that Horn had a dark side.

In 1892, Siringo was assigned to a case in Idaho, where he worked undercover to get information against corrupt labor union officials. Though he despised the labor union officials, he stood against a lynch mob to protect union attorney Clarence Darrow from being hanged.

In the late 1890's, posing as "Charles L. Carter," an alleged gunman on the run for murder, he infiltrated Butch Cassidy's Wild Bunch.

For over a year he severely hampered their operations but made few arrests.

After the Wild Bunch committed the 1899 Wilcox Train Robbery in Wyoming, he was assigned to capture them. He continued to work closely with Tom Horn on the assignment, though Horn was actually working for a cattle company at the time. Several members of the Wild Bunch were captured due to his efforts including Kid Curry, who would later escape only to be killed by a shootout with Colorado lawmen. During this time, Siringo also met lawman Joe Lefors, who later would arrest Tom Horn for murder. Later, he would say of Lefors that the man was incompetent and he greatly despised him. In the meantime, Butch Cassidy and the Sundance Kid fled to Bolivia, where they were later allegedly killed by Bolivian soldiers during a robbery attempt.

In 1890, Siringo's wife died, leaving him a widower with a five-year-old daughter. Three years later, Siringo met and married Lillie Thomas of Denver, Colorado and the two had a son in 1896. However, shortly afterwards, the two divorced soon after he was born.

After 22 years of successfully capturing hundreds of outlaws, Siringo retired from the Pinkerton Agency in 1907. During his career with the Pinkertons, Siringo participated in a number of other celebrated cases, including the Haymarket anarchist trial, the Coeur d'Alene miners strikes, and the trial of Western Federation of Miners Secretary "Big Bill" Haywood, who had been charged with the dynamite murder of former Idaho governor Frank Steunenburg. Although Siringo was a fine shot, the vast majority of his arrests were made without violence.

He then moved to a ranch in Santa Fe, New Mexico, where he began to write a second book detailing his experiences as a Pinkerton detective, entitled *Pinkerton's Cowboy Detective*. When it was complete, publication of the book was held up by the Pinkerton Agency who felt it violated a confidentiality agreement signed by Siringo when he was hired, and objecting to the use of their name. Siringo gave in, and deleted their name from the book title, instead writing two separate books, entitled *A Cowboy Detective* and *Further Adventures of a Cowboy Detective*, with fictitious names replacing real ones.

To vent his anger against the Pinkertons, Siringo wrote and clandestinely published a third book, entitled *Two Evil Isms, Pinkertonism and Anarchism* in 1915. Again, the Pinkerton Agency blocked publication, and this time attempted to have Siringo prosecuted for libel, asking that he be extradited from his ranch in Santa Fe, New Mexico to Chicago. However, the New Mexico governor denied the extradition request.

In 1916, Siringo began working as a New Mexico Ranger where his main task was to capture the numerous rustlers operating in the southeastern part of the state. After two years, he resigned when his ranch and his health began to fail. In 1919 he published *A Lone Star Cowboy*, which he said was to take the place of *A Texas Cowboy,* on which the copyright had expired. This was followed by *A History of "Billy the Kid"* in 1920. However, his health continued to fail, and that coupled with financial difficulties, forced him to abandon his ranch and leave Santa Fe in 1922.

He then moved to Los Angeles, California where he became a minor celebrity due to his well publicized exploits. While there, he sometimes worked as a film advisor on western film sets and even took an occasional bit part. In 1927, he released his final book, *Riata and Spurs*, a composite of his first two autobiographies. However, when the Pinkerton Agency intervened again to halt publication, the book became a whittled down version with many fictional accounts rather than the true accounts that Siringo had envisioned.

The next year, Siringo died in Altadena, California on October 18,1928.

Siringo's recollections of his life as both a cowboy and a detective helped to romanticize both the myths and realities of the Old West. Siringo's prowess as a cowboy and Pinkerton detective made him widely known in his lifetime; he met United States Senators, state governors, and national officials, as well as such diverse celebrities as Pat Garrett, Bat Masterson, Clarence Darrow, Charles M. Russell, Eugene Manlove Rhodes, William S. Hart, and Will Rogers, and numerous outlaws.

# "Texas" John Horton Slaughter

*Taming Arizona*

*"Unlike squalid old badge wearers such as John Selman and Wild Bill Hickok, John Slaughter was basically a very reserved sort of man. Nobody who wished to keep on calling terms with him overstepped that boundary."*

Judge Clayton Baird, who rode with Slaughter

"Texas John" Slaughter was a Civil War veteran, trail-driver, cattleman, Texas Ranger, famed Cochise County Sheriff, professional gambler, and an Arizona State Representative during his lifetime. Before he died at the age of 80, he was a symbol of the American West and much celebrated hero.

John was born in Sabine Parish, Louisiana on October 2, 1841 to Benjamin and Minerva Mabry Slaughter. However, when he was just three months old, his family moved to a land grant near Lockhart, Texas and began raising cattle.

John Slaughter

Though schooled in Sabine and Caldwell counties, Slaughter's formal education was brief. But the boy was a quick learner and found other opportunities to increase his knowledge such as learning how to speak Spanish and mastering cowboy skills from Mexican vaqueros. As a young man, he ranched with his father and brothers and just before the Civil War began, he enlisted as a Texas Ranger with Captain John Files Tom's company to fight the Comanches.

The diminutive 5 foot 6 inch man, with penetrating black eyes and a sometimes stuttering voice, was evidently determined to make his mark upon the world.

On March 9, 1862, he joined the Confederate Army, but by 1864 he was sent home because of an illness. However; after he recovered, he returned to service with the Third Frontier Division, Texas State Troops, in Burnet County, where he earned a reputation of a fearless fighter skilled with firearms.

When the war was over, he and his brothers established the San Antonio Ranch Company in Atascosa County, Texas, where they not only raised their own cattle, but also transported herds to Mexico, California, Kansas and New Mexico. They were some of the first to ever drive cattle up the Chisholm Trail. While he was in California on a cattle drive, he became an avid poker player, a compulsion that would follow him throughout his life.

On August 4, 1871, he married Eliza Adeline Harris and the two would eventually have four children, though only two would survive to adulthood.

In 1876, Slaughter was playing poker in a saloon in San Antonio, Texas, when he caught another player named Barney Gallagher cheating. When Gallagher won the hand, Slaughter challenged him with a gun and took back his losses. Later, the cheating man was so enraged that he followed Slaughter to his ranch where he told the foreman to call him out, intending on killing him. As soon as John came in sight, Gallagher took a shot at him but missed. Slaughter returned the fire and was not so unlucky. Gallagher fell dead on the ground with a bullet in his heart.

John Slaughter in later years

By the late 1870s, Slaughter felt that Texas had become too crowded and left his wife and children in Texas while he went to look for a new place to settle in New Mexico.

He spent the next two years buying cattle but didn't purchase any land in New Mexico. Leaving his cattle there, he then began to look for land in southern Arizona. This was evidently taking him some time and he soon sent for his wife and children who joined him in Tucson. However, his wife died shortly afterwards of smallpox in 1877.

Returning to New Mexico to get his cattle, Slaughter left his children in Arizona and traveled eastward. While camping on the banks of the Pecos River, he met a family named Howell, who had a 16 year-old daughter named Viola. John married the girl on April 16, 1878 and convinced the entire family to move with him to Arizona.

They first settled south of Tombstone before Slaughter bought the 65,000 acre San Bernardino Ranch near Douglas in 1884. Extending from Arizona down into Mexico,

Slaughter built a large and sophisticated operation that employed some 20 cowboys and 30 families who worked the farmlands. John and Viola did not have any children of their own, but adopted several children.

In 1886, Slaughter was elected Cochise County Sheriff, tasked with ridding the lawlessness of Tombstone and Galeyville. Working closely with Wells Fargo Express Agent and former U.S. Deputy Marshal, Jeff Milton, the two were deadly in tracking and capturing fugitives. During this time, Slaughter was known to have worn a pearl-handled .44 and carried a 10-gauge, double-barreled, sawed-off shotgun, which he called an "equalizer."

Slaughter also made the "mistake" of hiring Burton Alvord as a Deputy Sheriff. Though Alvord quickly earned a reputation as an excellent tracker, bringing in a number of cattle rustlers and other wanted fugitives, he also was a heavy drinker and would, within a few years, turn "outlaw."

One of Slaughter's first tasks was to bring in the Jack Taylor Gang, who had robbed a train near Nogales and shot at the train crew. He and his men heard the gang was hiding out at the home of Flora Cardenas. However, by the time they arrived the bandits had fled. They then traveled to Willcox, then Contention, where they found gang members, Manuel Robles and Nieves Deron sleeping at the camp of Manuel's brother, Guadalupe Robels.

When Slaughter shouted for the two men to get up, a gunfight ensued, in which Guadalupe Robles, who had otherwise been an upstanding citizen, joined in. He was immediately shot and killed.

Manuel Robels and Deron tried to run away while still blasting their six-guns. One bullet caught Slaughter's ear, who returned the fire, killing Nieves Deron. Manuel Robels; though seriously wounded by a shot from Burton Alvord, was able to escape. Soon, the leader of the gang, Jack Taylor, was arrested in Sonora, and Manuel Robles, along with Geronimo Miranda, were killed by the Mexican police in the Sierra Madre mountains.

During his first term, Slaughter also assisted the United States Cavalry against Geronimo's Apaches. So successful was Slaughter in his role of sheriff, he was re-elected in 1888.

In the meantime, the efficiency of Slaughter's deputy, Burton Alvord, as a lawman began to slip by 1889 as his drinking had increased. Frequenting the many saloons of Tombstone, Alvord started to socialize with some of the criminal elements and was known to get into frequent scuffles. As Slaughter began to chastise his actions, Alvord soured on both the sheriff and the law. Alvord soon moved on, but Slaughter would receive criticism for ever having hired the man, especially when he turned full-blown outlaw at the end of the century.

By 1890, the lawless Cochise County had been mostly tamed and Slaughter retired from law enforcement to tend to his ranch.

In 1906, Slaughter served briefly in the territorial assembly, but concentrated primarily on his business investments and his ranch. Eventually he bought a meat market in Charleston and two butcher shops in Bisbee. So wise were his investments throughout the years that he also began to act as a "banker" for his neighbors, loaning money for mortgages when needed.

In his later years, his health began to deteriorate as he suffered from eczema on his hands and feet and high blood pressure. He died in his sleep in Douglas, Arizona, on February 16, 1922, after complaining of a headache the previous evening. He was buried at the Cavalry Cemetery in Douglas, Arizona.

Imposing the law with his six-shooter and sawed off shotgun, Slaughter cleaned up Arizona Territory more than any other single individual. Along the way, he met and was much respected by other more famous Old West characters such as Wild Bill Hickok, Ben Thompson, Wyatt Earp, Big Foot Wallace, King Fisher, Sam Bass, Billy the Kid, and Pat Garrett.

One lawman who rode with Slaughter said of him, "He was like a spider spinning its web for the unwary fly."

Today, the Slaughter Ranch has been fully restored and serves as a museum.

## Thomas J. Smith, aka: Bear River

*Marshalling Abilene*

Thomas "Bear River" Smith served as a lawman in New York City, Bear River, Wyoming and Kit Carson, Colorado, before becoming marshal of the rough and tumble cowtown of Abilene, Kansas in June, 1870.

Thomas J. Smith was shot down in the line of duty while serving as Abilene's marshal.

Born in New York City on June 12, 1840, Smith grew up to be a middleweight professional boxer before joining the New York City Police force. However, after being involved in the accidental killing of a 14-year-old boy, Smith left the force in 1868 and took a job with the Union Pacific Railroad.

His new position soon took him westward where he landed in Bear River City, Wyoming, where he worked as a teamster. In no time, he utilized his boxing skills to gain a reputation as a tough man and he was soon appointed as the city marshal. However, trouble was brewing in the little city of Bear River after vigilantes hanged a murderer who worked for the railroad.

Soon, the man's railroad friends revolted against the vigilantes. Inciting a vengeful mob numbering in the hundreds, the lawless bunch torched town buildings and started a deadly shoot-out with citizens trapped in a storeroom

U.S. troops from Fort Bridger imposed martial law until the track-layers had passed. Bear River City soon became another railroad ghost town.

From Wyoming, Smith moved on to Kit Carson, Colorado, where he held a similar position before making his way to Abilene, Kansas. In June, he was appointed the Kansas Cowtown's first marshal, which was badly in need of law enforcement. He was paid a salary of $150 a month plus $2 for each conviction of persons arrested. One of Smith's first official acts was to ban all weapons in town without a permit. Within 48 hours, everyone had turned over their weapons to Smith, but he had to knock down two thugs before they surrendered their weapons.

Known as "No gun marshal," he gained a reputation for subduing assailants with his fists rather than a gun, and where lawlessness reigned supreme, he was forced to often use them. The decision to ban guns was unpopular with some members of the community and during the next few months he survived two assassination attempts.

Abilene, Kansas

On November 2, 1870, Smith was sent to a small settlement some ten miles from Abilene to arrest a man named Andrew McConnell, who was charged with murdering John Shea, a local farmer. However, when he arrived at McConnell's home, telling him that he had a warrant for his arrest, McConnell shot Smith in the chest. Smith returned fire wounding McConnell before falling to the ground. McConnell's co-conspirator in the original crime, a man named Moses Miles, then struck Smith with his gun, grabbed an axe and nearly chopped Smith's head from his body. Thomas "Bear River" Smith was buried in the Abilene Cemetery, where his body remains today.

The murdering pair of McConnell and Miles were soon captured and in March, 1871, both men were found guilty of murder and were sentenced to long terms in prison for their gruesome crime.

Afterwards, the town of Abilene returned to its lawless ways until the next marshal could be hired – that of James Butler "Wild Bill" Hickok in April, 1871.

Despite his reputation; however, Hickok did not do nearly as good of a job in the role as did Smith. Abilene eventually settled down when new railheads were built by Newton, Wichita, and Ellsworth, becoming the favored shipping points.

Years later, Marshal Smith would be remembered by another Abilene resident – none other than President Dwight D. Eisenhower, who said:

"According to the legends of my hometown he was anything but dull. While he almost never carried a pistol he...subdued the lawless by the force of his personality and his tremendous capability as an athlete. One blow of his fist was apparently enough to knock out the ordinary 'tough' cowboy. He was murdered by treachery."

## Wells Spicer

*Tombstone's Justice of the Peace*

Born near Monmouth, Illinois, Spicer was related to the Earp brothers. After becoming an attorney, he too moved westward where he worked as a lawyer and mining engineer at Salt Lake City, Utah. In 1875, he unsuccessfully defended John D. Lee when he was charged with the Mountain Meadows Massacre. Three years later, he moved to Tombstone, Arizona, where he worked as an attorney, mining broker, and U.S. Commissioner for Deeds. By the time the Gunfight at the O.K. Corral took place, Spicer was serving as Tombstone's Justice of the Peace. After Sheriff Johnny Behan arrested the Earp brothers – Virgil, Wyatt, and Morgan, as well as Doc Holliday, a pre-trial hearing was held on November 29, 1881 where Spicer decided that the defendants had been justified in their actions. His concluding statement read in part:

"In view of all the facts and circumstances of the case; considering the threats made the character and position of the parties, and the tragic results accomplished, in manner and form as they were, with all the surrounding influences bearing upon the result of the affair, I cannot resist the conclusion that the defendants were fully justified in committing these homicides that it was a necessary act done in the discharge of official duty."

Wells Spicer

Spicer immediately became a potential target for the Cowboy faction who began to take revenge. In December, 1881, he received the following threatening letter:

"Sir, if you take my advice you will take your departure for a more genial clime, as I don't think this One Healthy for you much longer As you are liable to get a hole through your coat at any moment. If such sons of bitches as you are allowed to dispense Justice in this Territory, the Sooner you Depart from us the better for yourself And the community at large you may make light of this But it is only a matter of time you will get it sooner or later So with those few gentle hints I Will Conclude for the first and last time."

Though Spicer wasn't killed by the Cowboy faction, his decision regarding the Earps brought his career to an end and he soon left Tombstone and worked as a mining engineer. In 1885, his body was found in the desert near Ajo, Arizona. He was thought to have committed suicide.

## Con Stapleton

*Deadwood Marshal*

Though the HBO series Deadwood shows Con Stapleton as a dim-witted card dealer at the Number 10 Saloon, who gained his short-lived marshal's position by begging Al Swearengen to appoint him, Stapleton actually was elected as the Deadwood Marshal by the miners on September 16, 1876.

Stapleton, who had immigrated from Ireland to the United States in 1871, was in Montana when word of the gold strike in Deadwood arrived. Along with the many others that flooded into the booming mining camp, Stapleton arrived in the spring of 1876.

When Wild Bill Hickok was shot down by Jack McCall in Nuttall & Mann's Number 10 Saloon on August 2, 1876, Stapleton was playing cards with him, along with Charles Rich, Carl Mann and Captain Willie Massie.

Afterwards, McCall was chased down the street and arrested. A couple of days later, a trial was held charging McCall with murder. However, because McCall claimed Hickok had killed his brother and he had only been taking revenge, he was found not guilty. Later the trial was found to be illegal and Jack McCall was arrested and hanged.

After the trail, on August 5, 1876, the men of Deadwood decided they needed law and order in the camp and elected Isaac Brown as Deadwood's first marshal on August 5, 1876. But for Marshal Isaac Brown, being a lawman would be a short-lived career. When he, along with the Reverend Smith and two other men named Charles Mason and Charles Holland were traveling between Crook City and Deadwood, they were ambushed and killed on August 20th. Leaving an open position, the miner's court soon met again on September 16th and this time they elected Con Stapleton as the new marshal.

Though he would only serve as the town's marshal for a little over a year, one of the most widely publicized events during his short tenure was the shooting of David Lunt. On January 14, 1877, Stapleton, along with Lunt and several other men were standing around talking at Al Chapman's saloon when a man named Tom Smith came barreling into the saloon with his pistol in the air. Shouting threats and leveling his gun on the saloon's patrons, he barked, "Anyone who moves gets shot!"

When the crazed man neared Stapleton's group, the marshal tried to disarm him and in the frenzy the pistol discharged, barely missing Stapleton's head and striking Lunt in the forehead. As the amazed crowd looked down upon what they thought was surely a dead man, amazingly David Lunt stood up, brushed himself and went about his business

Deadwood from Mt. Moriah, 1888.

like nothing happened. Stapleton then arrested Smith on a charge of shooting an officer and though Smith was found guilty he was soon released.

In the meantime, David Lunt continued on as usual, even though he had a hole that went entirely through his head. That was, until March 22, 1877, when he began to complain of a terrible headache. As he took to his bed at the Centennial Hotel, friends and staff cared for him, but it was to no avail. That night, some 67 days after he had been shot, he died. Afterwards, the doctor performed an autopsy and found that the bullet had carried a bone fragment deep into his brain, causing a large abscess and filling his brain with fluid. The doctor was amazed that he lived any time at all, much less for more than two months.

After Lunt's death, a new warrant was issued for Tom Smith for murder and the man was soon rearrested and taken to Yankton, Dakota Territory to stand trial.

In addition to his marshaling duties, one of Stapleton's favorite past times was organizing wrestling matches, most often at the Gem Theater. Sometimes he acted as a referee and at others as a participant.

In March, 1877, Seth Bullock was appointed as the Lawrence County Sheriff, and gradually assumed many of Stapleton's duties. On November 7th of the same year, the position of city marshal was eliminated altogether.

By the following year, many of the town's citizens had moved on to Colorado where another boomtown was forming in Leadville. Stapleton followed the rest in February 1878, but as to whether he did any prospecting in Leadville is unknown. Eight months later he reportedly died on September 10, 1879 in Denver, Colorado. He was just 31 years old.

## Dallas Stoudenmire

*Taming El Paso*

A gunfighter and lawman, Stoudenmire was born in Aberfoil, Alabama on December 11, 1845, one of nine children born to Lewis and Elizabeth Stoudenmire. In 1862, he joined the Confederate Army serving in the 45th Alabama Infantry, during which he was wounded a number of times and carried two bullets with him for the rest of his life.

When the war was over, he moved on to Columbus, Texas, around 1867, where he was said to have killed a number of men. Though definitely dangerous, the 6'4" man was said to have been quite a gentleman around the ladies, who found his handsome face and sharp dress quite attractive. However, Dallas had an extremely bad temper, especially when intoxicated. Continuing to hone his shooting skills, he became equally accurate with both hands and always wore two guns. During these years, he worked variously as a sheep farmer, a carpenter, wheelwright, and merchandiser.

Dallas Stoudenmire

Some time later, Dallas joined the Texas Rangers and in 1874 was serving as a second sergeant in J. R. Waller's company. Afterwards, he lived briefly in the Texas Panhandle, in Mexico during the days of Maximillan, and served a short stint as a marshal in Socorro, New Mexico.

While he was in Socorro, his brother-in-law, "Doc" Cummings, who lived in El Paso, Texas, convinced him that he should come there and take up the marshal's position. At the time, El Paso had a reputation as a violent town and the city hoped to bring in someone from the "outside" who had a reputation that was as "tough" as the town. Stoudenmire fit the bill. In early April, 1881, Stoudenmire traveled to El Paso and was hired almost immediately, starting his new position on April 11th. He was the sixth town marshal in just eight months.

His first task was to get the city jail keys from a deputy marshal who also just happened to be the town drunk. When Stoudenmire approached the drunken deputy, Bill Johnson, to get the keys, Johnson mumbled that he would go home and figure out which ones they were. However, Stoudenmire became impatient, demanding the keys immediately. When Johnson continued to delay, Dallas physically turned the man upside down, took the keys, and threw him to the ground. Stoudenmire wasted no time living up to his tough reputation, along with humiliating Johnson.

Just three days later, he was involved in one of the most famous gunfights in Texas, referred to as the "Four Dead in Five Seconds" gunfight. On April 14th, while Constable Krempkau was in Keating's Saloon, one of the worst pestholes in El Paso, Texas, he got into an argument with ex-City Marshal, George Campbell. Also in the saloon was one of Campbell's friend's, a man named John Hale. Hale, who was drunk and unarmed, pulled one of Campbell's two pistols, shouting, "George, I've got you covered!" Hale then shot Krempkau, who fell wounded against the saloon door. Realizing what he had done, Hale ran behind a post in front of the saloon just as Marshal Dallas Stoudenmire appeared with his pistols raised. Stoudenmire then shot once but the bullet went wild, hitting an innocent Mexican bystander. When Hale peeked out from behind the post, Stoudenmire fired again, hitting Hale between his eyes and killing him instantly. In the meantime, when Campbell saw Hale go down, he exited the saloon, waving his gun and yelling, "Gentlemen, this is not my fight!" However, the wounded Krempkau disagreed and though down, fired at Campbell, striking him in the wrist and in the toe. At the same time, Stoudenmire whirled and also fired on Campbell, pumping three bullets into his stomach. As Campbell crashed to the dusty street, he shouted, "You s.o.b., you have murdered me!" When the dust cleared, both George Campbell and Constable Krempkau lay dead. In less than five seconds in a near comic opera gun battle, four men lay dead. This gunfight was well publicized in newspapers in cities as far away as San Francisco and New York City and made Stoudenmire a legend.

Three days later, on April 17th, violence would erupt again, when the wealthy Manning brothers, who were friends of Hale and Campbell, convinced a drunken Bill Johnson to assassinate Stoudenmire. However, it took little convincing on Johnson's part as he was still suffering the humiliation he had felt at Stoudenmire's hands less than a week past. Johnson then hid behind a large pillar of bricks with his shotgun and waited. A short time later, he heard the voices of Stoudenmire and his brother-in-law, "Doc" Cummings. As he started to take aim, the drunken fool fell down instead, accidentally firing two harmless blasts into the air. The marshal wasted no time returning fire, sending a number of bullets his way and leaving Johnson dead on the dusty street.

This, of course, further enraged the Manning brothers who would eventually take their revenge. In the meantime, Stoudenmire continued to take a hard line against the lawless city of El Paso. Between the April shooting of Johnson and the next February, Dallas killed another six men in shootouts during arrest situations. The city's violent crime rate began to drop as Stoudenmire's legend grew.

In February, 1882, Dallas briefly returned to Columbus, Texas, where he married Isabella Sherrington. During his absence, on February 14th, James Manning killed Stoudenmire's brother-in-law and good friend, Stanley "Doc" Cummings. While Manning and Cummings were in the Coliseum Saloon, owned by Manning, the pair began to argue. The dispute escalated until gun smoke filled the room. When the air cleared, Cummings had stumbled outside the saloon door where he had fallen dead. Manning was arrested but at his trial, it was determined that he had acted in self defense.

With a jury filled with local residents, many who were friends of the Mannings, Stoudenmire was enraged. Unfortunately, the only man who had been able to control the marshal's temper was the now dead Cummings. The angry Stoudenmire also began to drink heavily and often confronted those people that he felt were responsible for Manning's acquittal. It became so bad, that many people avoided coming into town or visiting the saloons for fear of running into him. Though he had proved his effectiveness as a lawman, his actions began to turn the locals away from him. He was also a newcomer in a town where the Mannings had many friends.

City officials tried to control Stoudenmire, his drinking, and his actions by passing a law making it illegal for officers of the law to drink publicly and subject to a fine if caught. However, it was Stoudenmire himself who collected the fines, so the law failed and Stoudenmire continued to drink. In the meantime, his actions became more and more confrontational and bizarre. Sometimes, he was known to use the St. Clement's Church bell for target practice as he patrolled the streets, was suspected of spending unauthorized funds, and argued constantly with city officials. His list of enemies grew, including El Paso Times editor, George Washington Carrico, who alleged the city's crime rate varied inversely with the sobriety of its marshal.

By May 27, 1882, the town had finally had enough and the council announced they were going to fire the marshal. However, when Stoudenmire confronted them, drunk, and dared them to take his guns or his job, they backed down. However, two days later a sober Stoudenmire resigned. He then began to run the Globe Restaurant, which had formerly belonged to his brother-in-law, Doc Cummings. In July, he also accepted an appointment as a U.S. Deputy Marshal. This, however, did not stop him from using his gun to settle arguments and his ongoing feud with the Manning brothers continued.

In fact, the feud ran so deep that local residents prevailed upon Stoudenmire and the Mannings to sign a "peace treaty" that was published in the El Paso Herald. But, Dallas continued to make threats every time he was drinking.

On September 18, 1882, Stoudenmire and the Manning brothers – Doc, Frank, and Jim, met again in one of Manning's saloons to sign another "peace treaty." However,

Doc and Dallas soon began to argue about the first peace treaty and before you know it, they both had pistols in their hands. Doc fired first, shattering Stoudenmire's left arm and causing him to drop his gun. A second bullet hit Stoudenmire's shirt pocket that was filled with papers. Though it didn't break the skin, it knocked him backwards into the saloon doors and out on to the street. A two handed shooter, Dallas pulled his other gun and shot Doc as he came through the door, hitting him in the arm. Jim Manning followed and fired two shots, one going wild and the other hitting Stoudenmire behind his left ear, killing him instantly. Though the former marshal was very dead, an enraged Doc Manning proceeded to pistol-whip him with his own gun.

James and Doc Manning were arrested but were acquitted when the ruling was found to be self-defense.

Stoudenmire's funeral was held at El Paso's Masonic Lodge #130 and his wife had his body shipped to Columbus, Texas for burial. He is buried in the Alleyton, Texas cemetery.

The Mannings continued to live in El Paso, and soon their killing of Dallas Stoudenmire was all but forgotten.

During his life, Stoudenmire was involved in more gunfights than most of his better known counterparts, such as Wyatt Earp, Bat Masterson, Elfego Baca, Luke Short, Doc Holliday, and John Selman. He is credited with successfully taming one of the most violent town's in the Old West.

El Paso, Texas street scene, 1888.

## Henry Andrew "Heck" Thomas

*Tough Law in Indian Territory*

Henry Andrew "Heck" Thomas was one of the Wild West's most effective lawmen, apprehending dozens of notorious outlaws including members of the Doolin, Dalton, and Sam Bass Gangs.

Henry Andrew "Heck" Thomas

Thomas was born in Athens, Georgia on January 3, 1850 to Lovick and Martha Thomas. Reared and educated in Atlanta, he took on the nickname "Heck" at an early age. His parents wanted him to grow up to be a Methodist minister; however, the impetuous boy had other ideas. When the Civil War broke out, his father and two of his paternal uncles quickly joined and all three gained distinction with the Confederate Army. His father became a colonel commanding the 35th Georgia Infantry, his Uncle Henry also became a colonel and commanded the 16th Georgia Infantry, and yet another uncle, Edward Lloyd Thomas, commanded the 49th Georgia Infantry.

Before the war was over, Edward Thomas advanced to the rank of Brigadier General in command of the Thomas brigade. It was for his Uncle Edward that Heck served as a courier at the front of the fighting in Virginia when he was just 12 years old.

When the war was over, Heck's father became the first city marshal of Atlanta and Heck joined the police force at the age of 17. In 1871, Heck married his cousin, Isabelle Gray, the daughter of an Atlanta preacher, and the pair soon began a family. During his tenure as an Atlanta police officer, he began his career, gaining fame as a fearless fighter after having been wounded in one of the city's race riots.

In 1875, Heck moved his family to Galveston, Texas, where he went to work as a railroad guard for the Texas Express Company. Charged with guarding the Houston and Texas Central Railroad that ran between Denison and Galveston, the route was rampant with train robbery attempts. Just a year later, the Sam Bass Gang attempted to rob the train near the Hutchins Station, some twelve miles southeast of Dallas. In the inevitable shoot-out that occurred during the robbery attempt, Thomas was injured, but the gang got away with nothing, thanks to his foresight. Heck had placed the cash in an unlit stove, while stashing "decoy" packages in the safe. By the time the outlaws discovered the ruse, the train was safely gone. Afterwards, he was promoted to a Fort Worth detective for the company and by 1879 he held the position of Chief Agent.

In 1885, Thomas left his position with the Texas Express to run for the vacant office of Chief of Police. However, when he lost by a narrow margin, he went to work for the Fort Worth Detective Association. Continuing his success, he soon pursued brothers Jim and Pink Lee – two murderous members of the notorious Lee Gang. The gang of horse and cattle thieves had been plaguing Cooke County, Texas, and the Chickasaw Nation to such a degree that both the settlers and the Indians were up in arms. In May, 1885, when U.S. Marshal James Guy formed a posse to go after the gang, they were ambushed and four of the posse were killed.

Soon after, rewards totaling some $7,000 were posted for the capture of Jim and Pink Lee and Heck Thomas began the pursuit. After four months of continuous searching, Thomas leading a posse along with Jim Taylor, caught the Lee brothers off-guard in a hayfield near Dexter, Texas. Giving them a chance to surrender, as was his custom, the pair answered only with the sound of their Winchesters. In the ensuing melee, both bandits were killed, and the posse collected the reward. The newspaper proclaimed the next day: "The Lee brothers, the most notorious desperadoes in Texas, finally go down with their boots on."

Shortly after this daring deed, Thomas was appointed U.S. Deputy Marshal in 1886. Moving his family to Fort Smith, Arkansas, Heck worked under the infamous Isaac Parker, known as the "Hanging Judge." For the next seven years, Thomas would earn a reputation for being one of the most efficient deputies working the lawless land of Indian Territory. On his first trip out of Fort Smith, he apprehended eight murderers, a bootlegger, a horse thief, and several other hard case criminals. This would become the "norm" for Heck, who often worked single-handedly and would, over his tenure, bring more outlaws to justice than any other marshal working in Indian Territory.

Though his career was soaring, his marriage was floundering. Just two years after accepting the position as a U.S. Deputy Marshal, Heck's wife, Isabelle Thomas had become weary of frontier life and her husband's long absences. Before long she divorced him and returned to Georgia with their five children.

In 1888, while Thomas was recuperating from wounds received in the line of duty in Tulsa, Oklahoma, he met a schoolmarm and preacher's daughter named Mattie Mowbray. A year later, in October, 1889, the pair married in Arkansas City, Kansas and Heck soon began a second family.

By 1891, Thomas, along with two other Deputy U.S. Marshals – Chris Madsen and Bill Tilghman, began to work together to bring in some of the most notorious outlaws of the time. Soon, the trio took on the nickname of the "Three Guardsmen" and would become known as being largely responsible in bringing law and order to Indian Territory.

In 1892, Thomas and Madsen were pursuing the Dalton Gang who had been terrorizing Indian Territory with numerous train robberies and the ultimate shoot-outs that occurred during these attempts. On October 5, 1892, the Dalton Gang attempted to simultaneously rob two banks in Coffeyville, Kansas hoping to steal enough cash that they could "retire" from a life a thievery and escape to South America.

Chasing the Daltons was a little strange for Heck, as both Bob and Grat Dalton had once been Deputy U.S. Marshals like himself. He had also worked closely with their late brother, Frank Dalton, who was killed in the line of duty. However, these former ties to the Daltons did not stop him in his pursuit. In fact, Emmett Dalton would say that Heck Thomas was their "nemesis."

After the Dalton Gang had robbed a train in Adair, Oklahoma in July, 1892, Thomas had doggedly tracked them into the Osage Nation and located their hideout. Continuing to track the outlaws, he came upon their campsite about 20 miles south of Coffeyville. As he continued the pursuit, the news came that four of the Dalton Gang members, including Bob and Grat, had been killed in Coffeyville. Brother, Emmett Dalton, was the only survivor, having been severely wounded. Hearing the news, Heck continued to Coffeyville and identified the bodies for the Wells Fargo Company.

In 1893, the "Three Guardsmen" were tasked with taming Perry, Oklahoma, which had been born overnight in the Oklahoma land run of September 16, 1893. In no time at all, the settlement, which quickly earned the title of "Hell's Half Acre," was filled with some 25,000 people and 110 saloons. With the tidal wave of humanity that had converged on Perry, lawlessness, disputes, and mayhem were the "norm" of the day in this burgeoning city. Also operating in the area was the infamous Doolin Gang, whom the trio were determined to apprehend.

For four years, the Doolin Gang robbed trains and banks in Kansas, Indian Territory, and Texas, with the "Three Guardsmen" constantly in pursuit. Finally, in August, 1896, Thomas led a posse that caught up with Bill Doolin. When the outlaw was confronted, he tried to shoot his way out, but was killed.

While working the Indian Territory, Thomas arrested more than 300 wanted men in a dangerous job that felled fifteen other Indian Territory officers. During his tenure as a U.S. Deputy Marshall, Heck was known to go after the most dangerous outlaws, because the rewards were higher. Though his success in tracking outlaws provided him with the financial rewards he sought, he also paid a price when he was wounded at least six times during gunfights.

In 1902, Thomas moved to Lawton, Oklahoma where he would serve as the Police Chief for the next seven years. After a heart attack in 1909, finally he retired from law enforcement at the age of 59. Three years later, on August 15, 1912, he died of Bright's Disease. Henry Andrew "Heck" Thomas was buried at Highland Cemetery in Lawton, Oklahoma, where his grave remains today.

## Benjamin "Ben" Thompson, aka: Shotgun Ben

By W.R. (Bat) Masterson in 1907. ***Note***: The article that appears on these pages is not verbatim, as it has been very briefly edited, primarily for spelling and grammatical corrections.

### *The Career of Ben Thompson*

But all this is preliminary to the real purpose of this story, which is to tell something about Ben Thompson, the famous "gunfighter" of Austin, Texas. Ben Thompson was born in England and came to this country with his family when a boy. The family settled in Austin, Texas, and Ben learned the printer's trade and set type in the local newspaper offices of the city.

Ben Thompson

When the Civil War broke out he enlisted as a private in one of the Texas regiments and went to the front to fight the battles of the lost cause. He was only a boy in years when he enlisted, but was not long in showing the kind of mettle that was in him. While serving in General Kirby Smith's command during the campaign along the Red River, young Thompson performed many deeds of great daring, such as crossing into the enemy's lines and in carrying important dispatches for the officers of his command.

For the dash and courage he displayed at the battle of Sabine Cross Roads, just above the mouth of Red River in Louisiana, he was promoted to the rank of captain by his commanding officer. At the conclusion of hostilities between the North and South, Ben returned to his home in Austin, but did not remain long. The spirit of war was now upon him and he longed for more conflict.

Austin was too peacefully disposed for him, so he immediately set out for old Mexico, where Maximilian was just then having a lively time maintaining himself in his position as Emperor of Mexico. After getting on Mexican soil, Ben lost no time in reaching the headquarters of Maximilian's army, where he tendered his services in behalf of the invader's cause. He was instantly accepted and commissioned a captain and was soon wearing the uniform of the Emperor's army.

Ben, however, was not given much opportunity to achieve distinction in the invading army, for Maximilian soon after suffered a collapse and Thompson was lucky to get away from the Mexicans and reach his home in Austin with his life.

Ben Thompson was a remarkable man in many ways and it is very doubtful if, in his time, there was another man living who equaled him with the pistol in a life and death struggle. Thompson, in the first place, possessed a much higher order of intelligence than the average "gunfighter" or man killer of his time.

He was more resourceful and a better general under trying conditions than any of that great army of desperate men who flourished on our frontier thirty years ago. He was absolutely without fear and his nerves were those of the finest steel. He shot at an adversary with the same precision and deliberation that he shot at a target. He was a past master in the use of the pistol and his aim was as true, as his nerves were strong and steady. He had during his career more deadly encounters with the pistol than any man living and won out in every single instance. The very name of Ben Thompson was enough to cause the general run of "man killers," even those who had never seen him, to seek safety in instant flight. Thompson killed many men during his career, but always in an open and manly way. He scorned the man who was known to have committed murder, and looked with contempt on the man who sought for unfair advantages in a fight.

The men whom he shot and killed were without exception men who had tried to kill him; and an unarmed man or one who was known to be a non-combatant, was far safer in his company than he would be right here on Broadway at this time. He was what could be properly termed a thoroughly game man, and like all men of that sort never committed murder. He stood about five feet nine inches in height and weighed in later years, in the neighborhood of 180 pounds.

### *Wore Silk Hat and Prince Albert*

His face was pleasant to look upon and his head was round and well-shaped. He was what could be called a handsome man. He was always neat in his dress but never loud, and wore little if any jewelry at any time. He was often seen on the streets of Austin, especially on a Sunday, wearing a silk hat and dressed in a Prince Albert suit of the finest material. While he was not given to taking any unnecessary chances with his life, he would unhesitatingly do so if he felt that occasion demanded it. For example:

He had a falling out one day with the proprietor of a vaudeville house in Austin and that night, just at the busiest hour, went over to the place and fired a shot from his pistol into one of the big chandeliers that was hanging from the ceiling, which broke some of the glass shades and scattered the pieces of broken glass in all directions over the audience.

This, as might be expected, caused an immediate stampede of the patrons who rushed pell mell for the street. Thompson, when things quieted down somewhat, left the place without offering to do any further mischief. That seemed to satisfy Ben and in all probability the trouble would have ended then and there had the proprietor let the matter rest where it was; but he refused to listen to the advice of his friends and openly declared that he intended to get even with Thompson. As a matter of course, everything he said about Ben was instantly carried to him and, as is generally the way in such cases, some things he did not say were added to the story by the tale-bearers.

***The Threat of the Vaudeville Man***

At any rate, it got noised about town that the Vaudeville man was thoroughly organized for Ben and intended to kill him the first time he ever stepped inside his house. Of course, Ben was told what was being said about him by the hurdy-gurdy manager, but only laughed and said that he guessed if he didn't die until he got killed by the showman, he would live a long time. But reports of the threats that were being made against his life by the vaudeville proprietor kept reaching him with such regularity, that he finally began to think that perhaps there might be something in them. At any rate, he made up his mind to see for himself how much there really was in those threats that he had been hearing about for so long. So one night while the show was in full blast, he told a very warm personal friend of his by the name of Zeno Hemphill, that he had made up his mind to go over to the show and look over the arrangements he understood had been made for his removal from this vale of tears.

"Zeno," said Ben' "just fall in a few feet behind me and 'holler' if you see anything that doesn't look exactly right to you when I get inside that 'Honkitonk.' Remember, Zeno, I only want you along for a witness in case anything happens," remarked Ben, as he started to cross the street to the variety theater that was soon to witness a terrible tragedy within its walls. Ben entered a door that led to the bar-room from the street. This bar-room was a part of the theater, although the stage upon which the performance appeared was in another part of the building.

In order to reach that part of the building in which a performance was being given, it was necessary for Ben to pass along the entire length of the bar, then through a pair of swinging doors located about ten feet further on, through which it was necessary to pass before a view of the stage could be obtained. When Ben first entered the bar-room, he took a hasty survey of the surroundings, but saw nothing to cause alarm. In fact, he did not expect the attack to come from that part of the house, if indeed an attack was made at all, but was looking for it to occur after he had reached the theatre proper, which would not be until after he had passed the swinging doors.

Ben did not stop in the bar-room, but kept on walking leisurely towards the swinging doors and just as he was about to push them apart he heard Zeno, who had just then stepped into the room, cry out, "Look out, Ben." But before Ben could scarcely move, the bartender, whose name was Mark Wilson, had raised a double-barreled shot gun that he had lying along the mixing board back of the bar, and emptied both barrels, which were heavily loaded with buckshot, at Ben, who could not have been more than ten feet away.

Incredible as it may seem, Thompson escaped without a scratch. Mark Wilson, the bartender, was known to be a courageous young fellow who had on several occasions shown considerable fighting grit, and for that reason he had been selected to kill Thompson the first time he entered the place. Wilson, however, realizing that he was taking upon himself something of a job in agreeing to dispose of Ben Thompson, concluded that it would be best to get a little help, so he went to his friend Sam Mathews, and told him what he had made up his mind to do and asked him if he would help him out in the matter.

"With great pleasure," replied Mathews, and straightway went for his trusty Winchester rifle and immediately repaired to the variety theatre to help out his friend Wilson in putting Ben Thompson out of the way.

When Ben entered the bar-room that evening, he saw Mathews standing around the corner of the bar, but did not notice that he had a Winchester rifle leaning by his side; in fact, did not regard Mathews, whom he knew quite well, as an enemy and perhaps for that reason did not look him over very carefully. But to get to the point, the smoke from the shot gun had scarcely blown aside before Ben had whipped out his pistol and like a flash of lightning had shot Wilson dead in his tracks. Ben then 'noticed that Mathews had a Winchester rifle in his hand and instantly concluded that he too, was there for the purpose of aiding Wilson in killing him. Mathews seemed to anticipate what was passing through Thompson's mind, for he ducked down behind the bar instead of attempting to use the rifle, Thompson, instead of going around the end of the bar where he could see Mathews, took a rough guess at his location and fired through the end of the bar. The bullet struck Mathews squarely in the mouth and toppled him over on the floor.

### *When Case Was Called for Trial*

Ben then turned around and walked out of the place with his friend, Zeno Hemphill, who later on, when the case was called for trial, was the most important witness for the defense. Ben was kept locked up in jail pending the preliminary examination and was then admitted to bail and subsequently acquitted.

This is only one of a dozen of such occurrences that could be cited in the career of this most remarkable man. Wilson and Mathews were unquestionably men of courage, else they could not have been induced to enter into a plot to kill such a desperate man as they knew Thompson to be; but when it came to the scratch, they both lost their nerve and Ben was privileged to add two more names to the list of ambitious "gunfighters," who had sought to take his life. Thompson served a term as chief of police of the city of Austin and all the old-time citizens of the place remember him still as the best chief of police the city ever had. While Thompson was known throughout all that vast territory lying west and south-west of the Missouri River as the nerviest of men, and as unerring a shot with a pistol as ever lived; there were several men contemporaneous with himself who had the occasion arisen, would have given him battle to the death.

### *All with Nerves of Steel*

Such men as "Wild Bill" Hickok, Wyatt Earp, Billy Tilghman, Charley Bassett, Luke Short, Clay Allison, Joe Lowe and Jim Curry were all men with nerves of steel who had often been put to the test – anyone of whom would not have hesitated a moment to put up his life as the stake to be played for. Those men, all of them, lived and played their part and played it exceeding well on the lurid edge of our Western frontier at the time Ben Thompson was playing his, and it is safe to assume that not one of them would have declined the gage of battle with him had he flung it down to anyone of their number.

In making this admission, however, I am constrained to say that little doubt exists in my mind but that Thompson would have been returned the winner of the contest. Ben Thompson was murdered along with his personal friend, King Fisher, in a vaudeville theatre in San Antonio, Texas, in March, 1884.

Both he and King Fisher were killed from ambush by a number of persons who were concealed in the wings of the stage, and neither ever knew what happened. Ben was hit eight times by bullets fired from a Winchester rifle, and King Fisher was hit five times. All the shots were fired simultaneously and both sank to the floor dead as it is possible to ever be. It was a cold-blooded, cruel and premeditated murder, for which no one was ever punished by law.

# William "Bill" Tilghman

By W.B. "Bat" Masterson in 1907. ***Note***: The article that appears on these pages is not verbatim, as it has been very briefly edited, primarily for spelling and grammatical corrections.

## *Thirty Years a Lawman*

Notwithstanding the discovery of gold in California in 1849, and at Pike's Peak, Colorado, ten years later, the civilizing of the West did not really commence until after the close of the Civil War. It was during the decade immediately following the ending of the conflict between the North and South that civilization west of the Missouri River first began to assume substantial form.

Bill Tilghman

It was during this period that three great transcontinental lines of railroads were built, all of them starting at some point on the West Bank of the Missouri River. The Union Pacific from Omaha to Ogden, Utah, was completed during these years, also the Kansas Pacific, from Kansas City to Denver, Colorado, and the Atchison, Topeka and Santa Fe from Atchison, Kansas, to Pueblo, Colorado.

In twenty years from the day the first railroad tie was laid on the roadbed of the Union Pacific at Omaha, our Western frontier had almost entirely disappeared. There has been no frontier in this country for a good many years. The railroads long ago did away with all there ever was of it. Railroad trains, with their Pullman car and dining-car connections, have been reaching almost every point in the West of any consequence for the last twenty years.

On what was once known as our great American plains, which, a generation ago, furnished a habitat for the wild Indian, the buffalo, the deer and the antelope, today can be seen thousands of beautiful homes, in which none of the evidences of higher civilization are lacking. While it required but twenty years or so to bring about this wonderful change in this vast territory, the task was by no means an easy one.

Let the reader remember that in those twenty years, no less than half a dozen bloody Indian wars were fought, and that the scenes of those conflicts extended from the Dakotas on the north to the lava beds of Oregon on the west, and south to the frontier of Texas; and a fairly good idea of the magnitude of the undertaking will be gained. It was during those stirring times that nearly all of the famous characters of our once immense frontier, many of whom are now but memories, played a conspicuous part in this vast theatre of human strife.

James B. Hickok (Wild Bill) was perhaps the only one of that chivalrous band of fighting men, who composed the vanguard of western civilization, who had acquired fame before the period I have named. When this most remarkable man came to the West at the close of the Civil War, in which he had taken a conspicuous part, both in southwest Missouri and in the campaign along the Mississippi River, he brought with him a well-earned reputation for great daring and physical courage – a reputation he successfully upheld until stricken down by the assassin McCall at Deadwood, in June, 1876. But it was not of Wild Bill I started to write, but of one whose daring exploits on the frontier will not suffer by comparison.

The purpose of this article is to tell a story of Bill Tilghman, who was among the first white men to locate a buffalo-hunting camp on the extreme southwestern border of Barber County, Kansas, just across the Indian Reservation line, as far back as 1870. Billy Tilghman is one of the few surviving white men who reached the southwest border of Kansas before the advent of railroads, who is still in harness and to all intents and purpose as good both physically and mentally as ever.

It is now thirty-seven years since a slim-built, bright-looking youth, scarcely seventeen years old, pulled up for camp one evening on the bank of the Medicine Lodge River in southwestern Kansas, only a few miles north of the boundary line between Kansas and the Indian Territory. An Indian uprising, lasting more than a year, had been put down the year previous by General Custer, and, as a natural consequence, the Indians who had taken part in the uprising entertained for the white man anything but a friendly feeling.

Billy Tilghman, like others in that country at the time, became a buffalo hunter and was working along nicely until the Indians got after him. The Indians, by the terms of the treaty lately concluded with the government, had no right to leave their reservation without first obtaining permission from their agent.

It was therefore as unlawful for an Indian to be found in Kansas without government permission, as it would have been for a white man to enter the Indian Territory for the purpose of either hunting or trading whiskey with the Indians. The Indians; however, cared little for treaty stipulations at the time and often crossed over into Kansas for the purpose of pillage as well as killing buffalo.

The Indian, besides destroying the hunter's buffalo hides and carrying away his provisions and blankets while he was temporarily away attending to the day's hunting on the range, was often known to have added murder to his numerous other crimes, so that an Indian off his reservation got to be viewed with apprehension by the hunters.

It was a well understood thing among the buffalo hunters whose camps were located close to the Reservation line, that any time a hunter could be taken unawares by the Indians he was almost sure to be killed, if for no other reason than to secure his gun and belt of cartridges. The Indians had, in prowling around the country one day, come upon Billy Tilghman's camp, and, after pulling up what hides he had staked out on the ground for drying purposes, proceeded to set afire to those already dried and piled up ready for market.

When Tilghman and his two companions returned to camp that evening, after their day's work on the range, they found their camp a complete wreck. Besides the destruction of several hundred dollars' worth of hides, they also found that the noble red men who had paid their camp a visit during their absence had carried off everything there was to eat. But, as buffalo hunters found no trouble in making a hearty meal on buffalo meat alone, they did not despair nor go to bed on an empty stomach.

The day's hunt had resulted in the taking of twenty-five buffalo hides, and the question now arose what was to be done with them. If they were staked out to dry as the others had been, there was no reason for believing the Indians would not return and destroy them as they had the others. Tilghman's two partners were for moving away the first thing in the morning.

"We are liable to all be killed," said one of them, "if we stay here any longer."

"I think we ought to go about twenty miles farther north over on Mule Creek," said the other. "Besides, the hunting is as good there as it is here. And the Indians hardly ever get that far away from the Reservation."

"We will move away from here," said Billy Tilghman in his characteristically deliberate manner, "after I get even with those red thieves for the damage they have done us."

Billy Tilghman, although a mere boy at the time was the master-mind of that camp, and what he said was law.

"Ed," said Billy to one of the partners, "go and hitch up the team and drive to Griffin's Ranch and get a sack of flour, some coffee and sugar and a sack of grain for the horses and get back here before daylight in the morning, and Henry and I will unload those hides and peg them out to dry. Don't forget to feed the team when you get there and let them rest up for an hour or two, as you will have plenty of time to do that and get back here by daybreak."

Griffin's Ranch was fifteen miles north of Tilghman's camp on the Medicine Lodge River and the only place nearer than Wichita, which was one hundred and fifty miles farther east, where hunting supplies and provisions could be obtained.

Ed was soon on his way to Griffin's Ranch, which only took about three hours to reach. While Tilghman and Henry were busily engaged in fleshing and staking out the green hides, Billy remarked that if those thieving Cheyennes came again around his camp for the purpose of destroying things, there would likely be a big pow-wow take place among the Indians as soon as the news of what occurred reached them. "For," said he with some emphasis, "I don't intend to stop shooting as long as there is one of them in sight."

"But supposing," said Henry, "that there is a dozen or so of them when they come, what then?"

"Kill the entire outfit," replied Billy, "if they don't run away."

There was little else said on the subject before bedtime, but as Henry afterwards told me, it was not a hard matter to understand by Tilghman's actions, that the only thing that seemed to worry him was the fear that the Indians would fail to pay the camp another visit.

Before daylight the following morning, Ed was back in camp, having carried out his instructions to the letter. After breakfast that morning, Tilghman informed Ed and Henry that they would have to hunt without him that day, as he intended to conceal himself nearby the camp, so as to be in a position to extend a cordial welcome to the pillaging red-skins when they showed up.

Billy, as a precaution, planted himself before the other boys left for the hunting ground, so that in case the camp was being watched by the Indians, they could not tell if they had all left camp as they had done the previous day. About noon, and just as Billy was commencing to despair, one lone Indian made his appearance. He rode up very leisurely to the top of a little knoll where he could get a good view of the camp, and, after a careful survey of the surroundings, and discovering nothing to cause alarm, proceeded to make the usual Indian signals, which is done by circling the pony around in different ways.

Tilghman, who was crouched down in his little cache, was intently watching the Indian, understanding as well as the red-skin did, the meaning of the pony's gyrations. Directly, six other Indians rode up alongside of the first and proceeded to carefully make a mental note of everything in sight.

They soon concluded that there was no lurking danger and all rode down to the camp and dismounted. This was exactly what Billy had been hoping they would finally conclude to do. Now if they will only all dismount, said Billy to himself, as he saw the Indians riding down to camp, I will kill the last one in the outfit before they can remount. He got his wish, for they all hopped off as soon as camp was reached. Billy; however, waited for a while to see if they intended mischief, before opening up on them with his Sharp's big fifty buffalo gun that burned 120 grains of powder every time it exploded a shell. He did not have long to wait, for no sooner had one big buck hit the ground than he ran over to the sack of flour and picked it up and threw it across his pony's back, while some of the others started out, as Billy supposed, to cut up the freshly staked hides.

The big Indian who had swiped the sack of flour had scarcely turned around before Tilghman dropped him in his tracks with his rifle. This, as might be supposed, caused a panic among the other Indians, who little suspected that there was an enemy nearer than the hunting ground, until they heard the crack of the gun. In an instant, Billy had in another cartridge, and another thieving Cheyenne was sent to the happy hunting-ground. The first Indian that succeeded in reaching his pony had no sooner mounted him than he was knocked off by another bullet from Billy's big fifty. This made three out of the original seven already killed, and what was an unusual thing for a Southern Plains Indian to do, the remaining four abandoned their ponies and took it on the run for a nearby clump of timber, which all but one reached in safety. Billy managed to nail one more of the fleeing marauders before he could reach the sheltering protection of the woods. The shooting attracted the attention of his partners, who were not more than two miles away, causing them to hurry to camp, where they expected to have to take a hand in a fight with Indians, whom they had reason to believe were responsible for the shooting they had heard.

"The scrap is over," said Billy, when the boys got near enough to hear him, "and three of the hounds have made their escape. I told you last night, didn't I, Henry, that I would kill all that came if they stood their ground and didn't run away. Well," he said, in a rather disconsolate tone of voice, "I fell down somewhat on my calculations, as seven came and I only succeeded in getting four, but then that wasn't so bad, considering that they left us their ponies."

"What's to be done now?" inquired Henry, who was not hankering for a run in with the Indians at that time.

"Don't get frightened." said Billy; "and remember that we are in Kansas and that those dead Indians were nothing more than thieving outlaws who had no right off their reservation and if any more of them come around before we are ready to leave, we will start right in killing them."

There was nevertheless little time wasted in getting away from that locality. The camp dunnage was loaded into the wagon in a hurry, and the team headed towards the north, and Ed, who was driving, told to keep up a lively trot whenever possible. Billy brought up the rear, mounted on one of the Indian's ponies and driving the others.

"Look here, Billy," said Henry, as they were about to pull out of camp, "don't you think we ought to bury those dead Indians before leaving?"

"Never mind those dead Indians," replied Tilghman, "the buzzards will attend to their funeral; go ahead."

When dark overtook the party that night they were on Mule Creek, twenty-five miles from where they had pulled up camp at noon. The Indians reported the occurrence of the killing to their agent at the Cheyenne Agency, but received no satisfaction, and were informed that they were liable to be killed every time they left their reservation without permission.

That was Tilghman's first mix-up with the Indians, but it was not his last. He continued to hunt in that country, and as the Indians persisted in crossing over into Kansas, there were many clashes between them, which invariably resulted in the Indians getting the worst of the encounter.

***A Scout for the Government***

During the fall and winter of 1873-1874, there was practically no cessation of hostilities between the Indians and hunters along the Indian border, finally culminating in an uprising among the four big southern tribes, namely the Cheyenne, Arapaho, Kiowa and Comanche, which required almost a year for the government to put down. In this Indian war of 1874, Tilghman acted as a scout for the government and several times while carrying dispatches from one commander to another, had to fight his way out of mighty tight places with the Indians in order to save himself from being taken alive.

After the Indian uprising had been put down, Tilghman went up on the Arkansas River and took up a ranch close to Dodge City, where he lived for several years. In 1884 he was appointed City Marshal of Dodge City, and made one of the most efficient marshals the city every had. He was just the sort of a man to run a town such as Dodge City was in those days, being cool-headed, courageous and possessing excellent executive ability.

In the summer of 1888, a County-seat war broke out in one of the northern tier of counties in the state of Kansas, and Tilghman was sent for by one of the interested parties to come up there and try and straighten the matter out. Tilghman went and took with him a young fellow by the name of Ed Prather, whom he had every reason to believe he could rely upon in case of an emergency. Prather, however, proved to be a traitor, and one day attempted to assassinate Tilghman, but the latter was too quick for him, and Prather was buried the next day. After straightening out the County-seat trouble, Billy returned to Dodge and continued to live there until the opening up of Oklahoma Territory, fifteen years ago.

He was among the first to reach the territory, and took up a claim at Chandler, Lincoln County, where he still resides. Tilghman acted as a U.S. Deputy Marshal when he first went to Oklahoma and did as much if not more to stamp out outlawry in the territory as any other man who ever held office in that country.

***The Capture of Bill Doolin***

Tilghman has served four years as Sheriff of Lincoln County, and during that time has killed, captured and driven from the country a greater number of criminals than any other official in Oklahoma or the Indian Territory. His capture of Bill Doolin in a bath-house at Eureka Springs, Arkansas, single handed, was perhaps the nerviest act of his official career. Doolin was known to be the most desperate criminal ever domiciled in the Indian Territory and had succeeded for several years in eluding capture. A large reward was offered for his apprehension and a number of U.S. Marshals, with their deputies, had several times attempted to arrest him, dead or alive, but in every instance, Doolin either eluded them or, when too closely pressed, stood them off with his Winchester.

Doolin was credited with the killing of several Deputy Marshals. Tilghman got after him and trailed him to Eureka Springs, where he found him in a bath-house, and without calling on the local officials for assistance, affected his capture single-handed. Doolin was seated on a lounge in the bath-house when Tilghman entered, and before the desperado realized what was happening, he was covered by a 45-caliber Colt's pistol and ordered to throw up his hands. Doolin hesitated about obeying the order and Tilghman was forced to walk right up to him and threaten to shoot his head off unless he instantly surrendered. Doolin had his pistol inside his vest and directly under his armpit, and made several attempts to get it before he was finally disarmed. It was certainly a daring piece of work on the part of Tilghman, and he was lucky to get away with the job without being killed.

Bill Raidler was another notorious outlaw whom Tilghman got after, but in this case, the Marshal was forced to kill his man before he could take him. Tilghman and Raidler met on the road in the Osage Indian Country, and Tilghman ordered the outlaw to throw up his hands, but instead of obeying, he opened fire on the Marshal, who instantly poured a fistful of buckshot into the desperado's breast, killing him in his tracks. Raidler had been a pal of Doolin's and had been mixed up in several train robberies and had sent word to the U.S. Marshals that if they wanted him to come and get him, but to be sure and come shooting. Tilghman was too good a shot for him at the critical moment and Bill Raidler's life paid the penalty for his many crimes. [Most sources say that Raidler was injured, tried, and sent to prison.]

Thomas Calhoun, a negro, was another notorious outlaw and murderer whom Marshal Tilghman captured in the Territory, but not until after he had shot and broken the desperado's leg did he succeed in making him a prisoner. Calhoun was charged with the murder of a colored woman and a warrant for his arrest placed in Marshal Tilghman's hands. The Marshal came upon Calhoun and ordered him to throw up his hands, which he refused to do, and promptly opened fire on Tilghman, who, as he had so often done before, returned it with such good effect that the negro's leg was broken and he then surrendered, but died soon afterwards.

Dick West, known as "Little Dick," was perhaps the worst criminal in the entire territory outside of Bill Doolin. "Little Dick" was a member of the Doolin Gang of train robbers, and the hardest outlaw in the Territory to trap. He never slept in the house, winter or summer, and kept continually changing about from one place to another. Tilghman finally got track of him and ran him to cover, when a fight ensued. Tilghman, though shot at several times, escaped without injury and finally succeeded in killing his quarry.

"Little Dick," like his chief, Bill Doolin, had for several years made a specialty of ambushing and murdering U.S. Deputy Marshals in Oklahoma and the Indian Territory, and when the announcement of his death at the hands of Deputy Marshal Tilghman was made, there was universal rejoicing among the law-abiding citizens of that country. Space forbids that I go further into the career of William M. Tilghman at this time. It would take a volume the size of an encyclopedia to record the many and daring exploits and adventures of this remarkable man. His life's history has been aptly stated by a magazine writer as almost a continuation of the memoirs of Davy Crockett or the story of Kit Carson, as far as it relates to his adventures on the frontier of Kansas in the early seventies. After a career covering a period of thirty-seven years, spent mostly on the firing-line along civilization's lurid edge and after being shot at perhaps a hundred different times by the most desperate outlaws in the land, men whose unerring aim with either gun or pistol seldom failed to bring down their victims, this man, Tilghman, comes through it all without as much as a scratch from a bullet.

### *Sheriff for More than Thirty Years*

Billy Tilghman was born in Iowa in 1854, and moved to Atchison, Kansas, in 1856, and as a boy, passed through the reign of terror known in that country in those days as the Kansas and Missouri border war, which existed for a number of years along the frontier of those two states. It was a fierce and bitter contest between the pro-slavery influence of Missouri on the one side and the abolitionists of Kansas on the other, which finally culminated in the Civil War.

At the time Alton B. Parker received the democratic nomination for the presidency in 1904, Billy Tilghman was selected by the Democratic National Convention as one of the delegates to notify Mr. Parker of his nomination, and was last in New York at that time. He is still a resident of Chandler, Lincoln County, Oklahoma and will in all probability be elected Sheriff again there this fall. He is perhaps the only frontiersman living who has been almost constantly on the job for more than a generation, and who still lives on to tell the story.

***Note***: Bat Masterson could not have guessed when he wrote this article in 1907, that Bill Tilghman would, in fact, die from a bullet. At the age of 70, Tilghman was still acting as a lawman when he was appointed as the marshal of Cromwell, Oklahoma. After surviving decades of tough outlaws, he was shot and killed on November 1, 1924 while he attempted to arrest a corrupt Prohibition Officer by the name of Wiley Lynn.

## Dan Tucker

*Lawman of New Mexico*

Lawman and gunfighter, Dan Tucker, was born in Canada in 1849, but somewhere along the line, made his way to the American West, where he would eventually earn the nickname "Dangerous Dan," for his deadly shooting skills. He first appeared in Grant County, New Mexico in the early 1870s. Though some were suspicious of the slight, soft spoken man, who was rumored to have killed a man in Colorado before appearing in New Mexico, Sheriff Harvey Whitehill took a liking to him and hired him on as a deputy sheriff in 1875.

One of the first incidents that Dan was involved in was when two Mexican men got into a brawl inside Johnny Ward's Dance Hall, in Silver City in 1876. After one of the men stabbed the other, he fled from the saloon as Dan Tucker was approaching and the deputy shot him in the neck. The next year, Dan shot and killed a drunken man who was standing on the street throwing rocks at people as they passed by. No charges were filed against Tucker for the shooting.

In 1878, Tucker was sent to El Paso to assist in the chaos of the Salt War and in April of that same year, became the first town marshal of Silver City, as well as continuing to serve as a deputy sheriff. He soon put a stop to the discharging of firearms on the city streets. He also killed a thief as he was trying to escape and was engaged in a gunfight with three horse thieves inside a Silver City saloon, killing two of them and wounding the third. In November, 1878, he was shot and wounded during a shootout with a cowboy named Caprio Rodriguez when the man resisted arrest. However, in the end, Rodriguez lay dead. That same month, he resigned his position as City Marshal, but was reappointed the following year, on May 2, 1879.

Having tamed much of Silver's City's lawlessness, in January, 1880, he was more needed in the mining boomtown of Shakespeare, New Mexico. In May, he was dispatched to track down two thieves who had broken into a prospector's cabin. He returned two days later with all of the stolen property and reported that he had killed the two thieves.

The next year, Tucker became the City Marshal for Shakespeare, New Mexico, and in September, shot and killed cattle rustler Jake Bond. November was a busy month for the city marshal, as he killed a man who rode his horse into a local hotel dining room and arrested outlaws Sandy King and "Russian Bill" Tattenbaum, who were hanged by the town's Vigilante Committee inside the Grant House. Later that month, Tucker was sent to Deming, New Mexico on November 27, 1881, to calm down several outlaws who had basically taken over the town. Upon his arrival, he began to patrol the streets with a double barrel shotgun, and within three days, had shot and killed three men and wounded two more.

All in all, Deputy Tucker was said to have arrested some 13 desperadoes of a cowboy gang in 1881, killed several more, and brought order to the wild town of Shakespeare.

By March, 1882, Tucker's reputation had spread to such a degree, that when Doc Holliday and Wyatt Earp made a hasty retreat from nearby Tombstone, Arizona, they avoided taking the train through Deming, choosing to travel by horseback and avoiding Tucker's territory.

On August 25, 1882, Tucker became involved in the most controversial shooting of his career. The night before, in the mining camp of Paschal, New Mexico, Deputy James D. Burns was drunk inside Walcott & Mills Saloon and began twirling and flaunting his pistol. Though the town marshal, Glaudius W. Moore, and another deputy tried to disarm Burns, he refused, stating that as a law officer, he was entitled to retain his weapon. Burns continued to drink throughout the night and into the next day, going from saloon to saloon. By that afternoon he was in the Centennial Saloon, where once again Marshal Moore ordered him to give up his weapon and come outside. Also in the saloon was Dan Tucker. When Moore tried to arrest him; however, Burns drew his pistol and fired, though he hit no one. Tucker reacted first, hitting Burns in the ribcage and Moore also fired upon the drunken deputy, killing Burns. Because Burns was a popular deputy with the local miners, there was a public outcry for justice. Though both men were cleared, Moore was dismissed as town marshal. Though Tucker's reputation suffered, he retained his position.

Later that year, on December 14, 1882, Tucker was ambushed by a Mexican man as he entered a brothel in Deming to investigate a complaint, which turned out to be false. Though Tucker took a shot in the shoulder, he returned the fire, killing one man and a prostitute who had helped the would-be assassin.

By 1884, Tucker had opened a saloon across from the railroad depot in Deming, New Mexico. However, the following year, in October, he was appointed as a U.S. Deputy Marshal for the region. The next month he and another man were involved in a gun battle with Apache warriors west of Deming and were able to drive them off. On October 2, 1887, Tucker arrested a dangerous outlaw, Dave Thurman.

Described as "one of the best peace officers Grant County ever had," Tucker finally gave up his lawman responsibilities, resigned his position in 1888, and moved to California. The last time he was heard from was when he returned to Grant County, New Mexico for a visit in May, 1892. However, the short 5'7" ex-lawman had put on so much weight, his friends nearly didn't recognize him. Where he went after leaving New Mexico, is lost in history.

Recognized as one of the most dangerous and underestimated gunmen in the history of the Old West, Tucker was thought to have killed some 17 men during his lawman career.

## David "Big Dave" Updyke

*Crooked Sheriff of Ada County, Idaho*

David C. Updyke was born in the vicinity of Cayuga Lake, New York, about 1830. Said to have been raised in an upstanding family that boasted some of the leading citizens of New York, Updyke was a black sheep.

In 1855, he went to California where he was employed for two years by the California Stage Company as a stage driver. Three years later, he sailed to British Columbia to look for another kind of work, but finding nothing there that suited him, he soon returned to California spending two years in Yuba County, then two years in Virginia City, Nevada.

By 1862, word was spreading of the rich gold finds in Idaho and Updyke went first to Florence, then Warren, and by the fall he was in Boise County where he worked a valuable claim on Ophir Mountain.

By 1864, he had saved more than $1,500 dollars and went to Boise City where he bought a livery stable in the center of town. Though Updyke had committed no known crimes up until this point, he had begun to consort with a number of criminals. Before long, the livery stable became the rendezvous site for some of the Old West's most reckless bands of robbers and road agents.

However, this did not stop David Updyke from being elected Sheriff of Ada County in March, 1864. Though many of his cohorts were ruffians, they were a strong power in the Democratic party and Updyke won the election by a small margin.

Before long, Updyke was suspected of aiding in the circulation of stolen gold dust, as well as participating in a stage robbery near Boise City in 1864. So many rough characters began to hang about Updyke's stable that many of the citizens began to refer to them as "Updyke's Gang." However, he and/or his outlaw friends covered their tracks so well, nothing could be proven.

Soon after his election, he avowed to break up a vigilante organization of about thirty men, which had been formed in the Payette River settlement, some thirty miles from Boise City. This enraged many of the law-abiding citizens who felt the vigilante committees were their only protection from thieving and murdering road agents in the area.

But Updyke cared little about what those law-abiding citizens thought and somehow obtained all the names of the men in the vigilante group, procuring warrants for their arrests. While the proceedings and warrants were all perfectly within the law, Updyke and his "posse" secretly planned to shoot the vigilante leaders and maintain that they had resisted arrest.

The plan was that 15 to 20 armed men would leave Boise City, meet up with more road agents at Horse Shoe Bend, and then proceed with their warrants to the Payette River settlement. However, word leaked to the citizens of Boise City of the plan and they secretly dispatched a messenger to the Payette Vigilantes.

As Updyke's "posse" left Boise City about 4:00 o'clock in the afternoon to carry out the arrests, the thirty members of the vigilante group were assembling in self-protection. When Updyke and his men reached Horse Shoe Bend, they failed to connect with the country road agents and went on without them.

When the "posse" arrived at Payette River, they were surprised to find themselves outnumbered two to one. Forced to negotiate with the vigilantes, Updyke complied with their demands. The vigilantes agreed to go to Boise City to answer the warrants but they would not allow Updyke or his men to disarm them. After arriving in Boise City and obtaining an attorney, the complaints against the vigilantes were dismissed and they were discharged.

Afterwards, the humiliated vigilantes were obviously very bitter towards Updyke and began to closely watch his every move. The public soon began to believe the "Updyke Gang" was behind nearly every theft, murder and robbery that occurred anywhere in the area.

The next murderous outrage, in which the "Updyke Gang" was concerned, was the stage robbery in Portneuf Canyon, where four of its passengers were killed.

On July 26, 1865, Updyke, along with three other outlaws, robbed a gold laden stagecoach of some $86,000 in gold. In the melee, four of the stage passengers were killed, and the stage driver and another passenger were wounded.

The vigilante committee immediately went after the three other outlaws, but David Updyke was a different story. Having been duly elected as Ada County Sheriff, the vigilantes were more cautious and waited until the opportune time to punish him for his suspected wrongdoings. On September 28, 1865, the Payette River Vigilance Committee arrested him on a charge of defrauding the revenue and failing to arrest a hard case outlaw named West Jenkins.

However, Updyke made bail and knowing the reputation of the Vigilance Committee, he immediately left town, fleeing to Boise City where he had more influence. However, the citizens there too, were fed up with the criminal elements and began to form groups for the purpose of cleaning up the county. By the next spring, Updyke feared for his own safety and accompanied by another outlaw by the name of John Dixon, the two departed Boise on the Rocky Bar Road on April 12, 1866. Unaware that a vigilante party was following them, the two stayed overnight at an abandoned cabin some thirty miles out of town.

During the night, the vigilantes captured the unsuspecting pair and lead them some ten miles farther down the road to Sirup Creek. The next morning, as the vigilantes prepared to hang the men, they questioned Updyke about the whereabouts of the stolen cache. The crooked sheriff only glared at them in contempt, refusing to respond. The vigilantes then hanged both men under a shed between two vacant cabins. Updyke had only $50.00 on his person at the time of his death.

On April 14th, the bodies were found with a note pinned to Updyke's chest accusing him of being "an aider of murderers and thieves." The next day an anonymous note appeared in Boise that further explained the committee's actions. "Dave Updyke: Accessory after the fact to the Portneuf stage robbery, accessory and accomplice to the robbery of the stage near Boise City in 1864, chief conspirator in burning property on the overland stage line, guilty of aiding and assisting escape of West Jenkins, and the murderer of others while sheriff, and threatening the lives and property of an already outraged and long suffering community."

The gold taken in July, 1865, has never been found and many think it is buried somewhere in the City of Rocks.

## Stephen Venard

*Goldrush Lawman*

One of the most fearless lawmen during the California Goldrush, Venard began his life on a farm near Lebanon, Ohio in 1824. He received a good education as a child, attending Waynesville Academy and when he grew up, moved to Fountain City, Indiana, where he worked as a teacher. A man of strong morals, Venard soon became involved in the Underground Railroad and his life was threatened when slave owners put a price on his head. When gold fever began to sweep the country during the California Goldrush, Venard headed west in 1850. After prospecting on his own for several months with little success, he finally settled down in Nevada City, California, where he worked for wages on another miner's claim.

Over the next several years, he tried his hand at a number of ventures including a grocery store, the freighting business, and continued his mining efforts. However, none of these provided the financial success he was hoping for and in 1855, he took a job as a deputy under Nevada County Sheriff, W.W. Wright.

The following year, Sheriff Wright was killed, and when a new sheriff – William Butterfield, temporarily replaced him, Venard resigned, not having been on good terms with the other officer. That same year, the infamous Henry Plummer (who would later be hanged as an outlaw in Montana in 1864) became the City Marshal. In 1857, Venard ran against Plummer for the position, but lost, in what was said to have been a rigged election.

In the meantime, Venard continued to work in the area mines while sometimes working as a Nevada City police officer. After Henry Plummer had moved on, Venard became the Nevada City Marshal in May, 1864 and was regarded with respect, especially for his proficiency with his 16-shot Henry rifle.

On May 15, 1866, a Wells Fargo stagecoach was robbed near Nevada City by outlaws, George Shanks, Robert Finn and George Moore, who made off with nearly $8,000 in gold dust. A posse comprised of both county sheriffs and Nevada City officers was quickly formed to pursue the bandits. The posse split up to look for the desperadoes with Venard and Deputy Sheriff Lee, looking for the men near the headwaters of Myer's Creek. The two law officers soon came upon the fugitives and when gunplay erupted, Venard killed all three with a total of four shots.

Upon returning the gold bullion, Venard found that Wells Fargo had offered a $3,000 reward for the bandits. However, Venard refused to accept the entire amount, insisting that it be split up among the posse members. In the end, he accepted half of the reward and became an area celebrity for his bravery. Governor Frederick Low appointed Venard to his staff with the rank of lieutenant colonel in the National Guard and Wells Fargo presented him with a new gold-mounted Henry Rifle.

In June, 1866, Venard became a deputy sheriff working at the nearby boomtown of Meadow Lake City. However, the gold soon played out and Venard went to work as a shot-gun messenger for Wells Fargo. During the construction of the transcontinental railroad in 1869, he guarded the express coaches and served in the Mountain Division for two years.

However, by 1871 he was back in Nevada City, working as a police officer, where that same year, he played an important role in the capture of the John Houx Gang. It was not long before Wells Fargo asked him to come back as a detective when stagecoach robberies were becoming rampant in Sonoma and Mendocino Counties.

After serving for many years for Wells Fargo, Venard died of complications from a kidney ailment on May 20, 1891. Described as a "man of modest demeanor, thoroughly temperate, of the strictest probity and not afraid of anything," he unfortunately died so poor that his friends had to take up a collection to pay for his burial in Nevada City.

## William Alexander Anderson "Bigfoot" Wallace

*A Texas Folk Hero*

One of the most colorful and toughest of Texas' frontier characters was William Alexander Anderson "Bigfoot" Wallace. Growing up to be a backwoodsman, folk hero, soldier, and Texas Ranger, Wallace was originally from Virginia. Born in Lexington, on April 3, 1817 to Andrew and Jane Ann (Blair) Wallace he grew up to work in his father's fruit orchard until he heard that his older brother and a cousin, who had moved to Texas, had been killed in the Goliad Massacre in the spring of 1836. He then set out for Texas himself, in order to "take pay out of the Mexicans."

Wallace first settled near LaGrange, Texas in 1837 where he tried his hand at farming and quickly joined up with the Texas Rangers under Captain John Coffee Hays. In 1840, he moved to Austin, where he helped to layout the new town. While there, he was misidentified as an Indian named "Bigfoot," who had ransacked a settler's home. Though Wallace was soon cleared, the name "Bigfoot" stuck – an appropriate nickname for the six feet two inch tall, 240 pound muscled man.

In 1840, Wallace participated in the Battle of Plum Creek, and in the Spring of 1842, fought against Mexican General Adrian Woll's invasion of Texas.

Later that year, he volunteered for the Somervell Raid across the Rio Grande River and afterwards, joined a splinter group that was later called the Mier Expedition, to further penetrate into Mexico. However, the group was surrounded and captured by a force ten times their size. Forced into central Mexico, the men were able to escape, but were quickly recaptured and forced to participate in what became known as the "Black Bean Incident." This was a "lottery" in which black and white beans were placed in a crock, in a 1 to 10 ratio. Those who drew a black bean were executed, while a white bean meant prison. Wallace was one of the "lucky" ones, drawing a white bean and soon found himself on an 800 mile forced march to the Perote Prison in Vera Cruz. After a petition was signed by a number of U.S. Congressmen, he was released and after his return to Texas, joined in the Mexican-American War. After the war, he commanded a company of Texas Rangers fighting border bandits and Indians on the frontier. When the Civil War erupted, he was still helping to guard the frontier against the Comanche Indians.

Somewhere along the line, Wallace was granted a piece of land by the State of Texas, where he ranched along the Medina River. However, in his later years, he was living in Frio County, and when a small village was formed, it was named "Bigfoot," after Wallace, who had made a legend of himself during his lifetime.

Described as humorous, mellow, and honest, he became a teller of tales, which though sometimes embellished, were extremely popular among his visitors. In 1870, some of these tales were told by biographer, John Duval, in a best selling book called, *The Adventures of Big Foot Wallace, The Texas Ranger*, which further contributed to his reputation as a Texas folk hero.

Wallace died on January 7, 1899, and shortly thereafter the Texas legislature appropriated money for moving his body to the State Cemetery in Austin, Texas.

William Alexander Anderson "Bigfoot" Wallace

## John Joshua "J.J." Webb

*Lawman Turned Outlaw*

Serving most of his adult life as a lawman, John Joshua Webb (J.J.) was also a hunter, teamster, surveyor, hired gun, and member of the notorious Dodge City Gang in Las Vegas, New Mexico.

Born on February 14, 1847, in Keokuk County, Iowa, J.J. was the seventh of twelve children born to William Webb, Jr. and Innocent Blue Brown Webb.

In 1862, the family moved to Nebraska and then later, to Osage City, Kansas. Webb traveled west in 1871, becoming a buffalo hunter and then a surveyor in Colorado. He then drifted from Deadwood, South Dakota to Cheyenne, Wyoming, to Dodge City, Kansas.

Over the years, Webb would lead an adventurous life from lawman to outlaw, meeting numerous characters along the way, such as Wyatt Earp, Doc Holliday, Bat Masterson, and more.

The 1875 census of Ford County listed J.J. Webb as a 28 year-old teamster. Later he would serve as a business owner, peace officer, and a leader of Ford County's mercenary force on the side of the Atchison, Topeka and Santa Fe railroad in their battle against the Denver & Rio Grande railroad for right–of–way through the Royal Gorge in Colorado.

Numerous news articles from the Dodge City papers showed Webb to be a well–respected member of the Dodge City community. While there, he was deputized to ride in a number of posses. September, 1877 found him riding with Ford County Sheriff Charlie Bassett and Under-sheriff Bat Masterson to Lakin, Kansas in pursuit of Sam Bass and his gang who had recently robbed a Union Pacific train of $60,000 at Big Springs, Nebraska. Heading south to Texas, the posse assumed the gang would pass through southwest Kansas. However, their search was unsuccessful and Bass continued to elude lawmen for almost another year until he was finally killed on July 21, 1878 after an attempted bank robbery in Round Rock, Texas.

By January, 1878, Bat Masterson had been made the new Ford County Sheriff, and on January 29th, he deputized Webb along with two other men by the names of Kinch Riley and Dave "Prairie Dog" Morrow, to help him track down six outlaws who had robbed the westbound train at Kinsley, Kansas, two days earlier. Two of the gang members, Edgar West and "Dirty Dave" Rudabaugh, were caught within days by the posse. During the arrest, when Rudabaugh went for his gun, Webb stopped him and forced him to surrender. The other four accomplices were arrested later. Rudabaugh then informed on his cohorts and promised to go "straight." Rudabaugh's accomplices were sent to prison, but Dirty Dave was soon released, drifting to New Mexico and returning to thievery once again.

In September of 1878, southwest Kansas settlers were fearful and restless as word came that Cheyenne Chief Dull Knife and his band had fled from their reservation in Oklahoma and were headed to their home in the Black Hills. Exaggerated reports of killing and thievery committed by the Cheyenne on their journey began to be told in Dodge City. The bulk of the soldiers at nearby Fort Dodge were sent out to corral the Indians, leaving only about nineteen troops to protect the area. Unnecessarily frightened for their lives, Dodge City citizens wired the governor requesting arms and ammunition.

The weapons were received within days and Lieutenant Colonel William Henry Lewis, the Fort Dodge Commander, selected J.J. Webb, A.J. Anthony, Bill Tilghman, Robert Wright, and other experienced plainsmen, to scout the area. The men soon brought back word that some 200 warriors were in the area and the rumors of their acts continued to grow, with headlines screaming "Not a child or a woman in Kansas or Nebraska is safe." However, Dull Knife's band only wanted to get back to their ancestral home and soon removed themselves from the area and things finally returned to normal.

It was in 1879 that Webb worked as a hired gun for the Atchison, Topeka and Santa Fe railroad in their battle against the Denver & Rio Grande railroad for right–of–way through the Royal Gorge in Colorado.

Soon, John Joshua Webb moved on again to Las Vegas, New Mexico. Though J.J. Webb had been counted among the leading citizens of Dodge City, in Las Vegas, matters would take an entirely different turn. When he arrived, many of his acquaintances were there from Dodge including Henry "Doc" Holliday, David "Mysterious Dave" Mather, Wyatt Earp, and his old nemisis, Dave Rudabaugh.

Shortly after his arrival to Las Vegas, Webb partnered with Doc Holliday in operating a saloon, where Doc spent most of his time gambling. On July 19, 1879, the two were seated at a card table when a bully and former army scout by the name of Mike Gordon began to yell loudly at one of the saloon girls. A former "girlfriend," she had rejected him while he was trying to convince her to leave town with him. Furious, Gordon stormed out of the saloon shouting obscenities. When Doc followed the unruly man outside, a shot from Gordon's gun whizzed past him. Calmly pulling his revolver, Doc shot one time, leaving Gordon in the dusty street. Gordon died the next day and when word spread that Doc would be arrested for the killing, he fled to Dodge City.

In 1880, Webb accepted the position of Las Vegas City Marshal. In that capacity, he soon joined the Dodge City Gang led by Justice of the Peace Hyman Neill, known as

"Hoodoo Brown." The Dodge City Gang was firmly in control of a criminal cartel bent on thumbing their noses at the law. For two years, the members of the Dodge City Gang participated in several stage coach and train robberies, organized cattle rustling, and were said to have been responsible for multiple murders and lynchings.

The Dodge City Gang consisted of men formerly from Dodge City including Justice of the Peace, Hyman "Hoodoo Brown" Neill; City Marshal, Joe Carson, Deputy U.S. Marshal "Mysterious Dave" Mather, police officer John Joshua (J.J.) Webb, and a number of gunfighters and outlaws including "Dirty Dave" Rudabaugh, William P. "Slap Jack Bill" Nicholson, John "Bull Shit Jack" Pierce, Selim K. "Frank" Cady, Jordan L. Webb (no relation to J.J.), and a number of other hard cases. While Rudabaugh, Jordan Webb, Cady, Nicholson, Pierce, and the rest committed acts of thievery, Neill, Mather, Carson, and J.J. Webb, in their official capacities, helped to cover the outlaws' tracks.

J.J. Webb, shackled in the center of the photo, next to his jailers at the Old Town Jail in Las Vegas, New Mexico.

On March 2, 1880, Justice of the Peace, "Hoodoo Brown," learned that a freighter named Mike Kelliher was allegedly carrying about $1900 and the unlawful Dodge City Gang was determined to relieve him of the cash. The Ford County Globe of March 9, 1880, reprinted the report from Las Vegas Daily Optic:

About four o'clock this morning, Michael Kelliher, in company with William Brickley and another man, entered Goodlet [a member of the Dodge City Gang] & Roberts' Saloon and called for drinks. Michael Kelliher appeared to be the leader of the party and he, in violation of the law, had a pistol on his person. This was noticed by the officers, who came through a rear door, and they requested that Kelliher lay aside his revolver. But he refused to do so, remarking, "I won't be disarmed – everything goes," immediately placing his hand on his pistol, no doubt intending to shoot. But officer Webb was too quick for him. The man was shot before he had time to use his weapon. He was shot three times–once in each breast and once in the head... Kelliher had $1,090 [$1,900] on his person when killed.

Regardless of his status as a City Marshal, Webb was convicted of murder and sentenced to hang. On April 30th, Rudabaugh, along with a man named John Allen, burst through the Sheriff's office to free Webb. Though the jail break was unsuccessful, Rudabaugh murdered jailer Antonio Lino in the process. Webb's sentence was appealed and commuted to life in prison.

Rudabaugh soon fled Las Vegas along with another Dodge City Gang member, hooking up with Billy the Kid and his gang. However, Rudabaugh, along with Billy the Kid, was captured on December 23, 1880.

After Dirty Dave's conviction, he found himself in jail with J.J. Webb. Soon, the pair, along with two other men by the names of Thomas Duffy and H.S. Wilson, tried unsuccessfully to shoot their way out of jail on September 19, 1881. Duffy was mortally wounded and their attempt was unsuccessful. However, Webb, facing life in prison, and Rudabaugh, the threat of hanging, were determined.

Two months later, Webb and Rudabaugh, along with five other men, chipped a stone out of the jail wall and escaped out of a 7"x19" hole. Rudabaugh and Webb raced to Texas and then to Mexico where Webb disappeared and Rudabaugh was later killed.

Later Webb returned to Kansas, where he took the name "Samuel King," and worked as a teamster. Somewhere along the line he moved on to Winslow, Arkansas working for the railroad. In 1882 he died, of smallpox in Arkansas. John Joshua Webb never married.

## William Fletcher Wheeler

*Montana Territory Marshal*

A U.S. Marshal in Montana Territory, Wheeler was the son of a Methodist minister, born at Warwick, New York on July 6, 1824. Though the family moved around alot during his childhood, Wheeler received a good education and in 1843 became an apprentice for the Ohio Statesman as a printer and reporter under Samuel Medary. He remained in that position for three years, studying law in his spare time, and in 1848 was admitted to practice in front of the bar.

Wheeler moved to St. Paul, Minnesota, in 1856, and in 1857 he accepted an appointment as Territorial Librarian and private secretary to Samuel Medary, who by then was Territorial Governor of Minnesota. Wheeler continued in this position under Governor Sibley, the first state governor. Sibley commissioned Wheeler as a Lieutenant Colonel of the First Minnesota Voluntary Infantry in 1858. In the Spring of 1860, Wheeler projected and located the first telegraph line in Minnesota and incorporated a rail line from Duluth to St. Paul.

At the outbreak of the Civil War, Wheeler assisted in raising a company of volunteers which became part of the Fourth Minnesota Regiment, stationed at Fort Snelling. As the war progressed, he saw action at Cornith, Iuka, and Vicksburg. On the drive towards Chattanooga, Wheeler became severely ill and was discharged in the Spring of 1864.

After President Grant's inauguration, Wheeler was appointed as United States Marshal of Montana Territory on May 15, 1869, succeeding Neil Howie. In 1870, as Marshal, Wheeler wrote an extensive account of the Piegan War and coordinated the taking of the U.S. Census in Montana. Marshal Wheeler was also assigned as Superintendent of the United States Penitentiary at Deer Lodge in 1871. This duty consumed a great deal of time, as the prison had to be constructed from the ground up. Wheeler retained the office of U.S. Marshal until 1878, when Alexander C. Botkin replaced him.

Through the efforts of Wheeler and other early Montana settlers, the Montana Historical Society was formed; and in 1884 he was appointed it's librarian when the society became a state institution, a position he held until his death. He devoted much of his time collecting the reminiscences of old pioneers and writing their biographies. Wheeler was also the Crier of the United States District Court at Helena. He died at his home in Helena on June 24, 1894 due to heart and lung trouble which developed from pneumonia.

## Fred White

*Tombstone's First Marshal*

Fred White, Tombstone's first town marshal, was elected on January 6, 1880. In July, Wyatt Earp was appointed as a deputy sheriff for the county and the two formed an alliance to protect the town, as well as a strong friendship. White quickly established himself as a likable and professional lawman and contrary to many depictions of him in western film, he was respected by Clanton's Cowboy faction. In fact, he had arrested "Cowboy" members on a number of occasions, rarely having any problems when doing so. He got along particularly well with "Curly Bill" Brocius, often bantering and joking with the man. Overall, he was seen as an unbiased man, uninvolved in the politics of Tombstone.

But for White, he had a massive job on his hands, as the town of Tombstone, filled with rowdy miners and cowboys, was a lawless place, where violence was a common occurrence.

The night of October 27, 1880, was no exception, as several members of the "Cowboy" faction, liquored up and having fun, were finding sport in firing their six-guns recklessly in all directions on Allen Street.

At around 12:30 in the morning on October 28th, White responded to the sounds of gunshots, closely followed by Deputy Sheriff Wyatt Earp. He found Curly Bill Brocius and several other cowboys still shooting it up in an empty lot where the Birdcage Theatre now stands. Ordering the men to surrender their weapons, each of them gave up their guns voluntarily without incident until Curly Bill Brocius presented his six-gun to the marshal, barrel first. As White grasped the barrel of the gun the weapon discharged, shooting White in the groin. While no one knows exactly what happened, it is thought that the pistol's hammer was probably "half-cocked" over a live round when White pulled it from Brocius' hand.

Tombstone, Arizona in 1882.

Writhing in agony, White fell to the ground. An enraged Wyatt Earp then began to pistol whip Brocius before arresting him and taking him to jail for the shooting. Morgan Earp, also on hand, helped to bring in the other men who had caused the excitement, charging them with violating city ordinances. Upon depositing Brocius in a cell, Wyatt swore out a complaint against Brocius for assault with intent to murder. Though this incident is often portrayed including the Clanton and McLaury brothers, the newspaper the next day does not support this.

Boot Hill Graveyard today is a tourist attraction in Tombstone.

In the meantime, Marshal White was made comfortable and looked to by a doctor, who expected him to make a recovery. But it was not to be.

When the new day dawned, the rowdy makers went before the judge, were fined for violating city ordinances, and released. Brocius; however, asked for a postponement until he could get a lawyer. Later he appeared with Judge Haynes of Tucson, as his counsel, and as a lynch mob was forming in the camp to hang Brocius for the shooting of the popular marshal, whose condition had worsened and looked as if he might die, Brocius was ordered to be taken to Tucson to be held in protective custody. As Wyatt Earp and George Collins headed to Tucson with Brocius in a buggy, they were escorted out of town by Virgil and Morgan Earp.

In the meantime, Marshal Fred White, who had been steadily declining, lost his battle on October 30th and died. He was buried at Boot Hill Cemetery in Tombstone.

Brocius was said to have terribly regretted the shooting of White, whom he apparently liked, and maintained that the shooting was an accident, a fact that was supported by testimony given by White before he died, as well as Wyatt Earp in Brocius' trial.

Brocius was eventually acquitted of any wrong-doing, with Judge Nuegass commenting that the shooting was "Homicide by Misadventure" or, in other words, an accident.

Brocius was released from custody and despite Wyatt's statement that helped him to be freed, Brocius could not forgive Wyatt for the pistol whipping. This was just one more of the many incidents that increased the ever mounting tension between the Earps and the Cowboy faction.

After the death of "Old Man" Newton Clanton in July, 1881, Curly Bill became the leader of the Clanton Gang. After the Gunfight at the O.K. Corral in October, Brocius attempted to kill Virgil Earp and succeeded in assassinating Morgan Earp. Brother Wyatt, looking for revenge for Morgan's killing, reportedly caught up with Brocius on March 24, 1882, and killed him with a double shotgun blast to the chest.

# Appendix A

## Contributors

### Frank W. Blackmar

*Article:*

- Hamilton Butler Bell - Transforming Wicked Dodge City

Excerpted from the book: KANSAS: A Cyclopedia of State History, Standard Publishing Company, Chicago, Illinois, 1912

### Alfred Henry Lewis

*Article:*

- Bat Masterson - King of the Gun Players

Alfred Henry Lewis was a journalist and novelist who, by the late 1800's, had established a reputation as one of the foremost political writers of the country. In the first decade of the 20th century he started a short-lived Boston magazine called Human Life and hired Bat Masterson to write a series of articles on his gunfighter friends. However, Bat was not an autobiographer, and Lewis wrote this article on Masterson in 1907.

### W.B. "Bat" Masterson

*Articles:*

- The Career of Ben Thompson
- Bill Tilghman - Thirty Years a Lawman

Though most of us know that W.B. "Bat" Masterson was famous as a gunfighter and friend of such characters as Wyatt Earp, Doc Holliday, and Luke Short, many may not know that he was also a writer. After his many escapades in the American West, he accepted a post of U.S. Marshal in New York state. However, by 1891 he was working as a sports editor for a New York City newspaper. In 1907 and 1908 he wrote a series of articles for the short-lived Boston magazine, Human Life. Masterson died in 1921 of a heart attack.

### James Harvey McClintock

*Article:*

- Arizona Rangers

James Harvey McClintock was born in Sacramento in 1864 and moved to Arizona at the age of 15, working for his brother at the Salt River Herald (later known as the Arizona Republic). When McClintock was 22 he began to attend the Territorial Normal School in Tempe, where he earned a teaching certificate. Later, he would serve as Theodore Roosevelt's right-hand-man in the Rough Riders during the Spanish-American War and become an Arizona State Representative. Between the years of 1913 and 1916, McClintock published a three volume history of Arizona called, *Arizona: The Youngest State* (now in the public domain,) in which this article appeared. McClintock continued to live in Arizona until his poor health forced him to return to California, where he died on May 10, 1934 at the age of 70.

# Appendix B

## Lawmen by Last Name

### *"AKA" and "Nick Names"*

LEGENDS OF AMERICA

www.LegendsOfAmerica.com

Legends Of America has been exploring history online since 2003, with a heavy emphasis on the American West. Owner, editor, and author, Kathy Weiser-Alexander started the website as a hobby due to her deep seated love of history; but, it quickly grew into a business. She left her corporate job in 2004 to dedicate full attention to growing the content on LegendsOfAmerica.com, and along the way, found time to author books.

Great American Bars and Saloons, published in 2005, takes readers into the many watering holes of America's past, particularly the numerous saloons that sprouted up during our nation's Wild West days. This great photographic review displays hundreds of vintage photographs from California to Arizona, the mining camps of Colorado, and all the way to New York and its turbulent days of Prohibition.

In 2010, Kathy co-authored Greetings From Route 66 with various other Mother Road experts, which is the ultimate celebration of the Mother Road, providing history, roadside attractions, pop culture, historic photos, ghost stories – and even a few recipes from famous greasy spoons.

Meanwhile, her "web hobby" drew such a fan base, that husband, Dave Alexander joined Legends Of America full time in the fall of 2009. Now, working from their home base on the Lake of the Ozarks in Warsaw, Missouri, Kathy and Dave continue to explore American History and find new and exciting places to travel to and write about. At Legends of America, readers find stories ranging from the American Revolution, to Native American history, the Old West, to the early 20th Century, Route 66 and lots more.

While visiting LegendsOfAmerica.com, be sure to shop their stores for unique merchandise suited for history lovers, including Legend's Rocky Mountain General Store (store.legendsofamerica.com) and Legend's Photo Print Shop (photos.legendsofamerica.com).

Made in the USA
Lexington, KY
05 November 2019

56564832R00127